echoesuponechoes

New Korean American Writings

Edited by Elaine H. Kim and Laura Hyun Yi Kang

echoesuponechoes
New Korean American Writings

Copyright ©2002 by Elaine H. Kim and Laura Hyun Yi Kang

Library of Congress Number 2002113033

ISBN: 1-889876-13-5 (paper)
        1-889876-14-3 (cloth)

Publication of this book was funded in part by The Lannan Foundation and individual donors to The Asian American Writers' Workshop.

Book design by Purple Gate Design www.purplegatedesign.com

Published in the United States of America by The Asian American Writers' Workshop, 16 West 32nd Street, Suite 10A, New York, NY 10001. Email us at desk@aaww.org. The Asian American Writers' Workshop is a not-for-profit literary organization devoted to the creation, development and dissemination of Asian American literature.

Distributed by Temple University Press for The Asian American Writers' Workshop. To order, contact 1.800.621.2736 or go to www.temple.edu/tempress.

Editors' Dedication

To our students, who bring life to literature.

Acknowledgements

We want to thank Quang Bao, Cara Caddoo, Patricia Tumang, Andrea Louie, and Noel Shaw for their excellent work on this book and at The Asian American Writers' Workshop, which is so crucial to the discovery and support of Asian American writers.

The Editors

Elaine H. Kim is Professor of Asian American Studies and Associate Dean of the Graduate Division at UC Berkeley. Her current book is *Fresh Talk/Daring Gazes: Asian American Visual Art*, with Margo Machida and Sharon Mizota, forthcoming 2003. She is Executive Producer of Asian Women United of California's new video, *Labor Women* (2002), a 30-minute documentary about young Asian American women labor organizers.

Laura Hyun Yi Kang is Associate Professor of Women's Studies and Comparative Literature at the University of California, Irvine. She is the author of *Compositional Subjects: Enfiguring Asian/American Women* (Duke University Press, 2002).

INTRODUCTION
echoesuponechoes

What is the proper measure of a people and their writings?

A conventional mapping of Korean American writings might focus upon particular regions of "critical mass," such as the Koreatowns of Los Angeles, New York, or Chicago or KAL destinations spread afar in a global diaspora. Perhaps the unexpected places about and from which contributors to *Echoes Upon Echoes* write suggest broader and deeper Korean American imprints. The bleak and eccentric landscapes and mindscapes of alienation, obsession, conflict, and belonging in these writings attest to tension between habitation within and movement across strange terrains, communities, and languages. While many of the pieces in this anthology can be read as familiar explorations of lineage and identity, they also dramatize how the ties that bind become frayed, disassembled, and reassembled in and across time and space. We have grouped the writings under three pairings: arrival/return, dwelling/crossing, descent/flight. Each pair of words bears several meanings: location and travel, family genealogies and social relations, and acts of imagination and writing. We invite readers to chart the lines of affinity and dissonance among the pieces and the six sections.

Elaine H. Kim
Laura Hyun Yi Kang
March 2002

TABLE OF CONTENTS

arrival

return

dwelling

crossing

descent

flight

Contributors

arrival

STEPHANIE UYS

aN aPPLE...a pLANE...hOLDING A wOMAN'S hAND

1.
Once I was told you could divide your body
into two lives. But I got it wrong. I got it wrong.
She told me this and I believed, but he
only believed in one life, like one world... The possibility of one body
coming from that life to this life, to this world from that world
is possible, but she and I carry a single memory
carrying *the* memory, the memory of flight,
of fleeing one country...but no...no...I got it wrong.

2.
She runs in my body. I don't know her, but
my shoes are on her, and with each step leaves
press into mud, twigs into blades of grass,
flatten paths over the American landscape.

I do not know her, but I have learned to accept
Repetition. She speaks for patience
Eyes looking at eyes looking at brown iris looking at
Skin in skin in skin. An echo.

We feared for each other's safety.

3.

Last night, she dreamt she was a fish with a hook
in her mouth. She said, You are not Asian. Today you are White,
there is no American. Today I am you, and
since there is no American, You, an Asian,
are American. Therefore, I am not you,
you are *me* because I am white and white is American.

4.

He says to me, Please don't be that woman in the attic
and she agrees, but I say nothing.

From him, she learned about slight tremors,
bodies moving bodies, the predictability of flight patterns.
He thought. He thought if she spoke, she would become.
Become the I, but she left him before.

Then one day when the sun got up again
like a spot of dust again, doing tricks again, she
rolled over to me. *Every day you do the same action.*
I am not you. You are not me. And we fight for no reason.

But I like the friction. No the repetition.
Rely. Reliance. No Self. Relying.

It's impossible for two to live in one body.

She tells me she's tired
of eyes looking out not in
skin in skin the same skin the same echo
She says this time, this time
things will be different because a body
is only a body, not a part of memory
and I tell her I don't understand, but she wants
to understand, but we fail at communication.

5.
But see, I got it wrong. It wasn't fleeing.
She said being *taken away.*
Not fleeing. Not leaving in the middle of the night
fleeing, but leaving in the middle of the day, in all that light,
put on a plane holding hands with the social worker.
A Social worker.

That memory... an apple, a plane...holding the woman's
hand, not holding my mother's hand, not fleeing, being taken
away from one life to another.

She says they tried to separate us. I said we are together. She
says you are not me and I am you, but we are two
different people, but I say what about him? She says
skin in skin in skin. I don't understand. He doesn't understand.
Erosion. Corrosion. Disintegration.
I don't understand.

I am you, but you are not me. We are not together.
And still the same echo

6.

She has no body, but she is warm and white. My
body is dark, but he doesn't want me to forget
the memory. So they remember for us.

They remember darkness.
They say write poetry so that I *won't*
forget, but I keep writing
about forgetting, but she types out
YOU WILL NOT FORGET and I respond
forget what?

And she writes
for me about remembering,
but I want to forget
an apple…a plane…a woman
holding my hand…one country's
landscape shifting into another's.

DENNIS KIM

in america

my *umma's* hands are the smallest dam
in the world, holding back the deluge
from my transplanted yellow face
i am spared, dry, but still a son of a sea-jumping
tradewind-swimming immigrants
and i dream of floods
i dream of migration waves
i etch the phantom face of structural forces bigger than i
on the ionized chart of my skin to know myself

and my mother's hands are a driftwood dam
shielding my eyes from what she found
in my america's blood wet mouth
my mother's hands are rafts
on which i make my sorrow journey south
down the mississippi of my restlessness
trying to understand the privilege
burning my palms that my *umma*
bought with the sound of her porcelain
girlhood cracking into 53 bloodthirsty pieces:

one, for the halved peninsula
on which she was born
and has returned to but twice
since her departure

two, for the sons she squeezed
from her womb
born with petulant lips
and hearts as trembling soft
as peeled oranges

and two score and ten,
for fifty states of descending
madness. as a poet i loved
once said, "woman must cry
many times to be heard

in america."

in america

a fatherless child
is my father
and i am his child
child of his dreaming
of his ghosted parent
paring my face
into the woodcut image
of the hand he wishes
remembering, wishes
to remember, but recalls
only as the haziest
of gestures, a sheer
gauze memory that may be

but the residue of old papers
and photographs

yellow is the color of memory
yellow is the canyon of my *abba's* face

he is made of iron and i love him
love him without wondering why
i have unloaded my why
i have sheathed my questions
i have broken the neck
of my desire to know
what prompted this drama
we lock fists in
i have traced the rope
of this bout as far back
as it will go, tugged
until the mystery toppled
over onto me

and i am caught
in the *ugulhan* ribbon
of my father's eye
caught between my limping love
and thirsty words like why

DAISY CHUN RHODES
My Father's Voice

His teeth were strong enough to chew on beef ribs after savoring barbecued fat and meat. Tearing into gristle encasing bone, he chewed it into shreds until a "crack" sound occurred. Attention to bone marrow provided sucking sounds of delight. "*Cho-ta*," he'd say, showing how wonderful bones were, his flat Korean cheeks shaped into a broad smile of happiness.

I watched his eyes become slits of joy, a rare sight. Rare because most of his life was dedicated to work and his family, little for pleasure.

Once, in an unexpected moment of storytelling, my father said he had been so hungry when he was a young man that, in the brutal cold of a northern Korean winter, he dug in the frozen earth for roots to eat. "They were delicious," he told me. It was difficult to imagine the cold of ice until I defrosted the freezer of our refrigerator. I scraped a layer of ice with my fingernails and left my hands touching freezing cold and listened to drops melting into the kitchen sink.

One day my father said salt ships came into port, to his province of Pyung An, after the spring thaw. He said his *omanee* (mother) had died when he was a child, and his father had remarried. As soon as he was able to move on, he walked many miles until he could sail from Korea to the land of scented sandalwood, where it was rumored that money grew on trees.

Abagee (father) was among seven thousand men who arrived as laborers to work in sugar cane and pineapple fields. He was among the first Koreans to what was then the Territory of Hawaii. It was 1904.

Though he had four daughters and two sons, everyone was older than I. When *Abagee* began to teach me about my relationship to the earth, his words were few. Instead, he taught me by example to cut long green blades of grass with a sickle. The grass was then cut into tiny pieces with a sharp knife and mixed with chicken feed. Together we cleaned the chicken coop, mixing manure into the red dirt of Wahiawa, which the Hawaiians called a place of noise.

I was taught how to light matches to build fire for our baths, heating water from beneath a redwood tub *Abagee* had fashioned. Baths were fast and simple. Using small pans, we wet ourselves, soaped, then rinsed with only small amounts of water scooped from the tub.

Once, before the wood had turned into embers, *Abagee* tossed sweet potatoes into the fire, and we squatted together, quietly waiting and watching as smoke curled into our nostrils. "Is it ready?" I would ask, searching for his eyes. Finally, he shoveled up the hot root encrusted with ash. We partook of pure moments held together with layers of memories and savored the core of the hot yellow sweetness we shared together.

Abagee loved the small piece of land he owned in Wahiawa. With a small hatchet, he would chop out a fourth of a dried coconut. After removing meat, he would then fill the cavity with a mossy substance into which he stuck two pieces of stem. He hung the dried coconuts on the latticework he had built and watered them every morning. As the stems grew longer, leaves formed and then dropped. Buds appeared, and finally long stems of *hono-hono* orchids bloomed. They were hung in our living room, scenting our entire home with purple perfume.

An enormous tree showered orange *ohai* blossoms onto our front lawn. While lying on my fiber mat, I watched clouds of imagined dragons and white wisps of dancers pass over the tree I pretended was on fire. But the tree I still think of is the one bearing fruit that tasted like sweet and tender deep pink roses. It grew over the shed where the wood for our bath fire was stacked, not far from papaya trees.

In those days, nothing was wasted. When we killed chickens, I held the bowl into which blood was drained after *Abagee* cut a fine line on the bird's neck with a very sharp knife. The chicken never moved. It did not quiver. Sister number one made southern fried chicken, which we ate with kimchee and chopsticks. Our family ate some haole foods with Korean condiments.

The big noise came to our town when we were attacked by Japanese planes on December 7, 1941. Shortly thereafter, tuberculosis swept though our community. *Abagee* went into a sanatorium, and Sister number one died, followed by her newborn.

Weeds sprang up in our garden, and the orchids slowly withered away. Several neighborhood boys died when they examined a grenade. The explosion killed them. A white soldier and his Korean girlfriend wanted to get married. They killed themselves after her parents refused her marriage to an outsider.

Somehow, *Omanee* managed and coped until *Abagee* came home. He had the habit of reading the Korean newspaper at night before going to bed. In notes and chants, he sang the news of his brothers and sisters dying in Korea. The syllables rose into a crescendo and fell into a diminuendo. Staccato beats sang the news of his brothers and sisters serving as slaves to the Emperor of Japan.

The distinct, forceful sounds of his sing-song manner were clearly heard throughout the house. But I never heard him crying, even though he sang about the time Koreans lost their names, lost their dignity, lost their country.

Today, 118 years after the birth of my *abagee*, I hear his voice of pain in his now frozen stillness. The chants and sing-song sounds are of Chosun, land of the morning calm. He had been connected to his homeland until he took his last step off the ship, the *SS Korea*, on September 5, 1904 and became part of the Korean community in Hawaii. He married a picture bride who arrived in Hawaii on July 7, 1918 on the *SS Kawi* from Whang-hae Do, Korea.

He never returned to his place of birth.

Each spring, flaming red-orange *ohai* blossoms fall upon the headstones of my parents. Their names are raised to the sun and sky in Nuuanu. They say "Chun, Pyung Chan" and "Chun, Shin Ai."

SASHA HOM
Blue Fairyland

My name is Wol Soon Ann. I am female. I am of the Korean race. My date of birth is January 15, 1975. I know this because when I was found in front of #12 Bakdal-dong, Anyang, I had a sheet of paper with the accurate date of birth written upon it. Just like in the cartoons. An abandoned baby on a doorstep, with a note scribbled hastily, pinned to a basket. What a cliché.

She left me while she hummed a tune, enjoying the feel of the cold sun on her back, knowing that songs can last forever. She left me in a basket on a stranger's doorstep, or maybe he was a distant cousin, who found a package misdelivered, bundled me in his arms and hoisted me into the air like a damp featherless bird.

My name is Sasha Hom. My adopted parents couldn't decide what to name me. My mother wanted to name me Fanny or Lulu, impractical names for a round Korean baby. My father refused, and they settled on "Sasha" because my mother had heard someone calling their child Sasha in an empty museum. She said it sounded like the wind echoing off the cement walls.

My name is Tom So Lan, because the child must have a Chinese name, even if she is Korean living like a Chinese American. My grandmother gave me my Cantonese name before she was murdered. My grandfather did not cry, but I know that he was thinking, *We did not come to the States for this.*

Before I even had a name, my mother said that she used to pray for a child. She likes to say, "If you ask God and the universe for something, you will almost always get it, but you have to remember to be specific." So she drew a picture of a round-faced little girl with almond-shaped eyes, wispy eyebrows that just barely met in the middle, and an indentation right above the lip just tiny enough to place the tip of a pinky in, all perfectly symmetrical. She says that when she got me she couldn't breathe, because I looked just like the picture of the little girl in her dresser drawer.

My name is Sasha Hom. When receptionists and telemarketers ask me to spell my last name, I say, "H-O-M." They say, "Uh-huh? Go on." I say, "That's it," but think, *stupid white people*, even though I cannot see their faces.

My name is Sasha Gabrielle Hom. My name has been on many mailboxes, school rosters, checks, bills, invitations. It has been written on love letters, hate mail, recommendations, eviction notices, airplane tickets and veterinary bills.

My name is Sasha Hom. My uncle tells me I should reclaim my "original" name. I'm not sure what he's talking about.

My name is Sasha Hom, sometimes Sasha Ham when misspelled, but I answer best to "Hey."

In the fourth grade, I wore bells and keys around my neck on a chain. I wanted to sound like a dog when I walked, my I.D. tags jangling as I trotted around the playground with my pockets crammed with Milkbones. I carried Simon & Schuster's encyclopedia of dogs with me everywhere and had to identify the breed of every dog I saw on my way to school. Hence all the tardy slips hidden in the bottom of my plastic Snoopy backpack. In fourth grade, and perhaps even now, I believed I was born into the wrong species. I didn't believe I was being raised by the wrong parents, second-generation Chinese American hippies. Rather, I believed I was being raised by the wrong species, perhaps even in the wrong dimension and galaxy.

My school, Malcolm X Elementary, was a massive concrete structure surrounded by more concrete, patches of tanbark containing unsafe climbing structures and one elm tree. The hallways were wide enough for a truck to cruise across the linoleum tiles without ripping down the bulletin boards that were covered with graffiti and children's art. I'm sure the building contained asbestos and some kind of cancer-causing mold in the ventilation system. The basement was always dark, and the gray cement floors made it seem cool and damp even on a hot day. A fourth grader had once stabbed a fifth grader down there, and whenever I had to walk to the bathroom in the basement, I thought that I could still see blood on the floor.

One day I was in the basement bathroom, equally cool and frightening, when two girls came in while I was in one of the stalls. "Did you know that white people don't put toilet covers on the toilet seats?" one girl said to the other.

I was peeing, the little rough squares of toilet paper neatly arranged beneath my butt. My mother had told me that I was never to touch any part of the cold smooth toilet seat, or else I would catch a green germ that would leave moldy spots on my skin forever. So I would patiently lay each square down one by one, even if that meant peeing a little in my pants while holding my crotch, tap dancing as the squares of toilet paper slid off the seat. I peered under the stall door and saw little white bobby socks against smooth light brown skin.

"What do you mean?" asked the other girl.

"They just sit on the toilet seats without putting nothing down."

"Eww, that's nasty," said the other girl.

I flushed the toilet and walked out of the stall, acutely aware of the fact that I was not white.

"What's that girl?" said one of the black girls.

"That's that Chinese girl who thinks she's a dog."

I wanted to say, "I have a name, you know." But I didn't.

Background Information
Present Address: Foster Home in Seoul
Natural Parents: Both Unknown
My mother, Unknown, was an old woman who knew that age can be read in the gums, and the color of despair is off-yellow, like the meat of an apple that has stolen another tooth.

She was only 15. She liked to jump on tabletops and sing Elvis songs in broken English. Her favorite was the one about a dog.

My father, Unknown, I can't imagine. They say he had 22 children buried like land mines in the soil. He wore the heads of women across his back like a charm.

Place of Birth: Unknown
I was born by a river. I was born in a house with no doors. I was born in a hospital where records disappear when you ask for them. I wonder what name escaped from her lips as she let me slip out like a wet secret, a silent secret with no name.

THOMAS TESKA, AKA IN CHUN BAEK
Milk Carton Therapy

He still had trouble pronouncing his *r*'s and *w*'s. At 13, Jonathan Flynn, adopted, Korean, short and thin, flat nose and round head, athletic and smart, still pronounced *work* like *rock*, and *run* like *won*. His *l*'s were fine. He had no trouble with *love, little, ladybird*, etc. Jonathan's parents—Danny and Sara—had hoped that his speech would have improved by his tenth birthday. It didn't.

It was Jonathan's father, the son of strict but loving Irish immigrants, who believed that all it took was faith and hard work to fix what he called the "broken tongue."

And so, when Jonathan was seven years old, he was subjected to speech therapy class in school. He was forced to wear an empty carton of milk—split almost all the way down the middle and opened so it looked like a giant letter V—over his mouth and ears. The carton carried the lingering smell of sour milk and Palmolive (You're soaking in it). However, no matter how corny it looked, or how corny Jonathan felt wearing it, the carton did the job: He was able to hear how he sounded. *This is a totally humiliating experience*, he thought, the milk carton hanging from his face. A totally humiliating experience because he really wasn't as bad as the other kids in class. Kids who stuttered. Kids with horrible overbites or underbites. Kids from foreign countries like Brazil or Afghanistan or Holland, places where they don't even speak English! No, he didn't really belong there. *That* he knew.

Depending on the size and shape of a child's head, he or she wore either a half-gallon or quart. It was uncomfortable, but bearable, kinda like wearing cardboard headphones. Every noun, verb, adjective and pronoun, conjunction and infinitive, article and participle phrase, all were coming in loud and clear and in stereo! An interesting discovery: He could also hear himself breathe and wondered if it was the same for the astronauts who have to wear those big, bulbous helmets out in space. Or for the deep-sea divers who search the ocean floor for treasure chests, just like in the picture books he read. His face felt warm, wet and sticky from his breath. And his nose and ears itched something fierce!

During the lessons, which took place after school, the speech teacher, a tall, red-haired woman with big boobs and faux jewels clustered around her ears, would go around and help each student with his or her problem: a lisp, a stutter, a mispronunciation, an accent, whatever. She would stretch her mouth wide open like a python about to devour a small cow, to show where her tongue was and how it vibrated when she said, "la, la, la, la, rum." Just like that. Each student was asked to bring in a small hand mirror and use it during the class. Otherwise, how were they supposed to know if their tongues were in the right spot or not? Jonathan, while practicing vowels and whatnot, noticed something dangling from the roof of his mouth, way in the back, and asked the teacher what *that* was and if *that* was supposed to be there.

"Why, certainly, Jonathan," she laughed. "Didn't you ever see the inside of your mouth before?"

Jonathan thought for a moment. "No, I haven't."

"Not even when you're brushing your teeth?" she asked.

"I'm too short to reach the mirror in the bathroom."

"Well, *that* is important," she told him and smiled and winked, "So don't lose it."

And then the rest of the class checked to see if they had *that* too.

In class, she would say, always pointing and talking at the same time, something like: "See? Your tongue should go to the roof of your mouth, then down, then up, then down, up, down." Her tongue was huge and long, which was probably why the school had hired her, Jonathan surmised. To amuse the class, she would sometimes show how she could touch the tip of her nose with the tip of her tongue, a truly magnificent feat. No one in class could do that, no matter how hard he or she tried. But as any good teacher would do, she emphatically discouraged any of the students from attempting it, so as not to have any of the parents complaining to the school board. And when she talked, she talked slowly. It seemed, if you didn't know who she was, that the woman herself had some sort of speech problem. Also she had a habit of spitting when she talked: Little drops of saliva would jump from her lips, landing on Jonathan's forehead and nose; his mouth and cheeks were spared, protected by the milk carton.

The teacher had a name, of course. Jeannie Abrams. A former beauty pageant winner—Miss Oklahoma or Texas or somewhere around there. Her life had been one long road trip, accompanied by a bumptious mother who herself was a former pageant winner and prom queen, back in 19–. A string of messy relationships and unfulfilled dreams is what she would later tell her friends, who would swear that they knew her from somewhere...from where? Oh, yes, that commercial with the woman doing the laundry and buying the groceries and frying the bacon and never ever letting her husband forget that he's a man. *That* woman. No longer under the auspices of her mother, she decided at 32 to drop out of sight and start anew, leaving behind a couple of kids—Jack, 4, and Michelle, 6—with the doting, indulgent in-laws. She looked forward to a much slower pace of life without runways or tap dancing lessons. Dusty awards and medals with brightly colored ribbons cluttered one small shelf above the dresser in her studio apartment on Hudson Street, where a man had been shot the week before she moved in. It didn't make the local news.

Homework required that the milk carton be worn at least one hour each day, before or after, but never during supper. And two hours of practice on Saturdays and Sundays. Jonathan had to read aloud from a list of "trouble" words—words that escaped and challenged him. He practiced so much that the words themselves didn't make much sense. They lost their meanings, their sense of being. *Rumpled? That can't be right*, Jonathan thought. *Rumpled. Rum-pled. Rummmm...pled. That's right. Rumpled.*

After a year, he grew too old to continue milk carton therapy, but he continued practicing without the carton. What made matters even worse was that he firmly believed that he had inherited this horrible and unacceptable speech problem from his real parents, whoever they were. He had a Korean tongue to go with his Korean face. *Give me a normal tongue,* he would pray, *just like Mom and Dad's.* (Even his father had no traces whatsoever of an Irish accent. It was allowed to surface with much bravado one day out of the year, St. Patrick's Day.) Just like the mailman who comes around at noon. Just like his cousins and aunts and uncles. Just like everyone else. English, after all, was his second language. But he could not recall one word of Korean, his native language. *So,* he thought, *how could he have a second language if he couldn't summon up his first language?* This called for some serious thinking, some major problem solving. Jonathan gathered his notebook and pencils and went to his favorite place to think: the weeping willow in front of his house. And he thought *real* hard.

Somewhere, perhaps tucked away in his bedroom closet, was the only possession he had when he arrived in the United States at the age of three. It was something that wasn't expensive or meaningful. Just a colorful striped pouch with a drawstring to keep the things inside from falling out: coins, rings, marbles, candy. A simple object among the rest of his toys and clothes and games. *Throw it out and get rid of the problem,* he thought. Could it be that easy? A modicum of guilt surfaced, and he recanted that last thought. Reason is, he liked that pouch. Throwing it out would be...why, it would be like throwing out his favorite superhero action figure or one of his model cars, which he assiduously assembled and painted. It must be something else. Think...search....

Nothing. His mind wandered: He thought about his father, who showed him how to throw a knuckleball; about his mother's laugh and how contagious it was; and his go-cart painted bright red because red is his favorite color of all time. *These are a few of my favorite things,* he hummed to himself.

Lying under the weeping willow, Jonathan watched as the long, leafy branches swayed in the breeze, back and forth, touching momentarily, as if shaking hands before embracing. *How beautiful those branches are!* he thought. So thin and light yet strong enough that when bunched together he could swing like Tarzan. Rays of afternoon sunlight broke through like flashbulbs, taking snapshots of that moment and saving them in an album somewhere up in the clouds. The grass, still moist from the morning watering, tickled the back of his neck and legs. Jonathan felt the warm splashes of sunlight over his face, and his thoughts quickly dissolved from his lessons to the wonders of the universe. Nothing, it seemed, was more important than watching the leaves sway or perhaps taking a nap on a lazy Sunday afternoon. *Sundays,* he thought, *will always be Sundays. My pronunciation will always be my pronunciation. Miss Abrams will always be a speech teacher. My father will always be Irish. My mother will always tell my father to keep his elbows off the table. The kids in school will always tease me about my almond-shaped eyes and flat nose. The sun will always warm my face. The cap on my pen will always be left behind on the grass when my mother calls me in for supper.*

There, under the immense tree, in front of his house, on the dead-end street, in a town called Deer Park, somewhere in Long Island, Jonathan Flynn, adopted, practiced his *r*'s and *w*'s.

JULIA LEE
How Uncle Dan Got Himself a Wife

Act I: "Uncle Dan's American Dream"

Sponsored by my father, my uncle left South Korea in the spring of 1986 and moved to Los Angeles. Then, his name was *Eun Il*, but he soon adopted the American name *Daniel* in honor of his new country. He was 30 years old, a mild, nebbishy man with clumsy glasses, a flat face, bad teeth and quixotic ideals. He was inordinately shy. His lack of familiarity with the English language and with American customs rendered him even more awkward, more gauche around strangers. He was a confirmed bachelor, timid around women and even young girls like myself, prompting my mother to conclude, with devastating nonchalance, that he was an incurable "nerd."

Uncle Dan moved into our house upon his arrival in the States, ostensibly to help my father in his new business, a fast-food restaurant called Pioneer Chicken. But after three days of training, he quit, telling my father that kitchen work— *women's* work in Korea—just wasn't for him. Impulsively, he bought a ticket to Chicago, hoping to find a job there. He moved in temporarily with a recently married friend from Korea. After four months, though, he was back, driven away by the domestic discord of his friend's marriage and the lack of job prospects.

Chastened, Uncle Dan was rehired as a cook and prep attendant at my father's store, but four months later, he quit again, dissatisfied with the low pay and chafing under his yet-unfulfilled and undirected ambition. He bounced around from job to job in Koreatown, working as a stock boy, a supermarket bagger, a dishwasher. These jobs were all temporary, Uncle Dan insisted. Unlike most recent Korean immigrants who ran liquor stores and restaurants, Uncle Dan deemed such work too humble compared to his own lofty aspirations. So after a year of hapless underemployment, he enrolled in the local School of Oriental Medicine, determined to become a licensed Chinese herbalist and acupuncturist.

During his four years of study, Uncle Dan supplemented his meager income by apprenticing himself as a clerk for a Chinese herb wholesaler. On occasional weekends, my father would bring me over for a visit.

The store was housed in a shabby storefront in an especially drab section of Koreatown. Uncle Dan worked behind the counter, shoveling dried medicinal herbs and animal parts into plastic bags and weighing the quantities for waiting customers. Large, full-color pictures of deer stags and bears and dancing ginseng roots covered the walls, advertising three of the more popular ingredients in Chinese medicine. The antlers of male deer, dried and sliced into round woodlike chips, were said to promote male virility and potency; the gallbladders of bears, ground into a dark powder, were alleged to aid circulation; and the roots of ginseng plants, shredded into sinewy strips, were said to endow the body with recuperative strength and energy. Often, Uncle Dan would scoop together a complimentary bag of *hanyak*, or "healthy herbs" that my mother would then boil for 24 hours in a rigged-up Crock-Pot. The black stew that emerged, thick as crude oil and vilely odiferous, was then forced down my throat. I would hold my nose, cursing my uncle as I gagged on the foul mixture.

Uncle Dan eventually earned his license in Chinese medicine and acupuncture in the early 1990s. He opened a small Chinese herb store in Van Nuys, California, just in time to be hit by the recession. Unable to pay his rent, he closed shop within the year. My exasperated father enjoined him to settle down, citing his fickleness and shiftlessness, but Uncle Dan had another plan. He hadn't yet abandoned his dream to own his own Chinese medicine and acupuncture clinic. Not at all. Rather, he had slightly altered his plan. Several months later, he broke the news to my incredulous father: He was opening up an Oriental medicine shop in Clarksville, Tennessee.

Act II: "Clarksville, TN" or "Uncle Dan's House of Herbs"

Clarksville, Tennessee, is not a place where you imagine there are lots of Korean people. With a population of about 100,000, the town is located in the northern part of the state. The local tourist board hypes it up as "Historic Clarksville," with townies dressed in 18th century garb, hefting around muskets and spinning wheels. A diminutive Korean man is a little odd here, amid the costumed and bewigged ancestors of early American settlers.

Clarksville, however, is only a few miles away from Fort Campbell, an army base on the Kentucky border. Home of the 101st Airborne Division (known during World War II as the Screaming Eagles), the base sustains a substantial population of military officers and personnel previously stationed in countries like – yes – South Korea. When transferred to Fort Campbell, these men brought with them their newly acquired Korean wives, young women transplanted from provincial Korean towns to America's Deep South.

A population of Koreans, however displaced, or confused or small, meant a potential customer base for Uncle Dan. Sure, the U.S. Army provided complete medical care to its servicemen and their families, but that was Western medicine. What Fort Campbell needed was an Oriental medicine specialist. Spying an untapped market, Uncle Dan moved to Clarksville, set up shop and ordered fresh herb supplies from abroad. His only competition was a sole rival acupuncturist. Still, Uncle Dan nearly failed again, giving up once, moving back to Los Angeles, and then returning to Clarksville for another go at his business. The second time proved the charm, and Uncle Dan established a steady, if small, client base among the Korean wives of American servicemen. The women came in regularly for their own customized blend of *hanyak*, and I imagined their husbands' horrified expressions as they boiled the strange herbs in their tiny kitchens and then quaffed the nasty stew.

Although his customers were predominantly women, Uncle Dan was still awkward with the ladies. He was well past 40 now, still single, and still painfully shy, though no longer so impoverished or unsuccessful. On his own, he had sub-scribed to Korean matchmaking services in the hopes of wooing a potential mate, but to my father, he complained that Korean women always snubbed him. Even now that he was steadily employed, he wasn't so compelling a catch; he made an exceedingly modest living that barely allowed for the support of another person. So Uncle Dan continued to live as a bachelor, frugally and solitarily.

In 1997, more than 10 years after he arrived in the United States, Uncle Dan became a naturalized American citizen, finally and firmly joining himself to his new country. He now ran his own business, leased a small single-family home near the army base and drove his own car. In honor of his newly won citizenship and his modest American success, Uncle Dan allowed himself a minor indul-gence, an indulgence that would eventually and dramatically complete his American dream. With a portion of his savings, he purchased a new desktop com-puter and a subscription to AOL.

Act III: "My Aunt Olga" or "email Order Brides"
A year passed, and Uncle Dan sent my father an email. He had important news, he announced. He was getting married. To a woman he had met through an inter-national matchmaking service on the Internet.

"Mail-order brides"—or "email-order brides"—conjures up images of doughy, white-trash American guys and desperate but nubile women from China or Korea or Vietnam, women who latch onto an American, eager for that green card and the chance at a new life. My uncle was an American man, but not white. His mail-order bride was foreign, but not from East or Southeast Asia. No, Uncle Dan's bride was from the Ukraine. Her name? Olga.

In the past several months, Uncle Dan explained, he had registered with a matchmaking service and had initiated email correspondence with three or four Ukrainian women. At the urging of the head of the service, he had booked a trip to Odessa, spending a few days "getting to know" his email pen pals. How much communication occurred is difficult to gauge, given that the Ukrainians did not speak English and my uncle did not speak Russian, but at the end of the visit, my uncle had taken a liking to Olga, a 27-year-old college graduate employed as a chemist. She liked him too, apparently, and they decided to get married just as soon as she arrived in the States.

In the end, it took almost six months for Uncle Dan to fill out the necessary paperwork to get Olga home to Tennessee. There, the relationship did not get off to an auspicious start. Uncle Dan was a parsimonious bachelor, vigilantly aware of expenses and waste of any sort. Olga heedlessly left lights on and water running. Dan spent his free time at home, watching TV or tinkering with his computer. Olga only wanted to go shopping so she could "buy more cosmetics." Dan had difficulty understanding Olga's Russian-accented English, and Olga had trouble deciphering Dan's Korean-accented English. My uncle complained to my father, who responded, "If it's so bad, then send her back!"

So Dan tried. He told Olga that things weren't working out, that he would pay her airfare back home. But Olga wept, wailing that she would kill herself if Dan forced her to return to Odessa. She vowed to contain her indulgent tendencies and pleaded for a second chance. In the face of such earnest contrition and desperation, Dan hesitated, retreated, contemplated. He wrote my father a terse email, concluding, "Now I have to marry her. I have no choice. She'll kill herself if I don't."

Uncle Dan set a late August wedding date. The proposed location for the ceremony? Where else? Las Vegas.

Now *I* began to wail. "Dad!" I yelped. "That's so tacky and wrong! I mean, why Las Vegas? Tennessee is bad enough, but *Vegas*?"

"Uncle Dan thinks that's where Americans usually get married," my father explained.

I pouted, then announced, "You know what? If we were white, we'd be white trash. But we're not, so what does that make us? Yellow trash?"

The rest of the family treated the news with similar astonishment and disapproval. "She's only marrying you for the green card," my aunts warned Dan. "She'll leave you as soon as she gets her American citizenship," my uncle is cautioned.

In the end, angered by his family's lack of support, Uncle Dan ditched the Las Vegas wedding altogether. Instead, he had a quickie ceremony at the local courthouse, informing us via email that it was too late to stop him. He was now legally married in the state of Tennessee, and the ceremony happened to be free, to boot. He sent us wedding pictures with the email, but they took so long to download that my father deleted the files rather than waiting to get a look at his new sister-in-law.

In the months following the marriage, Uncle Dan lapsed into sullen email silence, maintaining sporadic communication with one of my aunts in Korea but remaining estranged from the rest of the family. I placed bets with my sister on how long the marriage would last. "Three months," she guessed. "Six," I responded. "Do you think we'll ever meet Aunt Olga?" she asked. "No," I scoffed.

Postscript: "My Tennessee Cousin"
Over the summer, news about Uncle Dan filtered back to us through the aunt in Korea. Aunt Olga, it turns out, was pregnant. She was due to have a baby girl in September.

Surprised and uncertain, my aunts and uncles debated how to respond. Ashamed at their previous lack of graciousness, they quietly assembled baby clothes and money to herald the imminent birth, tentatively taking the first steps toward welcoming Aunt Olga and Uncle Dan back into the family.

My father asked if I would like to contribute anything to the package. I hesitated, but he gently reminded me of my high school graduation and Uncle Dan's gift to me back then.

I had forgotten. It was the spring of 1994, and Uncle Dan was about to leave for Tennessee for his second and final attempt to establish a Chinese medicine shop. At the last minute, we had invited him to my graduation, and at the reception, a tea dance held on the school's front lawn, Uncle Dan had stood uncomfortably on the lawn's periphery, dressed in an ill-fitting suit with a program clutched tightly in his hand. I remember seeing him there, sweaty and stiff, surrounded by 80 recently graduated girls in white voile dresses reminiscent of debutante ball or wedding gowns, and I remember thinking, "That man is in hell."

Uncle Dan endured the postgraduation socializing for several minutes before skirting out. But before leaving, he awkwardly approached me with a graduation gift wrapped in heavy, glossy white paper and tied with a gold ribbon. I tore off the wrapping and opened the package. Inside was a heavy black bottle of Chanel No. 5 perfume.

It was an odd gift to give a 17-year-old girl, strangely intimate and endearingly earnest, but wildly inappropriate given my adolescent tastes. Spritzing some on my wrist, I inhaled the musky fragrance of middle-aged matrons, wealthy dowagers, Rodeo Drive socialites. Thanking Uncle Dan and watching him leave, I turned around and gagged at my sister, who laughed in response. The bottle lay untouched on my dresser as I returned to my drugstore fragrances, my juvenile Tea Rose and Calyx.

Now I berated myself for my ingratitude and wondered if Uncle Dan had ever bought Aunt Olga perfume. I was certain she would respond with greater appreciation. I thought of Uncle Dan's new daughter, my cousin: American-born, half-Ukrainian, half-Korean, to be fed on Chinese herbs and raised in the debutante terrain of Tennessee. The unlikelihood of it all made me laugh. Uncle Dan had fulfilled his American dream, albeit in an unexpected, even absurd, fashion. He had remade himself. The hopeless bachelor's life was now full of women, and I heartily wished him luck.

And then, of course, I pitched in for the baby gift.

return

ISHLE YI PARK
Maehyangri

Here the road curls into shoulder of rice paddy,
window air drunk against my hair. The taxi driver
jerks and stops, jerks and stops, over loose gravel, hesitant
to take us any farther. You students, hiss, like danger.

Mesh tent billows over terracotta dust and 700 students
sit in hunched waves, fingers wet with subak,
singing minyohs memorized years before I arrived:

there, the barbed wire, wrapped with pink tissue
like blooming kosmos, and through its looped folds
an expanse of green outstretched lover, limbs
supple, Maehyangri; she lies breathless,

sun a white disk in indifferent sky
I snap pictures of do-or-die students, handkerchiefed against tear gas,
dressed to go to Orchard Beach more than a rally....

There, a woman in front of barbed fence, baby strapped with blanket
to bent back, and northwest, a farmer poking police
an arm's length away from her trodden crops

and the students are rioting, riot boys brandish
their sapling sticks and branded with confusion we swing at each other,
each crack stippling my ears, we swing at each other:

my young Korean brother, of split cheekbone and torn shirt,
my young Korean sister, fingers scissored with wire cuts,
we are killing each other again. Helenah, hold my hand

 a young man stumbles out, eyes feral and wild,
I hold him up gently, blood seeping through my fingers,
soothe him with banmal, yah, illu wah, genchanah, and we
inhabit a quilted space, cupped moment of healing.

And I realize, what I want is this:
a moment for his split wood carving cheek to heal
respite, for this bruised, beautiful valley to heal
for the marrow of my people tainted with pollution
and shaking from vibrations of dropped U.S. bombs, to heal

for babies with cotton-stuffed ears,
for children who lull to engine hums of 747s,
a silence so clean it baptizes.

Here is the sun, a white eyelid indifferent
to the dust rising from its fields. An ajumma,
baby backwrapped and tending to the mound graves
of her loved ones. Han Lae Sook. Here are my sister's palms
shredded like blossoms.... Hold them. Tight. Like this.

SUN YUNG SHIN
Lessons from Mr. Kim

We American girls took a night taxi with Mr. Kim
to a strip club in Seoul.
Mr. Kim laughed and put his hand on our legs.
We knew Koreans were supposed to be affectionate....
We drank *soju* –
and never knew potatoes could be that lethal –
while near-naked women danced in glass cages
suspended above our heads,
traveling on a track around the dark room
like a motorized mobile of giant dolls.
Mr. Kim pointed to the red curtains,
men parted them like private lips
and disappeared.
He laughed as though he would never stop –

Back home his wife washed dinner dishes,
his gray-haired mother slept,
the daughters studied.
I was not his daughter, but
oh, I was studying, too.

PEGGY HONG
Red Ginger

Honolulu, 1968

The classroom door is still locked. A girl hangs on the bars of the jungle gym. *Ab-ba* brings me here, then drives away. I wait until Miss Okino comes. The girl waves to me and calls me over. I am not yet used to my "American" name. She's not Korean like me, but she's something like me. This morning she waves me over.

She's something like me. She looks like she would understand my words. But I know she will not. I remember her from Miss Okino's class. The girl climbs to the top of the jungle gym and she waves. Miss Okino says I'm "the new girl."

My words seem strange here. As strange as my favorite red shoes and the *kimpap Om-ma* packs for my lunch. My clothes are funny and stiff. I listen, but keep my own mouth shut. The girl waves me over. I climb halfway up the monkey bars. Her mouth moves in ways I've never seen. She calls me by my American name. She hangs on the bars of the jungle gym talking and chewing.

Her tongue is red, her name is Marie. Marie gets dropped off early each morning. She is alone on the monkey bars when *Ab-ba* brings me here, then drives away. I listen to her words, I watch the shapes of her mouth, her bright red tongue the same color as my shoes.

She hangs upside down, then pulls her dress up and tucks the skirt between her knees. Her arms hang down. A little plastic sack of something red in her hand almost touches the wet grass. Her name is Marie. I am "the new girl." She swings herself up, opens the bag and holds it out to me. She is something like me, but she is not like me.

"Ginger," she says. Then she repeats, slowly, when I do not respond. "*Gin-ger.* You like some?"

She shows me how to eat it. Her tongue is red, her name is Marie. She takes a pinch in her fingertips as red as her tongue and puts the red strips into her mouth. She licks her fingers.

"You like?" she asks again as she chews.

I take a pinch and chew like she does. I ask, "*Ginger?*"

This thing in this new land. This girl on the jungle gym. This taste in my mouth. The teacher is not here yet. The grass is still wet. This red ginger, sweet, hurts my teeth, and spicy, burns my mouth. I chew a long time, wondering what to do with it. *Ginger.* I am not yet used to my American name.

Everyday, these words.

It burns when I swallow. Marie watches me chew and holds the bag out again.

Everyday, more words. *Ginger*, Marie's red tongue. The shape of her mouth as she talks and chews. *Ab-ba* brings me here, then drives away. Miss Okino says I'm "the new girl."

Marie laughs, says, "Just swallow it!" and offers me more. She talks and chews. I listen, take more. My red shoes get darker from the wet grass. I chew, I swallow.

HUN OHM
Michigan Tryptich: 1977-78

I. Sister

Narae is not a smart girl and has to try hard in school, just to get checks. But sometimes getting pluses is not the only thing, and then she's all right. In fact, she's just fine.

Like the time when we are down near Haystock's pier, when there are three big silvery kings who have lost their way and are flopping in the shallows. It is my sister who takes off her red buckle shoes and chases those fish back into deeper water, a little cowgirl mermaid soaking herself up her knees, a shimmering blue in a deeper blue that leads to indigo and green and black. She is a shepherdess and doesn't think twice about saving some fish that are bound for the cannery anyway.

She is a funny girl in a lot of ways, but then again, she's my sister, and maybe siblings have stories of expansion and contraction, of distraction that make them real to no one but ourselves. Which is too bad, because it is private, then, and it is boring.

But then there is the time when we are at our friend Park's—a mutual friend because my sister and I are close in age and young and still new in the neighborhood and limited in friends—we are in the basement and look at old paintings that the dentist father has squirreled away in order to sell later in life at auction, forty thousand dollars for the most prized. There is a dust in the basement that covers everything, and cobwebs hang in the strangest way in every corner. But we are young and accomplices and unafraid of horror show filth. We explore the terrain and make fingerprint masterpieces on dusted canvas.

My sister moves next to me and whispers in my ear. She tells me that the dust that covers everything is not dust at all, but really one trillion people, shrunk to size, so small that we need telescopes to see them cry.

But why, I ask her. Why are they small, like stars, like a shiny pin that no one knows in the bottom of a tube that no one sees? How can they grow so small?

My sister wrinkles her eyebrows and waits a while. I wait for her answer, because I will believe her. She is older and knows these things. She has the right to tell. It's because they aren't people like we know, she says. They're old, from ten million years ago. And they came here from Pluto on sailing ships.

I lean back onto a table and don't say anything. My sister is telling me about things I don't know, and I'm not about to interrupt.

And on the way, she goes on, on the way they started to shrink, because it's really cold in space and the sun is so far away that it's like a piece of corn.

She measures out a kernel of corn with her fingertips, to show me what she means. Between her dusty fingers, the space is very small. I am convinced that it must've been cold.

And my sister continues, because she knows I am listening. During the journey, she says, many people died because they forgot to bring blankets, and others died because of sadness, thinking they would never see the people, the friends and cousins that they had left behind. When the survivors finally reached the sky on earth, they dropped the dead bodies from the ships, whole communities wrapped tight in white tape, because this was their tradition on Pluto, and they watched the bodies fall down to the ground and waved good-bye.

My sister gathers the dust with her fingertips and lets it sprinkle down on our canvas a little at a time. She takes a hold of my fingers and then lifts them up gently, out of the dust, one at a time. This was the first time it snowed on earth, she says. And every year since, the dust people take all their dead and bring them up to the sky and let them fall back to the ground as they say bye-bye.

She is done with the story and looks at me. She nods her head to show me that it is true. I just stand there in that basement and look at those old paintings all faded and dying, choking on Pluto people who have no home, who have become so small that no one can see them unless they look really hard, through telescopes that can't even make a dot of light as big as corn. I feel a little dizzy, but maybe it's just the air in the basement. It's really musty here, and I tell my sister I want to go home.

Out in the open air, it's snowing, because it is January and we live in Michigan, and my sister and I start to walk along the road that leads home. And then, all of a sudden, I start bawling, I don't know why, maybe because I'm six and only a kid, or maybe because I've forgotten my scarf and my cheeks are cold. Either way, I can't stop, and I just stand there in the road and cry to kingdom come.

So my sister, she bends down and wraps my arms around her neck. And then she lifts me into the air, on her back, above the ground, and she carries me down the road. She can do this, because she's my older sister and bigger than me, and just a little bit stronger too. And she keeps going, even though it's snowing like crazy and my face is buried into her neck because the wind is blowing and stings my tears really bad. And when we reach our front porch, I look up, finally, and see the snowflakes still falling, though actually now, on my front porch, I see that they don't fall at all but really that they float, slowly, softly, in a drift, one-two-three, quiet, and then gone. And my sister, she stands next to me, looks me over. She brushes off the snow and says it's time to go inside where it's warm.

Narae is a strange girl, and she's not beside me anymore. But even though she's far away, in a place bluer than cold, she's my sister, and I love her.

I just wanted you to know.

II. Stars
For Callisto and Arcas
The Great Bear and the Bear Warden
My mama says that she's a bear, waves her hands like paws, her broken fingernails like broken claws, in front of my eyes so that I might see how a mama bear might wake her sleeping cub. And the forest outside still dreaming in the color of dew, because it's before morning and sunshine and even the little sparrows sleep with

one eye closed, one eye open like this, see? And then day comes before you know it, and you might miss it after all if you sleep too late like I like to do. You might miss the day that follows night like a kite tail, behind its footsteps, inside its tracks my mama saying little one, still dreaming, are you?

Little bear baby with eyes like the dark. Hair standing straight like I'm kitty cat scared by scary things even though I'm not, because I'm a big boy and can sleep by myself and could always, well not always, but for a long time like ten trillion years. So I'm not even a little bit scared. It's just that my mama cuts my hair because she can, and we don't have to pay $6.50 for Joe's Little Man-Big Man, Back to School-Back to Work Special, even though Johnny Park says that you get a green gum ball if you're good and don't say ouch when Joe snips your ear because he's too busy looking at your mommy's boobies.

But sometimes my mama's not a bear waving her paws for minnows inside a stream. Sometimes she's a red rainbow bending across the sky, and with her arms outstretched she is reaching and reaching because there are three gold coins underneath the deep sea, and you might find them, yes, if you can hold your breath real long. Which I try until my mama smacks my bottom and says I look all silly turning cherry like the sun. But well, that's not all she can do.

Because sometimes in the market near the pig heads stand, or next to the kitchen stove where she cooks me tasties that I like to eat, my mama's not just a rainbow sinking down into the silent sea. No, she's the whole blue sky who says she won't ever fade away, tells me my papa is flying across to faraway lagoons where the mermaid sings, not coming home soon because he must work so hard and through and through. And why?

Because he's your papa and will always love you more than dried seaweed rolls with soup. This you remember, don't you?

And so my mama says when she gives me rice in water mixed with Spam, third time today because I'm always hungry and ask for more, or when she watches newlyweds whoop about refrigerators, five-thirty sharp on channel five, seven o'clock next if you missed it first time. But my mama never misses no, not ever, so we get to watch together two times not one, and that's the best because we're champions and through our crystal balls know all the answers second time round.

These gray mornings inside the old stone church with its arch and spiral, behind the wood bolt doors that lead to heaven, where Luke and Mark and that little one Jesus stare in gold and diamonds, my mama takes me to light a candle in grace's corners. And I don't have to wear no Sunday best, because my mama says I'm beautiful just the way I am. Yes, I am, I'm beautiful like a baby bear, with eyes so small you might miss them shine unless you don't forget to look real close like this, with one eye closed through a telescope, see?

And what if I want to blow out all those candles, more than I've ever seen?

Or when I hide underneath the pews when my mama talks so quiet to the old priest in black and says there's another one coming, what can she do? It's OK, dear Papa, who is art and heaven, I won't ever tell I've seen the sad moon of you. But I'll hold you deep inside my belly button like this until it grows hot air balloon round like my mama's middle, and then I'll float so high and fine I might disappear. Into these nights when you're still sleeping in the dark dark shadows, with your crescent face so skinny because sometimes it is, and the clouds around your eyes like purple grapes you can't see through unless you suck off the skin. You'll say, Oh, I've been asleep so long it's like a dream. And it will be because I'll be out of sight of your beams like a bear in night's dew.

Over there in a corner, with her hands stretched forward, my mama kneels before the kingdoms just how she's learned to do. And here's me, writing in the Bible book because they have little pencils here cut so short it looks like I have Big Man hands, and I can draw dear Jesus, words in pictures like the naughty pharaohs do. Here's a donkey blind in the winter's desert, and there's Mary waiting for sweet providence to guide her to the stable. And the sky's so big it can eat stars and has room for more, seconds and thirds because right there, and there and everywhere there's a bunch of black light that growls like my mama's tummy when it hurts bad at night, because it's kicking and growing even when she sleeps.

And if she can't sleep even at three o'clock, I lie next to my mama who has arms like a jungle gym with crossing bars I can hold real good so we won't fall down and skin our knees when we dream. Which happens sometimes, and hurts even though I don't ever say so or cry, because I am big enough and can hold so tight that I must close my eyes and count to 892 while the moon flies bye-bye like a kite broke loose into the wind. Sinking deep and deep in my mouth like moon gumdrops so sweet until I spit.

When my mama crosses herself before the altar, she says a prayer. She says, Father, bless your children, who are lost and frightened without you. And then she clasps her hands together and says amen. But dear Papa not me, not ever me, though I might disappear underneath the new lights of day. Not even on these moonless nights though they might hold me tight like there's no tomorrow.

Because with your eyes closed we're shifting, won't you see these glowings?

So high in the soft sky, even after three. See my hair like fur full with dia-mond's dust and gold. Tipped with honey and straight, so straight through the clouds like rainbows and spires and candle's grace. See me sleep, my eyes black pearls, drifting slow and deep to sunken ships and sea horses and seaweed beds, swaying gently in the wake like a mermaid's tale, dreaming this life our own above the bottoms of the sea. Where I don't need to leave for breath. No, I won't ever say good-bye.

And during these mornings, my mama, she tells me things. Says she's spoken to God who sees everything and knows, knows just how we're doing. She says, Angel, wake up, you can't sleep like this underneath the pews.

Well, sometimes my mama doesn't talk like a great bear, or a rainbow, or a small bear even, and sometimes she misses, I think, maybe more than me. But that's alright, I hold onto her fingertips just the same. We're all by ourselves, you see. In telescopes. Clear nights.

These stars.

III. Snow

Believe it or not, it was true. It was the end of December and there hadn't been a snowflake for the whole of winter. No icicles, no snowmen, nothing but dry yellow grass. There was some grown-up talk of an Indian summer, but us kids knew better. Mid-Michigan winter had something waiting. We knew he wouldn't let us down.

When it first started that afternoon, you couldn't ask for a prettier scene. Big, white flakes the size of Susan B. Anthony's, floating down from the clouds in that big lazy way. Driving the yellow bus back from Cook Elementary, Mrs. Pinkle had to stop twice and slop the windshield clean with her flannel sleeves. But even she didn't seem to mind the weather. We watched her look up at the sky, counting out loud, mapping the path of the cold front with her coal eyes. She stuck out her tongue and caught a few like a winter princess. Not that there was any mistaking her for the crabby battle-ax that she was. Mrs. Stinkle is what we called her. A million years old with her gray grease hair wrapped loose in a bandana. Still, the way she was smiling through her tobacco teeth as she gazed at all the whiteness, you could've sworn she was a kid like us some century ago.

By evening, it was plain we wouldn't be going anywhere the next day. My sister and me pressed our noses against the family room window and breathed fog onto the glass. There was a foot and a half on the ground, and it was getting colder. My sister said all the Christmas lights would be veiled by white that year. I wasn't about to disagree. Our mama brought us hot cocoa in Santa Claus mugs and smiled when she saw the fingertip drawings we had made in our breath. She told us it was nice like this, quiet without any wind to talk over. A grown-up thing, I guess, I didn't care one way or another. All night long I thought of the snowmen we would dig from the ground. I dreamt of our school bus disappearing forever, blanketed by the unmelting snow.

No one knew how it all began. Maybe it was when he stumbled through the front door full of rye fumes. Or there's the story of how it was really the other women's snow he tracked in with his Ski-Doo boots, over and over, paying no mind to hide it for all those years. No one knew for certain, but Mrs. Pinkle did it that night. She hacked him up, her old man. Bless her heart, she sent him off to the Promised Land.

Some said it split clean like a melon rind. Others said it was more a splattering of sorts, like she was using the thick, block end. Who knows, that was all later, after the snow melted and they found him stiff-backed behind their propane tank. There wasn't much of him by that time—something had found him first and gnawed off most his skin. But one thing was for sure. The man was dead, six times with a hatchet atop that old geezer head.

When they brought her in to ask why she'd done it, Mrs. Pinkle didn't give it much thought to say, No, it wasn't me. She just shrugged and curled her greasy locks around a withered finger. She said it was about time for snowflakes that winter. She said she'd been waiting for them to fall a long, long while. Then she stood up tall and proud. She nodded her head, and they led her away.

I don't know, maybe it was the older kids in the back of the bus who started it. Maybe it was just a nursery tale. But back then, there was a saying that started going around. "If you're looking for a bit of snow," it began, "just make sure you don't bring it in with you from the cold. Because slam-slam thank you ma'am, it'll melt all around you in the end." They made a song of it. They taught it to the little ones, to my sister and me. And we laughed. We sang it from the top of our lungs.

Funny, that's the way she and I made sense of it all.

Everything in Michigan, I mean.

SOO JIN OH
Landscape, Five Years Later

This is our landscape.
Bourgeois, heartbreakingly suburban;
                    these are the ashes we rise from.
                        Charles Wright

1.
Day after a night long high,
out your window looking toward Beta House,
spring comes late to Chenango Valley:
willows threading green,
sunlight paring down.
Cigarette hand half-in, half-out:
we watch ashes flicker down to parking lot
where parents are packing children into cars,
a flow of *good-byes* and *nice meeting yous*,
the parents familiar with each other
for being strangers in this rural town.
Their summer suits and dresses
are rumpled, their tans darker
for sitting through four hours
of name roll calling by Taylor Lake.
The graduates peer behind sunglasses,
smile for the video cam.

This, after finals and senior week parties:
classic rock, Old Milwaukee,
cardigan sets, ties and navy blazers
discarded on beer floors. There is the sense
of everything being discarded: fold-up chairs,
the choir disbanding, professors stripping
out of doctoral robes. And even the grass,
watered with champagne and last fall's cider,
will be cut tomorrow. The graduate smiles
are rather old, saying *glad to leave.*

2.
You say to me:
Doesn't it make you sad, you know.
The parents. They look so young.
It makes me angry.

3.
1990, we arrived.
From Queens, New York, we arrived.
A babble of tongues we arrived.
From hooky days, cigarette bathroom floors, fenced in schoolyards we
arrived.
Black jeans, black shirts, black shoes, black hair, black eyes we arrived.
From concrete night discotechs, all night cafés we arrived.
A jangle of ads ads ads plastered ten stories high on our foreheads we
arrived.
With a plethora of words out the mouths of street con artists and ready-made
money we arrived.

From our parents we arrived.
Our parents' fingers ringing the cash register we arrived.
With our parents' stories of failed small businesses, street vendors, con
artists, fast lost money we arrived.
Walking the streets searching for our parents' stories until our bodies
wearied we arrived.
With lost tongues we arrived.
Parentless, we arrived.
Parentless, we graduated.

4.

What have we graduated from?
The year we arrived, the willows were ready-old
and diseased, cut down early October
before the first snowstorm. Spring,
a once classics major now financier alumni
donated saplings, a genus which winter stripped
bare to red branches. We walked
between the willows, sometimes together,
mostly alone, up Cardiac Hill to Academic Quad.
The chapel's domed Golden Nipple
shone like its own moon and sun. Once
I laid a hand, hesitantly, on the new bark –
white flesh just under: veneer that summer greyed,
bark the years toughened. Is it worth noting
that something like that grew in a place like there?

5.

Flushing, Queens,
your father lay dying until he did die.
You flew the body to another country,
to a severe landscape.

BENJAMIN H. HAN
(words are loose)

Bullet in the head. 1950. Korean War. What do you do? He clutched his head roughly. His fingernails entering his skull. Eyes tightly shut, but mouth wonderfully open. Yellow-white teeth. Scream until the mountains burn. GET OFF MY LAND! Scream louder. THIS IS MY LAND! THIS IS MY LAND! They don't seem to care. Maybe you should give them your land. Be Quiet! Do not speak and maybe they will not kill you.

Fine, then just rant and let them shoot your head off. They would have anyway.

In 1996 Mommy is dying. She's possessed by the words of her grandfather. I can tell because she is yelling. She never yells. Mommy is kneeling on her bed clutching her head and then pulling out her hair. Her brain is bleeding. She is crying because the pain is too awful, and words are flowing from her head to her mouth, profusely in Korean.

Curse me, Mother, for I do not understand these words.

I cannot understand any of the Korean words of my great-grandfather and mother. They are familiar, but I cannot translate them. I do not really want to know them. When I sit on a bus in Korea, I see these words. When I pick up my father's newspaper, I see them again. Whenever I see Korean words, I see the same words my great-grandfather yelled before he was shot, and the echo my mother yelled. Words in a different language, words that are so familiar, but completely out of my reach. These are words that have carried themselves through time to surround me.

Can a bullet travel through time? No, but words can. Watch:

Point a gun to my great-grandfather's head. Listen to his words. Pitiful, isn't he? Can't he die like a man? Shoot. Yes, just shoot. His words are gone, are they not? Where did they go? Can they just disappear? My mother is watching. Staring because that is all a six-year-old can do. Destroy a head. Migrate. Shoot a head. Move.

One week later my mother is with her grandmother 500 miles south of the farm. Actually, 502 because they are sitting on a dark boat off the coast of Pusan, waiting for the Korean War to end. They cannot speak on the boat. There are forty other people on the boat, and no one can speak. My mother sits on the dark boat, eyes wide open, and the only words on the boat are her grandfather's.

Three days on the wooden boat was enough time for the words to lodge themselves nicely between the neurons in my mother's head. Sleeping. Dormant. It would be 46 years until they exploded in her poor skull and curiously land into my arm. It would take 46 years, missed opportunities, and extensive traveling throughout time.

The words should have detonated a lot earlier if not for my own powers. By the time I was nine years old, I was able to create earthquakes. One day, out in the backyard of our house in bucolic Ohio, I began banging the ground with my aluminum bat. I hit the ground hard with all my anger to prove my power. Then it started to rain, and I went inside, leaving my strength in the ground. The television was on inside, and my father was watching the local news. He told me there had just been a slight earthquake in Southern Ohio. I did not know it then, but the words were too scared to leak out, they had to wait.

I was born in Cincinnati, Ohio, so it was my land, but I hated my land. And it did not like me. The town I grew up in was tiny and filled with woods. I use to run through those woods, finding arrowheads and running through my backyard until I got to the small, brownish, warm pond. Perfect for skipping rocks or finding frogs. I would stare at the pond. I wanted to know what was beneath it, to see if I could escape my town to another place below. I was aching to get out, and the words knew that. The arrowheads knew that.

THIS IS MY LAND! Words spoken in Korean. Words caught in my mother's head. Delicately stuck between her brain cells. But before they found a place in her head, they had displaced her, 500 miles south and eventually to the United States. They had caused her migrations and were waiting to be released ever since my birth, to physically move me and cause my own movements. The problem was, I wanted to move.

The words could not have anticipated my family's move back to Korea, the motherland. It was 1995, and tension within the Korean peninsula was making headlines across the world. North Korea had its nuclear weapons, and South Korea had its economic power. It was a coarse homecoming for my mother, with her grandfather's land in enemy territory north of the 38th parallel, the Demilitarized Zone. But the words in my mother's head had no intention of going back to the family farm. There was nothing there but a body with a silenced head. A dead body cannot move. Can decaying bodies force others into movement? No, but words can.

We settled in Seoul, in an apartment building high above a city that was once farmland and was now littered with neon lights. My parents were finally home after years of movement, migration and places. Korea had changed since they left, with its rapid modernization, economic growth and money. Things were growing too fast in South Korea, and my parents were quick to join in. It seemed like there was something there that had been waiting for them all those years. Meanwhile the words of my great-grandfather, still resting in my mother's head, could not even begin to grasp the full circle that was taking place. The words were back to where they were constructed. Words do not like circles, they like progression, and my great-grandfather's words especially love movement.

I was bound to be next. The one to carry on the words forward through time and place. It was my great-grandfather's way of holding onto the land, instead of losing it again and again throughout time. I was the obvious choice. I came to Korea not knowing a word of the Korean language. There were no words for me to speak in Korea. Pretending to be reticent, but in fact being awkward and silent. Taxi drivers lectured me on not knowing Korean, my relatives yelled at me for having no Korean words, and even the Burger King cashiers wondered why I could not ask for American food with the proper words. I had no Korean words, and a magical force was going to give me some. I am family.

Someone should have been able to guess that South Korea could not hold its quick economic ascent without consequences. I could not have been able to guess that my mother's head would hemorrhage for no apparent reason. Even the words could not have guessed they would finally be freed from my mother's skull.

Between 1995 and 1996, things were quite literally falling in South Korea. A major bridge collapsed and killed three dozen people during the early morning rush hour. A pink department store collapsed to the ground one hot summer day, killing many people. Crumbling quickly to the ground. Korea was not able to hold its own because it had grown too fast. I sat in my apartment with things falling all around me, and I did not care. One year removed from the United States, I was homesick, angry and mute. But I wanted to stay put because America was too far away then, and I wanted things to fall. I wanted my apartment building to fall. In my unhappiness, I did not want to move. I wanted to fall. I was satisfied watching U.S. Army television and not moving. I was not nearly as strong as I had been in Ohio. My great-grandfather's words felt betrayed that things were falling apart in Korea and that I wanted them to. It was time, but I did not want my mother to die.

There it comes again, my mother's screams. Her grandfather's words finally decided to explode that year, to remove themselves from uselessness, from just watching, and to rise up in a wondrous cloud of destruction:

Bleed. Let blood flow and let the words out. Slip out between the hiding spots in my mother's head, cut your way out, slit holes, brain cells are just brain cells, and pain is just pain. She is dying, and I am the only one who can hear her screams. She does not sound like a woman. She does not sound like a man. She does not sound like my great-grandfather. She sounds like words escaping. On her bed kneeling as her brain is imploding or exploding. Holding her head just as my great-grandfather did almost fifty years before, she screams for hours until she lands perfectly on the bed. Her bloody brain empty of the words of her grandfather, which had occupied her head for so many years. And I cannot take this. I cannot sit still anymore, mute, wishing for things to fall down. I run out the door. It is morning already, and I have been up all night listening. Letting the words chase me. I run down the stairs. I pass the singing milkman. And I run to the river and I sit, letting the words infiltrate.

But there's a problem – I do not understand the words.

I could not sit still in Korea while my mother was dying. I should have sat by her hospital bed before she had brain surgery. But I was stuck with all these words, now free to roam around me, and almost forcing me elsewhere. I needed to get out. I needed to flee. Random almost. Migrating anywhere. The words were awful. They were moving me away from one dying person to another.

I met her at the largest tree in the world. She continuously tried to cover her skin because she burns easily. I bought her a bottle of lime soda, and we drank. On the ride back to the city, a short woman pushed me off the train. I landed on dark dirt as the crowded train moved along. She got off the train with me. We went to see Mother Theresa, but she wasn't there. She was in Rome, and so we decided to work until she came back.

Home of the Dying. Or was it Millet's Angelus?

At the home, I made friends with a dying man. He was young, and all he had were broken bones. His body was frail and cold. We talked for hours about people who die. He told me that words were meant to haunt people. Words hexed him. His brother yelling at the top of his lungs as he drove his motorcycle to his death. My friend never forgot those words, and now he was starving to death. I told him that words cause migrations, trade patterns, and movements across nations. He did not believe me. All he said was, there is nothing you can do but sleep on the streets.

Then he died in the middle of my great Ernie Banks 500th home run story. He was going to die anyway, but I suppose he didn't want to listen to my America anymore. But I wanted to know more about his words. He asked me to buy him some cigarettes. I went out and bought a pack of imported cigarettes with a bottle of lime soda. The nuns yelled at me and removed the presents from my hands. That's when I started with my Ernie Banks story, empty-handed.

His body was wrapped in white sheets. I carried it out into the street. It was heavier than I thought it would be. His body was filled with words, and now I have some of them. What could I do with all these words? They weren't in me yet, but they were tormenting me. Did someone die? Maybe it was wrong of us to do what we did that night. I had just met her earlier that day at the big tree, and death usually is followed with a sense of austerity.

Jumping off the walls.
Liquor diffused in our brains. Jump.
Two foreigners in India.

Ha!

Made love in the bathroom. Turned the water on so the dead wouldn't hear. So the words wouldn't hear. Did someone die? She told me that I had to transgress, to distinguish sad from happy, and forget from forgot. Was my mother dying?

There was nothing I could do but listen to my dead friend. I slept on the streets later that night. I wandered to a giant bridge over the river. A man asked if he could clean my ear. It's too dark, I told him. He left me alone. I slept on the streets with dusty ears, alone.

I went back to Korea and forgot all about the words; my great-grandfather's words, my mother's words, and my dead friend's words. I thought about dead bodies and dead motorcycles. My mother had survived her brain surgery with only a small amount of brain damage from the escape route of the words. Her hair was shaved off, and a scar was left from the exit the words had taken. Where had the words gone?

One week after arriving home in Seoul, life was wordless. Nothing was falling down. My mother was alive, but my friend was dead. I missed him. Then my arm started to grow larger and larger with an infection. The words had found a place in my arm, and it was my turn for surgery.

The doctors told me a spider had bitten me, but I knew better. They cut out the overwhelming amounts of yellow and white infection from my arm. During the surgery I passed out, landing on the hospital floor, seeing nothing but static. I thought I was dying. The doctors made an error by leaving a one-inch hole in my arm, where the infection had been. Now there was an empty space just waiting for something to fill it. And something would occupy the small rounded rectangle in middle portion of my arm. There was only one thing that really could.

THIS IS MY LAND! My great-grandfather yelled in Korean before he was shot in the head. These are the words that began migrations in my family. The words that made my mother flee south and eventually to the United States, because she had lost her only sense of home. The words found a semipermanent location in her head, sleepy and tired. I believe they would have stayed lodged in her head if she had not migrated back to Korea. Eventually they would have filtered into American soil, thousands of miles away from my great-grandfather's small farm in northern Korea, whenever my mother would inevitably die. But by moving to Korea, she had gone almost full circle in time and in place. Something was disrupted, and I would be next in line to receive the words.

So now I have these words in my arm. Words that are accustomed to moving. I want to move with them. Sometimes I move, and sometimes I let the words move. With the words, I am aware of movement. I am reminded of death, and sometimes my friend haunts me after all these years. His words are also in me, in my arm, and I appreciate them because that means he is still alive.

I am certain that the words will never explode in my arm to escape like they did in my mother's head, even though I have many more words than she held in her skull. That's because I can never go full circle, since I never really had a land. There is nothing for me in Ohio but displaced arrowheads. If I go back to India, he is dead, and she is no longer there but back in Europe. I have no real land. That makes me fortunate, because if I did, the words would kill me.

Riding in the taxi in Seoul, Korea. I roll down the window as it stops directly behind a bus. Ephemeral. I do this to smell the exhaust from the bus. Prosaic. I do this because it reminds me of Korea. It is funny because I am in Seoul and yet I still need to be reminded that I'm in the city. I do not need this to sustain myself, but sometimes the words do. So we roll down Seoul's city streets together. I point my face out toward the neon red crosses. I try to breathe with regularity, artificial wind blowing at my face. I can't, because we are moving, and I know we are.

DOMINIC CHOI
Friday the Day I Hate Being Korean

The torment of the alarm only to be saved by the 10-minute intervals of snooze was the only sanity left in his life. Good thing I'm Korean, thought Jaewook. He had taken his shower last night like every Korean does, and with a quick brush of the teeth, head under the sink, he was out of the house within 10 minutes. Traffic was heavy that morning, and all he could do was think about closing the Burkard bank deal. As he smoked his Marlboro Lights, Jaewook's attention shifted to his father and how sickly looking he had become. "Was it the cigarettes or working twelve hours, six days a week?" He spoke out loud, but once he saw the tower of glass looming from the highway, his attention focused back to closing the bank deal. He had once thought only white people could work in those glass towers, while Koreans would be on the ground floor, managing the deli or the dry cleaners. Then he laughed as he thought of how far he'd come.

Jaewook never remembered being left in Korea at the age of one while his parents established their lives in the States. Nor did he remember being shipped at four by total strangers to parents he had not seen most of his life. The whole family was proud that he had made it into that glass tower seen from the highway. Now, all the aunts could brag to their *ah gee ma* friends about how important he was, including the eldest aunt who had married the American serviceman from the Korean Conflict and had brought the family here.

Navy blue-suited Jaewook to a tee. He stood tall and at times looked down on people in the elevator if they were not dressed in suits. "Where is the Burkard report I asked for, Liz?" he screamed to his white assistant. She was always nervous around Mr. Choi, which is what he insisted she call him. "It's coming over the fax right now, sir. I have your tea and bagel ready for you." He was the master of making numbers look appealing, of making them dance for clients. He could have a client in his grasp, as if he were leading the waltz at some grand ball.

"Damn right! Who's the king?" he'd yell at the top of his lungs, so that everybody on the floor knew something big was going to happen. "You are, Mr. Choi." replied Liz, glancing at him for his approval.

Power lunches were never his thing. Yes, he processed all the manners and knew what to order, but deep down he was never happy unless he was eating *bahp* and *kim chee gegah*. The day was almost done. All he had left was to get congratulations from the CFO, and he was out of there. Then he remembered it was Friday. "Shit I'm late!" he yelled as he ran into his office to change his clothes. "Hey, where are you off to?" asked one of his buddies. "Going to help a friend move," Jaewook replied, ashamed to admit that he had to work at his parents' fish store. He had to cut across town on Friday, the busiest day for traffic known to man, without being late. He smoked as if it were going out of style, one cigarette after the other, since he knew he would not have many opportunities after he arrived at the fish store.

6:15 P.M. He parked his car. Seeing the line in the fish store, he knew it was going to be a busy night. Jaewook put his cell phone on vibrate and stuck it into his front left pocket. Then like some trained seal, he stuck the half-empty pack of cigarettes in his front right pocket and walked in. As he fought his way through the crowds of blacks waiting impatiently for their fried fish, he looked over to his *ahmma*, who was smiling, happy to see her eldest son. His *ahpah*, on the other hand, gave him a look that said, "Why are you late?" knowing he had to cross over the Woodrow Wilson bridge on Friday. Jaewook went straight to the back, took off his sweatshirt, and donned the apron he always wore. The customer base in his parents' store was mostly black and that didn't bother him.

He would put his head down and as he cut fish, ripping out the guts and chopping off the heads. The whole time he would ask himself, *Why me?* He worked for a Fortune 500 company, brokering multimillion dollar deals, and now he was cutting fish. He had wondered why his parents couldn't just hire someone, but he knew them and knew no one would work with them. As the evening progressed, he would hear the black patrons belittle his parents and himself with comments like, "Do you understand what I'm saying, do you speak English?" The whole time Jaewook would think, *I'm busy and I have to sell to people like you?* There would be times when altercations about orders would arise, and he would be the aggressor. He would hear, "Chink, I want that shit fried hard." Then he would turn around with a look that said, "I'll see you outside when I get off," and the whole time he hated being there.

Time would tick as slowly as traffic. Occasionally, he'd sneak into the bathroom to smoke or make calls to friends to see what he'd be doing if he weren't working. Jaewook's parents had a good system. One person would take the orders while one person gutted and cut the fish and placed them into the deep fryer. The last person checked the fish in the deep fryer and then packaged it and called out the number. His mom usually took the orders because she spoke English better than his father. His father usually cut and gutted the fish because he was fast. Jaewook would package it and hand it to the customer. He considered himself the fish Nazi like in some *Seinfeld* episode. He demanded that the customers give the money quick and get out of the way till their numbers were called. There would be times when someone would say something to his *ahmma* that would make him flip out. The regular customers knew the drill. Jaewook wasn't going to take any shit, and most of the time his mom didn't even know what was said. Yet his dad and mom would ask him why he was causing trouble. Jaewook considered himself the most hated man in D.C. He thought to himself, *One day someone is going to shoot me.* But he didn't have any fear. His hatred ran too deep.

It was about 9:30 P.M. Jaewook knew it was close to closing time. He would stock all the sodas so that his father didn't have to lift the heavy cases. He would usually convince his parents to close a little early. After the last order had been filled, they would start cleaning up. That was really why Jaewook came to work on Fridays. He felt that it was his duty, being eldest son and all. He couldn't bear to imagine his broken dad, who had made him his first sled, carried him on his shoulders, kissed him to show how much he loved him, taking out the trash. As Jaewook would do every Friday, he smoked his last cigarette as he took out the trash and felt grateful for being Korean.

dwelling

SUIL KANG
Sungbook

It was about this time, near the beginning of the summer I turned 11, when Uncle Song started to build a wall around his yard. Uncle Song was a day laborer. He was one of many laborers who worked in building a new Korea, laying asphalt roads and constructing apartments and large glass buildings.

He was a small man. He wore dark trousers and light cotton shirts that always looked one size too large for him. He had high cheekbones that looked polished and highlighted his dark bronzed face. He did not look straight at you, as if a thin film closed over his eyes.

Mr. Song's house stood next to the main road that started at the foot of our hill, wound up to our village and continued higher up. The house was about a hundred yards from the crossroads where the main side street in our village, the street by where my house stood on one side and Ayoung's house stood on the other side, crossed the main road.

None of the streets in our village had names. Everyone who needed to know knew where the streets were and how they weaved and forked, so there was no reason to name the streets. The few newcomers or visitors could find their way around easily enough. All they had to do was to ask anyone in the village.

Mr. Song's house had a large yard. The place where it stood was once considered the end of our village. His yard included land that was cleared before more people moved into the mountainous area beyond and around his house.

The house itself was small; two rooms connected by a wooden floor. An enclosed kitchen was attached to the main room, the larger one where Uncle Song and his wife slept. A fireplace, where charcoal briquettes were fired in winter, was dug in the earth beneath the hinged door of the smaller room.

A stepping-stone abutted the wall below the kitchen doorsill. Another small stepping-stone was laid before the wooden floor. Save a long wooden pole that propped up a sagging clothesline that extended from a corner of the kitchen, the large yard was empty.

The rumor was that Mr. Song was planning to build a real Western house and sell his new house for a handsome profit. The first Western house that I had seen was near the bottom of our hill, across the stream. It was nestled against the opposite mountain, a little below the Buddhist temple, almost directly opposite the waterfall.

Large stones cemented together in a mosaic pattern formed the firm foundation of not-so-tall gray walls. Chestnut trees and elder branches hung over the walls and screened a handsome two-story red brick house, as if the house was conscious of its beauty and tried to tone it down in modesty. I had imagined warmth and a spontaneous and joyful family life inside the panels of large glass windows on the upper story.

I did not think Mr. Song's new house would be as pretty as the first Western house by the waterfall. His house would stand in our village, on a bald mountain, whose small streets had been paved hastily, recently. Mr. Song was a day laborer, not a magician. Besides, I could not imagine another house so pretty, serene and in harmony with its surroundings as the house where the top Korean movie stars had come to film a movie. That was when I had just begun to explore the mountains near our village with Kyonghee.

The older brothers and sisters in our village knew of the filming before us, the kids in the village. They ran down the hill shrieking and shouting. We followed right behind their heels. Hiding behind rustling branches and jostling for a better view, they pointed toward the waterfall and rattled off the names of top movie stars. I strained to see, but could not match any of the names with the figures by the waterfall.

You had to know what to look for before you could find what you were supposed to see.

I did not even think that Mr. Song's house would be as nice as the new ones on the opposite mountains, which I could see if I stepped into the middle of our yard: large houses with tiled verandas, panels of windows and shiny black automobiles. However, the idea of a house with indoor plumbing and a bathroom in our village excited my imagination. Perhaps each of the houses in our village, especially my own house and Ayoung's, one by one, could have indoor plumbing someday.

I had been to the house of one of my mother's old friends near downtown, where taxis and buses honked and crowds bustled. In Aunt Kim's house, you went into a little room, sat down on the toilet and flushed your feces away. I did not have to steel myself up for the stench or be vigilantly careful how I placed my feet on the creaking wooden panels.

Once a month, or twice a month, I went to the bathhouse, far below my school, Sungbook Elementary. On these occasions, I sat in the large tub of steaming water until my whole being down to my innards warmed. Mother or Aunt Jung then scrubbed me hard until my skin turned pink.

I loved the hot bathhouse. It was embarrassing too, because I imagined that on these occasions everyone in my village knew I was coming from the bathhouse and knew the last time I had been to the bathhouse. A tiled bathroom in my own house and hot water spewing out of a faucet were the apex of elegance that I imagined modernity promised.

On a cheery day in late May, I washed my canvas shoes by the washstand in the middle of our yard. I dabbed a worn toothbrush against a bar of soap and scrubbed the soil from my canvas shoes. I set them against the wall under sunlight. They would be dried before the evening arrived. Meanwhile, I would check out Mr. Song's house.

Mr. Song had built a three-foot-high wall of cinder blocks all around his yard. His trousers were rolled up. The muscles in his calves flexed firmly when he hoisted a sack of cement upon his shoulders. He mixed the sand and the dark gray cement powder little by little with a long shovel. When the mixing was done to his satisfaction, he scooped a lump of cement on a wooden palette, which he held with his left hand. His right hand troweled the wet cement on the top of five or so cinder blocks lightly and quickly.

Mr. Song placed and set an additional block across the top of two others. He scratched off the oozing cement with his trowel and mixed it with other wet cement. He built up his new wall, firmly gluing together the cinder blocks. As he worked in mixing and laying the blocks, his eyes were deep and focused, clear like marbles.

The older of his two boys was about five years old. He cleaned the water pail and brought out fresh water. He anticipated the tools his father would need and made them ready for easy pickup. The younger brother trailed behind the older one, then started to poke the sand mound with a thin wooden stick. He seemed pleased to see how easily he could slide the grains of sand.

I felt funny watching Mr. Song and his kids. I did not want to be an intruder. I pretended that I had an errand to run and was stopping by on my way. I started to climb up toward the higher part of BookAk mountains. I would go home after reaching the next ridge of the mountains, around the next village.

The sun was up high in the sky. White, cotton clouds drew pictures of fantastic birds and faces. I identified the faces of Jesus and God the father. I closed my eyes then opened them to see if they moved or stayed still. Perhaps Minister Jang was right; Jesus and God the father were up in the sky.

Could I see the face of my father? He would not be up there. Minister Jang had said only the believers, the Christians, would be up high in heaven. Aunt Jung had told me that my father could not hurt a fly. It would not be fair if my father were not in heaven. Even if God's rule was strict, and my father was wrong to not believe, how about all my grandparents, well, my great-grandparents, if some of my grandparents were still alive in North Korea? It would not be right to punish them in hell, when they had not even known about Jesus and God the father. Minister Jang must have forgotten to tell us the whole story.

I went by Mr. Song's house again about two weeks later. He had added two rooms, one large one next to the kitchen and another one next to the smaller room. The walls of these rooms had a new concrete look. The houses on the opposite mountains were built with red bricks and large, pretty stones. I had expected that Mr. Song's house was not going to be as nice as those houses, but I was disappointed at the concrete look.

However, each of the new rooms had nice sliding windows on the sidewalls that faced the yard. I liked the dark wooden encasements and the sashes. Curved black metal bars encased the windows like the ones I had seen in a picture of an Italian village. I was pleased with the windows.

Ayoung had told me that the inside was reworked so that you could take a hot bath in a room between the kitchen and the new large room. The kitchen was revamped so that you could stand while you prepared food. Ayoung's father, Uncle Chun was the elder of the village, so she had heard a lot about Mr. Song's house. Her voice rose and her eyes animated as she told me about the bathroom. I saw the same desire in her that I had about indoor plumbing and being able to soak in hot water until your skin turned soft.

In the next two weeks, Mr. Song extended the wooden floor. His new house was now about twice the size of his old one and was no longer open to the yard. It had a balanced look, and a door with a golden doorknob closed off the inner living space from the outer yard. The black tar roof had been replaced with red roof tiles. Only a new gate needed to be attached to the two pillars that Mr. Song had built up at the open ends of his new wall.

I imagined nice little tiles all along Mr. Song's new kitchen and bathhouse. Perhaps he could really make big money on it, I thought.

One afternoon in early July, I was sweeping the yard, and Aunt Jung was preparing water kimchi. She had bought large radishes, scrubbed them clean and brought out hot red pepper powder. She sliced and cut them into thin tile sizes and handed me a piece to taste. It was crunchy, juicy and sweet. The radishes would make good water kimchi.

All of sudden there was a commotion. Young kids ran up the main road. A woman's screeching cries, bawling wails of children and loud thumps shattered the calm afternoon. I ran up the hill to Mr. Song's house.

A crowd of adults and kids stood wide-eyed, unable to believe the dust that rose and swirled about Mr. Song's new house. A large, ugly gap had appeared in Mr. Song's new wall. Two men with huge sledgehammers were attacking the new room next to the kitchen.

Aunt Song moved between the two men, stretching her hands and arms to stop the blows and not knowing which sledgehammer she had to block first. The men pushed her off. Aunt Song shrieked, "Somebody, somebody help us!" The men worked in silence without a break. Aunt Song, exhausted and unable to further resist, sat on a broken cinder block by a corner of her house. Her black hair, which was always put up in a tidy bun, was disheveled and drenched in tears, sweat and dust. An aunt from the crowd brought out a cup of water and urged Aunt Song to take a sip.

Some of the kids in the crowd started to whimper and make crying sounds. The adults hushed them. The crowd dispersed, in ones and twos, in silence, as if their thick silence could push away the dust and crumbling walls and place them back to the hour before the blows of the sledgehammers.

I stood there and watched. The two men razed Mr. Song's wall.

Uncle Chun heard from the district office and explained that the office had dispatched the two men because Mr. Song did not have the right to build up his house. The land on which his house was built belonged to the government.

It was said that our whole village was on the government's land. If you wanted to build a house, you needed a permit from the government. A permit was possible only if you owned the piece of land where you wanted to build your house.

No one in our village or in the new villages that sprawled around us owned the piece of land on which his house stood. People just moved in and built their low houses. The aunts of our village explained to each other in agitated whispers and in worried tones. All the houses in our village were illegal. The government could come in at any time and claim its land.

A heavy blanket of silence weighed down our village. After flurries of explanations, the aunts just stopped talking. They did not meet each other's gazes. The streets became empty. People hurried into their own little house, as if they were afraid to be seen outside, and all would be alright if they stayed quiet, unseen.

I was terribly upset. I did not ask any adult for further explanation. My mother was away. She did not know what happened in our village. She did not know Mr. Song. Aunt Jung never saw anything that she could not accept. She would shrug her shoulders and go about doing her duties at Uncle Choi's household.

No one could persuade me that it was not wicked and malicious to knock down Mr. Song's house when it was almost done. Our village was built without permits long before I was born. No district officer had ever cared whether someone put up a gate, a wall or new additions to their houses. As I remembered it, most of the walls in our village were built in the last couple of years.

Everyone in the village knew that Mr. Song was building up his house, and the district office must have known it for a long time. If they were going to destroy his new house, why did they have to wait until it was almost finished?

Someone must have been really jealous of all the money that Mr. Song was going to make. That person must have bad-mouthed Mr. Song to someone at the district office. I had thought all the uncles of our village were good and decent, even if they were poor. Being poor wasn't their fault, but which uncle or uncles could have betrayed the common decency?

I could not pinpoint, but my doubt kept resting on Uncle Chun, because he, as the elder of the village, had the closest tie to the district office and knew more than anyone else about Mr. Song's new house. Couldn't he have prevented the disaster? I shook my head and swept aside my doubt.

Perhaps Mr. Song did not have any money to hand out envelopes to the officers at the district office. And, perhaps, he ignored warnings and exacerbated his situation with his temerity.

If you wanted to rise above your station in life, you needed someone strong who would protect you. Failing that, you had to assure those who felt superior to you that they would remain superior. It would also be wise to reassure your fellow sufferers that your new position would not be any better than your old one. Perhaps, Mr. Song was too proud to take these precautions.

I shuddered at the memory of the two men who demolished Mr. Song's new house. They seemed to relish their job, expending their energy to bring the house to rubble. They were day laborers like Mr. Song. Shouldn't they empathize with Mr. Song's plight? Would the district office have cared whether they thoroughly destroyed Mr. Song's house? The two men had worked hard to completely demolish Mr. Song's house.

They were like the guard who had whipped Kyonghee, Ayoung and me when we craned to look at the beautiful house by the twin bridges years ago. The house was built on a field where large, old cherry trees grew. Before the house was built, we climbed and hung from the branches of the cherry trees. There were more cherries than we could ever eat, and we stuffed ourselves with sweet black cherries.

The new house was bigger than anything we had seen. We heard that it had a beautiful rock garden. We held onto the steel bars of the front gate and poked our heads to see the garden. We were also curious to see our cherry trees, if there still hung the sweet black cherries.

As we admired the beauty of trimmed trees and exquisite rocks and pointed to our trees, a guard sneaked up to us and cracked his whip on our hands and faces. We shrieked, falling backward, stunned at the sharp stings at our fingers and cheeks.

The guard could whip without worrying about the consequences. He reveled in his power over us. Sometimes the hired hand acted out viciousness that his owner would hesitate to show and looked meaner and more despicable than those who used him.

About two weeks after the ransacking of Mr. Song's house, when our village seemed to have settled back into normal routine, Ayoung told me that Mr. Song was building up his house again. I admired Mr. Song's determination. At the same time, I wondered if Mr. Song had gotten permission from the district office.

On a sultry August day, Ayoung and I went by Mr. Song's house on our way to buy paper dolls in a local entertainment house. When no household in our village had owned a television, and at times like—I could recall the dreamlike memory—when I saw two men with bulbous helmets and padded suits place an American flag on a crate of sand dunes, people packed the entertainment house to watch the black-and-white television set on a tall dresser.

With President Park's new village movement, half of the households in our village obtained their own televisions, and the entertainment house changed its business slightly. The owner, Aunt Kwak lent out more cartoon books and martial art novels; wonderful stories of martial artists who could climb walls and create gusting winds from their palms. She also sold thin carton papers on which perforated, colorful pictures of a princess and her clothes were printed.

Uncle Song had cleaned the rubble and amassed broken bricks on one side of his yard. He was building up the room next to the kitchen. He did not have the easy dexterity with which he had handled the bricks, the cement and the sand at the beginning of the summer. His face seemed strained and stiff. His wife watched him with a pleading glance.

Ayoung told me that Mr. Song did not have the money to finish his house. He bought additional materials he needed on credit, promising to pay the debt when he finished the house and sold it at a profit.

Mr. Song finished his second house by the beginning of September. It was not as nice as his first. The wooden floor that had extended the old one and the golden doorknob were gone. The two additional rooms were rebuilt, but without the extended floor and an inner door. There were two more plain cement side-walls for each of the additional rooms. Two small hinged windows replaced the handsome windows that I liked in Mr. Song's first house.

Nevertheless, Ayoung had assured me that Mr. Song's house still had the indoor plumbing and an in-house bathroom where hot water came out from the faucet. Perhaps, Mr. Song could pay off his debts and have a little left for him and his family, even if he would not make as much as profit as he would have made from the first one.

Two men from the district office showed up again, and Mr. Song's second house was demolished to rubble.

I happened to pass by his house late one afternoon. Aunt Jung had told me to get some tofu and bean sprouts for the evening. There was a little shop between our village and the next village up the hill. The prices were higher than in the shops down below near the twin bridges, and the items in the shop—dry goods, a few types of fruits, vegetables and fish—looked dingier than in the markets down below, but it was convenient, especially when you wanted to buy just a couple of items.

Mr. Song's house was open as it had been before it was built up. Mr. Song was drinking the strong rice liquor in his yard. His two little kids squatted about three yards from him and played with stone pebbles. Their concentration was not in the game. They fidgeted about each other and kept turning toward their father. His wife attended house chores. She seemed careful not to arouse Mr. Song's anger. Her face was puffed as if too many tears had gotten stuffed under her skin.

Toward the end of the summer, Mr. Song was building up his house again. People in the village tried to not notice it. No one made a comment. His third try looked shabby, and terribly sad in the recent memory of his first brilliant new house. No one from the district office came the third time.

I hoped that Mr. Song would not snap like some people do when life frustrates their aspirations. I had heard that my father died when all our money was lost in the stock market. He studied music and could play wonderful piano, but he could not keep a job and support the family. He died poor and sick. I hoped also, without faith, that Mr. Song would find a way to avoid becoming a lifelong construction worker.

SUE KWOCK KIM

The Korean Community Garden in Queens

In the vacant lot nobody else bothered to rebuild,
dirt scumbled for years with syringes and dead
weed-husks, tire-shreds and smashed beer bottles,
the first green shoots of spring spike through –

bullbrier, redroot, pokeweed, sowthistle,
an uprising of grasses whose only weapons are themselves.
Blades slit through scurf. Spear-tips spit dust
as if thrust from the other side. They spar and glint.

How far will they climb, grappling for light?
Inside I see coils of fern-bracken called *kosari*,
bellflower cuts named *toraji* in the old country.
Knuckles of ginger and mugwort dig upward,

shoving through mulched soil until they break
the surface. Planted by immigrants they survive,
like their gardeners, ripped from their native
plot. What is it they want, driving and driving

toward a foreign sky? How not to mind the end
we'll come to. I imagine the garden underground,
where gingko and ailanthus grub cement rubble.
They tunnel slag for foothold. Wring crumbs of rot

for water. Of shadows, seeds foresung as *Tree*
of Heaven & Silver Apricot in ancient Mandarin,
their roots tangle now with plum or weeping willow,
their branches mingling with tamarack or oak.

I love how nothing in these furrows grows unsnarled,
nothing stays unscathed. How last year's fallen stalks,
withered to pith, cleave to this year's crocus bulbs,
each infant knot burred with bits of garbage or tar.

Fist to fist with tulips, iris, selving and unselving
glads, they work their metamorphoses in loam
pocked with rust-flints, splinters of rodent-skull –
a ground so mixed, so various that everything

is born of what it's not. Who wouldn't want
to flower like this? How strangely they become
themselves, this gnarl of azaleas and roses-of-Sharon,
native to both countries, blooming as if drunk

with blossoming. Green buds suck and bulge.
Stem-nubs thicken. Sepals swell and crack their cauls.
Lately every time I walk down this street to look
through the fence, I'm surprised by something new.

Yesterday hydrangea and chrysanthemums burst
their calyxes, corolla-skins blistering into welts.
Today jonquils slit blue shoots from their sheaths.
Tomorrow day-lilies and wild-asters will flame petals,

each incandescent color unlike: sulfur, blood, ice,
coral, fire-gold, violet the hue of shaman robes –
every flower with its unique glint or slant, faithful
to each particular. All things lit by what they neighbor

but are not, each tint flaring without a human soul,
without human rage at its passing. In the summer
there will be scallions, mung-beans, black sesame,
muskmelons, to be harvested into buckets and sold

at market. How do they live without wanting to live
forever? May I, and their gardeners in the old world,
who kill for warring dreams and warring heavens,
who stop at nothing, see life and paradise as one.

FRANCES PARK
Around the Block

Strolling you past the ice cream parlor and the historic inn where morning glories wrap around ornate iron gates, past shops that offer all the tokens of a seaport town—shells, stones, watercolor postcards—I'm thinking what a breath of heaven we have here. This is our home, where we eat and play and drift to sleep while boats rock outside our windows. Everything feels like waves forever. Of being carried off to sea. Winnie, wherever you go in life, I want you to walk around with this picture of the world and blow it up larger than life. Like the skies are opening up for you. Promise me you won't wither from fear, or shrink from the footsteps behind you, or grow into a crooked tree.

The summer I turned 12 my family moved from a college town in Massachusetts to suburban Virginia, to a street called Lilac Lane, where dreams never left the block and the nation's capital, a nine mile shot up the highway, was as far off as the moon. No one saw beyond the trees—the kick balls and birdies flying, the swings and seesaws, back and forth. When we moved in everything stopped in midair. Why, you wonder? Because we were small and dark, and we huddled over dishes of strange food. Winnie, this was ages before Benetton and ethnic Barbies and places like The Fortune Cookie Café, where pink parasols open like flowers over tables and waiters stroll dim sum around in rickshaw carts. This was 1966!

Your uncle Tommy and I were the only Orientals in our school. We were born in America and we could recite the Pledge of Allegiance like all the other children, but our parents' mild manner and voices—not to mention the way they squatted in the front yard to pick weeds—were painful reminders that we weren't American at all. Not to mention the neighborhood name-calling.

Hey, Chop Suzy! Hey, Won Ton Man!

Sometimes the sound of footsteps from a quarter of a century ago creep up to me, and I'm back on Lilac Lane, scooting Tommy home.

Wait up, Moo Shoo Dorks!

"Why do those boys always say that?" Tommy would frown.

"Say what?" I'd shrug.

Poor Tommy would look up to me—he was, after all, four years younger—and see nothing but my stone face. What a disappointment I must have been to him! Nothing but a stone-faced sister! I had no backbone; no vines, no roots. Winnie, I was a weak little unwanted tree.

It was those times when I'd yearn most for Massachusetts, for the town where ivy climbed up old stone buildings and foreigners gathered in a bakery called Athena's. I always felt at home whether I was eating baklava from a bag or counting all the colorful flags that were posted in the hallway of the political science building where my father was known as Professor Lee. Even my mother joined the Wives Club, a group that exchanged recipes and bowls of spicy food.

And then there was Lilac Lane.

Not long after we moved in, someone left a pair of chopsticks on our doormat. When I found them I ran down the yard and tossed them down the sewer like a stick of dynamite. They weren't the copper kind we used at home but the wooden ones from Ding Wow's Carryout. We weren't even Chinese!

We were Korean.

School started, and I soon learned that there were three girls my age who also lived on Lilac Lane. Betty, Joni and Jan. Even though we were all in the same sixth-grade class, they made a point of looking through me like I wasn't there. I was dust, if that. A thing in saddle shoes. It's true, sleepy girl, I accounted for nothing in their universe, and their universe was Lilac Lane.

What did they look like? They were bony little girls with stringy brown hair and anemic complexions. They looked like they lived on a diet of gum and soda. They walked around in patent leather shoes and ratty macramé tights. From the window I could never tell who from who, but up close Jan stood out with her braces and big bumpy nose. Of course, she was boss.

Tommy soon found a friend named Matt who got into the habit of picking him up every morning for school, so I usually ended up walking alone. And every morning I would listen for other schoolchildren, their footsteps behind me. Bully footsteps. Betty, Joni and Jan footsteps. No matter how early I left the house, I could feel their collective hate breathing down my neck, ready to grab my ankles. I'd wait for them to pass me like I was some mutt in their path.

Ew, something smells!
What could it be?
Pollution!
Ew!

But there are some boundaries that can't be crossed; some spaces—like the ones in our heart and soul and character—that we try to keep sacred. Since my heart and soul and character were barely sprouts in the ground, my only boundaries were the front and porch doors of our Cape Cod home. The backyard where my father had put up a tall fence, then built a rock garden on a rolling hill. And my bedroom.

My bedroom was a corner of the world where I found some semblance of peace. A converted attic, a big airy room. I liked the way the ceiling slanted over my bed as snow fell in fat patches outside my window and branches scratched against the house like the fingers of skeletons wanting in. I liked the way, after I used the toilet in the middle of the night and ran up the bare wooden stairs with ghosts after me, the rug felt warm and woolly on my feet. I liked the way the garden looked from my window, so earthy and permanent, the quartz glinting through clumps of petals and leaves after a spring shower. I liked my bedroom, for a corner of peace meant that someday I might have a grander corner, far away from here.

But it was hard to look beyond the trees when most of the time I was too chicken to venture outside. In broad daylight? That was like stepping off a curb and into a speeding car!

Hey, Suzy, play 'Chopsticks' for us!

I remember wishing I was invisible. Or dead. Winnie, wake up, do you know what that does to a child? It makes you grow up smiling at strangers just so they won't call you names. It makes you grow up looking into eyes like windows, wondering whether they'll let you in. It makes you grow quiet because you'd rather cough up blood than the truth: The whole world hated your guts.

Why didn't my parents do anything? I didn't want them to do anything. The spoken word would make it too real, too awful; it would echo from here to eternity. Better to keep it to myself, like some murderous secret. Once I was in the door, I shut out Lilac Lane. I went up to my room and studied my science and social studies books even on nice days like today, Winnie, when there is sunlight on the sidewalk. Tommy soon found two more friends—Pete and Lance—and my lack of them made me move back from the window and close the curtains and lay in bed so still I wouldn't hear my mother calling me down for dinner. Don't ever do this, Winnie; don't ever withdraw from the world. It's like a part of you is already in your grave because your heart is only barely beating.

My parents probably didn't understand what was going on anyway, at least not fully. Bombs and bloody screams from the outbreak of war still went off in their heads. What was common prejudice compared to a soul full of scars? My parents lived in America, but their thoughts floated across the ocean.

My father, now a professor in Washington, was a famous man in South Korea. He had secret political ambitions. I remember whispers and late night phone calls. While he was arranging his rock garden today, he was laying out plans for tomorrow. He was a quiet man of earthquakes.

My mother, on the other hand, lived back in time, at the moment of invasion when she and two cousins escaped across the Korean border, from north to south.

Her parents, who were frail and frightened, told her to leave, packed her bags and practically pushed her out the door in a communist storm. She was only a school-girl. She believed she would be coming back home when peace was restored. She believed the storm would blow over. But now, nearly two decades later, her home-land was still split and in shambles, and she was slowly realizing she would never see her parents in North Korea again. What a sight, that grief-stricken look that invaded her eyes when she was alone and deep in thought. She might be picking weeds or making dinner. Winnie, that look was the boundary between us. She lived her life in limbo. How could she love me when her heart was halfway around the world?

My parents only socialized with diplomatic types who lived in other neigh-borhoods. There was a lot of hushed talk at their dinner parties because my father was planning to save his country from dictatorship—yes, even if it meant over-throwing the government—when the time was right. How could he have known the time would never be right? How could he have known he would die long before his time, leaving my mother to wither in America? Winnie, I want you to know something and hold it close to your heart like a locket….

Even though your grandfather tended his garden as though every seed he sowed was a seed from his heart; even though every bud that flowered was a tiny monument of his soul; even though he had the character to see beyond trees, the garden is gone now.

Toward the end of the school year, a new student joined our class. The principal brought her to our classroom and introduced her to us as her daughter Courtney. The girl had a glamorous, grown-up air about her, like she knew all the answers but was keeping them to herself. She had wavy auburn hair, a mole above her lip and blue eyes that poked through long dark eyelashes. So decorative compared to my plain two-toned face. She seated herself in the empty desk next to mine and stared at me all morning. At lunchtime—we ate in our classroom because the cafeteria was overcrowded—she turned her desk around to face mine.

"Can I eat with you?"

I was so used to eating alone I didn't know what to say. Now there was a desk, a face.

"Sure," I fidgeted.

"I like your dress," she said. "It's pretty."

"Thanks. I like yours, too."

"Thanks!"

We ate silently against the noise of crumpled bags and milk through straws. Winnie, you may never have memories of this morning, but the smell of warm bologna and mustard on white bread will always bring me back to that class, that day. She bit into her sandwich and asked,

"Are you Chinese or Japanese?"

"I'm Korean," I said so quietly I wasn't sure she heard me.

"Korean," she repeated airily. It was like a globe was spinning in her head. "Want some Fritos?"

"OK," I said.

She held open a baggie of Fritos for me. I reached over and dug out a handful even though I wasn't really hungry anymore. I think I was full of hope.

"I'm Courtney," she breathed.

"I'm Suzy," I breathed back.

"I wish I had your hair, Suzy," she said in the most earnest voice I had ever heard. "It's so long and shiny."

When I walked home from school that afternoon, the trees parted like clouds down Lilac Lane. I couldn't believe it, Winnie. I could see beyond the trees. I had a friend!

Courtney and I became best friends overnight. The next day, she brought me an orange from California, and it seemed to me we'd been peeling oranges together all year long. The next minute we were up in my room, listening to records and gossiping about the kids in our class.

"In India, they'd be called the Untouchables," she shuddered.

"What does that mean?" I asked.

"It means you wouldn't touch their cooties with a ten-foot pole!"

Her parents were divorced, which in those days was practically unheard of in middle America—not exactly scandalous, but enough to raise eyebrows. My parents thought they had cause for concern. What kind of woman was her mother? What kind of *principal* was she? Was this girl Courtney a normal child? You have to understand the warpedness of war and culture, Winnie. A country might split in two, families torn apart, spirits broken and bodies dismembered, but marriages? Never! That was taboo.

Courtney had been living with her father in California, but something happened, something I suspected was awful and abrupt and not within the confines of our friendship to ask. Why else would she leave so suddenly? Why else was she here?

"My father took me to Hong Kong last year," she said proudly, stirring brownie batter in my kitchen. "It's like a great big Chinatown. The teeny tiny streets with the teeny tiny people with their big straw hats."

I clammed up. Was she making fun of them?

"The best part was the food," she said, licking her fingers, then giggling. "My father would say, *Have a plate of eyeballs and intestines, honey*. And I'd just close my eyes and eat and eat and eat."

Outwardly we didn't have much in common. While I came to school in scuffed saddle shoes, Courtney was a preteen dream in velvet headbands and starched blouses. While I was shy, self-conscious and bookish, she was mature and mischievous and talkative, to me at least. I know now that Courtney gravitated toward me for all the reasons no one else had—I was foreign and friendless. But beyond that, we both had inner stigmas and secrets and an alienation of the heart that brought us together in an antisocial bond. Against whom? The All-American family. They were the enemy.

Courtney lived with her mother in a home in the country, a 40-minute drive to school. So I still shrank from the footsteps behind me on Lilac Lane, the psychological spits in the face—*There's that crummy dish from Ding Wow's!* But they couldn't touch me the way they did before. There was a fence between us. After all, I had a friend who ate *mandoo* soup with me, who taught Tommy how to win at Monopoly, who spent many nights at our house. And who sometimes cried in her sleep.

Winnie, I hope someday you find a friend who will stay in your thoughts for the rest of your life, a friend who forms some philosophy in you so that even when you're feeling like a crooked tree, you remember to stand tall because she was there once, to water every part of you.

"Get lost!" she shouted at some boys who were making fun of me on the blacktop during recess. They were making slant eyes and buckteeth faces. "Don't pay any attention to them, Suzy. They only act that way because they're low class."

I froze. This wasn't like walking down Lilac Lane. This was a public stoning. "What does low class mean?"

"It means their dads are drunks," she stated matter-of-factly, like she plucked this from an encyclopedia. "Not like *your* father, who's a professor, or *my* father who's an international businessman."

Now the boys were closing in on us, circling us. I was cracking into a million ugly pieces. Courtney shouted, "Disappear or I'll have my mom expel all you fools from school!" They scattered across the blacktop like marbles.

Whenever anyone made fun of me, I would pretend not to notice. I'd look away or lower my eyes, wishing I could just blink and disappear. The problem with this, Winnie, is that you don't learn to love yourself. But Courtney tried to change that.

"Don't let them make you feel ashamed of who you are," she said as the bell rang and we started back to our classroom, "You're *better* than them. Take those three," she said as Betty, Joni and Jan ran by us holding their noses, "They're just going to grow up to be hicks—*hell-raising hicks*, my father would say—believe me. Now *you're* going to grow up to look like all the beautiful rich ladies in Hong Kong. You should see them in their silk dresses and pearls."

Courtney was the first person who ever told me I would grow up to be beautiful, and she told me this all the time, as a given. I would stare into the mirror and pray for the day. Silk dresses and pearls, silk dresses and pearls. Even bullies love beautiful ladies, I told myself, not knowing this was a dangerous way to think. Years later, men would love me for all the wrong reasons, and I would do everything in my power to poison their lives for having poisoned mine when I was a homely schoolgirl. And poor Courtney would marry men who would disappoint her, each one more than the last, until I painfully realized that she had been more troubled than I all along. But I'm getting years ahead of myself. I'll save those stories for you when you're older, Winnie. Today I'm remembering the ugly years. When I stood alone and unchosen during square dance time. When bullies would make slant eyes and buckteeth faces across the classroom. When I would hear, *What's cooking, Chop Suzy?* all the way home.

Betty, Joni and Jan were furious that I had a friend. A friend with authority. The principal's daughter. They would *hmmmph* by me on the way to school, mumbling under their breath. And I would say to myself, *hell-raising hicks*. I think maybe they could read my mind, because one morning I heard their footsteps ganging up on me. They were fast and deadly. On a mission. I quickened my pace, pretending to be late for school. But in a rush of arms and elbows and kicks, they knocked me to the ground. I remember the fall in slow motion—my books flying, me bumping into bushes, then hitting the pavement. Winnie, I was a twig, a broken branch. I wanted to run home and up to my room, close the curtains and think of ways to die. Instead, I ran to Courtney.

She marched up to them on the blacktop. I stood behind her, wishing I'd kept my mouth shut.

"You're all in big trouble," she announced.

Jan squinted evilly. "Why are you friends with *her*? She's ugly as sin."

Yeah, ugly as sin, Betty and Joni chimed.

"She wears those same ugly saddle shoes every day. You know what everyone calls her behind her back? The Sweet and Sour Dork."

The Sweet and Sour Dork, Betty and Joni cracked up.

Courtney walked right up to Jan, face-to-face. She didn't bat an eyelash. "You have a gross nose," she said.

Courtney reported the incident to her mother, who then called their mothers in for an after-school conference. As punishment, the girls had to stay in during recess and wash chalkboards for the rest of the year. But school was almost out, and I was dreading the summer more than ever now. What would happen to me, alone on Lilac Lane? How could I keep the image of me in silk dresses and pearls alive? Surely it would fade away before fall. Courtney came up with an idea at lunchtime.

"Let's run away from home."

"What?" I said. "Why?"

"So we can get away from *here*," she explained as she cut up a cupcake on her desk. "From them," she pointed to our noisy classmates.

"Courtney, I can't! My parents would kill me!"

"I just mean for the summer. We'll come back."

"Where would we go?"

"To California. We can stay with my father."

"How would we get there?"

"Hitchhike," she shrugged, her hands covered with crumbs. "Everyone's doing it."

"No! I can't!" I was horrified.

She smiled strangely. "I'm just joking."

"Oh," I nodded, not sure.

She inched up to me and whispered, "But do you think your parents will let me stay at your house when my mother goes on vacation with her boyfriend?"

"I think so," I said, growing excited.

"I'll help your mother in the kitchen and your father in the garden. I won't be a pain to have around. I promise."

My parents did let her stay at our house when her mother went on a week-long vacation although, again, they thought they had cause for concern. Why isn't her mother married to her boyfriend? Why didn't they take Courtney with them? What kind of *principal* was she that she dropped Courtney off at our doorstep like an orphan? I didn't have any answers. I didn't *care*. As far as I could see, adults existed on the fringes of our lives. They loved you from a distance, even in your own home. Courtney and me, our lives were each other.

Tommy said some boys were calling him *Hiroshima Head* and *Tokyo Tom* when he rode his bicycle around the block. Sometimes they chased after him with squirt guns and water hoses. So Courtney and I took to sitting on the front lawn while he rode up and down the limits of Lilac Lane.

"In California, surf's up every day," she said. "You ride waves instead of bikes."

"Neat. Can you surf?"

"No, but my father's going to teach me how."

I held my breath. "When?"

"When you and me move there," she decided. "California is so cool. You've got the Pacific Ocean, and when you're skateboarding on the boardwalk it's like you're surfing down the coast."

I grew excited, I don't know why. "Can we get an apartment?"

"A beach house is better," she said.

A beach house! Those were the times when I could see way beyond the trees, Winnie. My face grew dreamy like yours after a lick of ice cream. Just then Courtney leaped off the lawn.

"Suzy!" she gasped.

I looked down the street and saw some boys about Tommy's age on either side of his bicycle. They were heckling and shoving him. Tommy was trying to balance himself; he was trying to ride away. By the time Courtney and I got there, it was too late. He was already on the ground, already bleeding. The boys were nowhere in sight. It's like they slid down the sewers! Tommy looked up at me with that frown of his, and what did I do? I looked away.

Yes, it was heartbreaking to witness my little brother in that situation and yes, I think he was bruised badly, meaning skin-deep, but I was still willing to close my eyes. Pretend it had never happened. That drove Courtney crazy. She wanted to kick, scratch and blacken eyes. After supper we sat up in my room. We flipped our flip-flops off the bed and fanned ourselves with comic books.

"Quit being a goody-goody Mouseketeer! Stand up for yourselves!" she said.

"Shhh!" I pleaded. I didn't want my parents to hear.

"Suzy! It's not like they were teasing some fat boy at the pool! Those little Ku Klux Klanners wanted to *kill* him!" She fanned herself furiously, then calmed herself down. "Ever since it happened, Tommy looks kind of different, I don't know, he looks kind of..."

Unforgiving, Winnie. He looked kind of unforgiving. Like he didn't believe in God anymore—or big sisters. Of course it would pass, he would get back on his bicycle, but I do believe he lost an ounce of faith that day.

"He's all right, Courtney," I said. "He's got other friends. They just don't live on our street."

She rolled her eyes and cornered me. "So you're going to let everyone walk all over you? Squish you like ants?"

"What am I supposed to do?"

She paused, her face turned funny. "Barf on them!"

"Barf on them?" I cried. "Gross!"

Then we lapsed into laughter about who had the funnier looking feet.

I lay in bed that night, dreaming of escape. There were no safe borders to cross, only the ironies of life to face. My mother had wanted to stay in North Korea but was forced to leave; I wanted to leave Lilac Lane, but was forced to stay. Winnie, what a tragic parallel that your grandmother and I led separate lives on the wrong side of the line. Peace was a myth.

The next morning, we discovered that our house had been teepeed. My parents were in the front yard scratching their heads. They didn't understand the meaning of toilet paper streaming through bushes and trees. I felt sick, like I'd swallowed some horrible pill, one that wouldn't kill, just slowly poison me for the rest of my life. Courtney stood beside me and never before was I so grateful for her presence, her American face. Otherwise I'd have to live with the memory of my Korean family cleaning up the yard while our neighbors watched from their living room windows.

"Don't worry, Dr. Lee," she spoke up, "Kids do this all the time. Suzy and I will clean it all up."

My father went to his morning lecture, and my mother began to pick weeds, talking to herself. Tommy was still in bed. Courtney and I cleaned up, working our way to the backyard. She was so quiet I thought she was going to explode. When we opened the fence to the backyard, she did just that.

"Look! Look what they've done!"

I couldn't believe my eyes. I was seeing the opposite of a mirage. My father's garden! Rocks had been turned over and tossed, and his beloved marigolds and pansies lay flattened like corsages on a mound of dirt. It looked more like a grave than a garden.

I trembled. "What are we going to do?"

"We clean up," she said soberly.

We spent most of the day picking up rocks and weeding out dead flowers. Tommy helped us by hosing dirt off the rocks. Fortunately, none of the flowering shrubs had been harmed, and so the azaleas and rhododendrons gave the garden a blossoming look, at least. When my father came home that evening, the damage must have looked minor to him. He didn't act too upset. But who could really tell, Winnie? He was a quiet man of earthquakes.

Neither Courtney nor I could fall asleep. We were both in shock over what had happened, too shocked to even talk about it. Finally she got up and opened the window. She was burning up. It was the middle of the night.

"It's Us versus Them, Suzy. It's war."

"War?" I said.

"Next thing you know they'll set your house on fire."

"No, they won't," I said. My heart was beating so hard I could hear it. I wanted to move to California. I wanted to move back to Massachusetts. I wanted to be anywhere but here.

"Yes, they will!" she whispered. "We have to show them up. Otherwise they'll do it again and again! You know it's true!"

Yes, I knew it was true. This time I couldn't hush it away. They had gone too far; they had jumped the fence and crossed the boundary. It wasn't Courtney's war, but she was on my side; she wanted to fight. And something suddenly seized me—I didn't want to be a quiet girl of earthquakes anymore. We got dressed and sneaked out of the house.

First we ran up and down Lilac Lane, spitting on every lawn. Spit! Spit! Spit! Winnie, it felt like nothing else, just running and spitting in the summer darkness. I felt removed and on the prowl, as though a marvelous, monstrous part of me had crawled out of my soul.

Next we crept into backyards, our shadows larger than life on picket fences. We trampled on flowerbeds and dug up bulbs. We knocked over flowerpots and kicked bricks. We cursed everyone to high heaven, hiss, hiss, hissing. The exhilaration! Courtney, earth in her fingernails, hair bouncing in her frenzied face. Me, uprooting snapdragons like I was yanking limbs out of joint, then stomping on their corpses. Making graves out of gardens. Yes, yes, yes! This was my night to spit back on the world in front of the God who had put me here, then looked the other way. I wanted the night to go on forever, but it didn't. It stopped when I saw Courtney wavering in the moonlight. Was she sobbing?

"Courtney?" I said.

"He didn't want me anymore, Suzy!"

"Who didn't want you?"

She shook her head. "My father! He didn't want me living with him anymore!"

I caught my breath, I didn't know what to say.

"That's why I'm here!" she cried.

I remember that speechless moment, how it all made sense to me, although had this happened the night before or the night after, who knows. Maybe the night was crystal clear because I knew just then that it all came down to this: What had brought us together, what made this night happen, when she would rally all her anger and then crumble to the ground, was a feeling of being unloved, but never uttering the word. Why? Because it would echo from here to eternity.

Your grandfather lived long enough to plant more flowers in his rock garden, but after he passed away nothing ever grew there again. We watered, it rained—nothing. It's true, Winnie, you have to believe me. Don't limit yourself to the sights and sounds of a seaport town.

And yes, Courtney and I got into trouble for what we did, and we'd get into a lot of trouble after that. That was the beauty of it! You have to live for those moments when you're drunk on your own blood and your fever drives you out the door. Winnie, we conquered the world! We spat on and we tore up and we murdered Lilac Lane!

I'll never forget how the skies opened up for me, and I caught a glimpse of Courtney, her face in years to come—gorgeous and rebellious and smoking with rage—while I broke branches like I was breaking every bone on the block. God, the liberation! Even now, when I'm feeling beaten and weakened and stalked by the footsteps behind me, I go back to that night when I felt more powerful than the tall trees around me, when my heart and soul and character came to life.

MIJIN LEE
A Collective Voice

Skin

My skin is pale, showing every freckle, beauty mark, bump and knick. It has shed the tan I grew up with in California, after my family moved to Korea. I am embarrassed to wear shorts for fear of blinding people. When I visit my aunt in California for the first time since we've moved to Korea, she looks at me and says how *bboyae* my face is, how clean and glowing. She says she can see my face well.

When I am in middle school, a boy I do not know slaps me in the face. My skin stings from shock then becomes numb. I don't understand why he hits me and I hold my cheek; I can't say anything until he has walked away. I yell at his back, words that I hope will break his bones, but he continues to walk as if he cannot hear me.

When I am in high school and whenever I fly home to Korea during college, my mother and I visit the *mogyoktang*, the bathhouse, once a week. We sit on pink plastic stools at faucets next to one another. We turn our stools so that she is sitting behind me. She dips the small rough towel into the bowl of water and scrubs my back until it turns red. All the sweat and dirt roll off into gray eraser marks, which are then rinsed off with the shower head. The dead skin cells slough off, allowing the layer of fresh skin underneath to breathe. My mother runs her soapy hands over the curves of my blades and down the deep crease along the center. She rinses again until my back is smooth and clean. We both turn around, and I do the same for her.

My skin is prone to cuts and bruises, but over time they always heal. My skin protects; it questions anything that comes near—a light touch, grip, a warm breath, spit, a gaze, glare, music, noise. My skin inhales and exhales, deciding who and what to absorb.

Eyes

My father tells me I shouldn't buy *Seventeen* magazine, because I am not seventeen yet. I argue that all of my friends subscribe and their parents never say anything. He gives in, but says it's junk and not good for me. My eyes devour the bright-colored photos of tall slender models with flawless skin, long legs and large round eyes framed with shimmery eye shadow. I turn the glossy pages for hours until my stomach feels sick from the desire to look like every girl in that magazine. My father becomes angry when he catches me letting my younger sister flip through *Seventeen* for the first time. Now I know why.

My eyes have no creases; my eyelids fold under and disappear when I blink. I never realize that this is what makes my eyes different from the magazine eyes until I hear of my friend's operation. She has just graduated from high school, and I've graduated from middle school. She comes to church wearing sunglasses, and I try to see through the tinted lens to see how her eyes have changed. Finally she takes the shades off, and I try not to gawk at her eyes which are red and swollen as if she has cried or someone has hit her. There are visible incisions in her eyelids like red thread patching up a tear, woven in and out of her delicate skin. They call it the *ssangkapul susul*, the "double-lid surgery." My classmates in college have no idea what I'm talking about when I mention this procedure. I explain to them the words, "double eyelids" and "creases." The only person who already knows what I'm talking about is an Asian Pacific American woman in that class. The others come up to me and examine the upper rims of my eyes then stare at each other's eyelids to make the comparison. "Oh, I see," they say, "now I see."

Do you? I ask with my eyes.

Ears

"*Ching chang chong.*"

"Why don't you go and make your computers?"

Different voices enter my ears and try to slice my throat from within. When I am young the words are easy to react to; I give Joey the finger with a "fuck you" to go along with it, and I shove that middle-school boy into the wall for asking me about computers. Joey runs to get Mrs. Lincoln, our fourth-grade teacher, telling her, "That girl just said a bad word."

"Is this true?" she asks me.

I nod my head then tell her why. Mrs. Lincoln bends down to tell me that sometimes I have to let words go through one ear and out the other. But I still hear them—hundreds of variations—and they hardly ever pass through as if taking a harmless stroll. Instead, the words enter both ears and push their way down my throat, through my chest and into my stomach. I am learning to shit the words out, telling myself that nobody has the right to make me feel this way, that those words are just a clatter of noise. But the noise never ends, and my body continues to work.

My ears listen for truth-words to live on, words that resound. They listen carefully to my relationships, my people and my self.

My ears have their own language of sounds that are my home.

These are the familiar sounds of scraping spoons and clicking chopsticks, my mother talking of cooking and new recipes, my father's steady voice that rarely ever rises above a certain level, my sister's songs and my brother's winged laugh. My friends build nests within me. Their voices and the absence of their voices roost like birds that stay, migrate, but always return.

Nose

In fourth grade I do a report on Bill Cosby and notice we have the same flat nose. So I brag to my friends that I have a Bill Cosby nose. On TV I watch an Asian girl look at herself in the mirror taping her eyes wide open and pinching her nose with a clothespin. I hear other Asian Americans complaining their noses are too flat. I hear about nose surgeries that involve breaking the bone of the bridge, replacing it with an artificial structure and splicing off any flesh that flares beyond three quarters of an inch. In Korea my sister and I play a game of pointing out women who have this surgery, cringing at the unnatural dents and pinched appearance of their noses. Now we play the guessing game of pointing out the women who have no surgery, wondering if their faces are really natural.

I have my dad's nose—a *manil koh*, garlic nose. In college, my nose smells home when I am near the scent of bean paste, garlic and dried salty seaweed wrapped around white rice. I am unfamiliar with spices such as oregano, paprika and basil; I can never smell the difference. So I stick to *gkochu-gkalu* or red pepper, sesame oil and soy sauce to give my food flavor.

Mouth

My family eats Korean food almost every night. When we live in California my mom cooks American food every Friday, and I look forward to these nights. They are special, because I feel like a normal American kid. In high school I discover the perfect combination of kimchee and spaghetti. My father tells me, laughing, that I will get a hole in my stomach if I keep eating such spicy foods. Korean food is only eaten at home, at *hanshik* restaurants and at church. In ninth grade I hate the foreign exchange students who speak Korean so loudly in the center of campus and eat *gimbab* in class, bringing Korea to school. But in eleventh grade I begin to learn to take my home with me wherever I go. Strong smells of kimchee and *japchae* linger among Mr. Byrd's lectures of *Tess of the D'urbevilles* and *The Scarlet Letter* as I share my lunch box with classmates.

When my family sits at the dinner table, we each have our own rice and broth. In the center is a huge hot pot full of thick spicy stew and side dishes like kimchee, *namul* and *gkaenneep* we share. Our spoons dip into the stew, our chopsticks into the *banchan* – the taste of my family settles into my tongue.

When I first learn to speak, my tongue becomes comfortable practicing the dance of *gah nah dah lah mah bah sah, ah jah chah kah tah pah hah*. I am three and I run my finger over the black-printed words of a storybook, translating them into a language of my own, of words I've picked up from my parents and love to say.

Then I am five years old and learning how to speak in complete English sentences, blowing air out through my two front teeth and bottom lip to say my *f*s. Every Wednesday the students who can't speak perfect English get pulled out of class to go to speech therapy where we receive lollipops for improvement.

People think it strange when my parents speak to us in Korean and my sister and I respond in English. Before kindergarten I always speak Korean, because it is the language breathed at church, among my relatives, and in my home – the only three places I am familiar with at this age. When I begin to attend school, we learn to speak the American language of Smurfs, hula hoops and hopscotch. We bring into the house pieces of America. Worried, my mother makes us go to Korean language school on Saturday mornings because our tongues are forgetting how to shape the sounds and patterns of Korean, her language. But we complain that we hate the school, that we don't need to know Korean in America. That was then.

In ninth grade she hears me ask her, yelling, why don't I feel American, as I'm washing the dishes the hot water stinging my hands. She can't answer and watches me, not understanding why I'm almost crying.

In elementary school I made jokes in class, because I had control when I was able to make others laugh. When my body and face began to transform into an awkward adolescent, I refused to attract attention. I began to hear the words – quiet girl, shy and reserved. So I believed those words were me, and the silence took control, my voice becoming lost.

I was once divorced from my parents when I wanted to be fully American. I wished they would whisper when speaking to me in public, their Korean sounding loud and out of place. But now I love to hear their tongues dance variations of *gah nah dah lah mah bah sah, ah jah chah kah tah pah hah*. Now I speak

Konglish—a mixture of Korean and English, both existing in the same sentences. I realize boundaries are created to indicate who belongs where or where belongs to whom. My identity straddles the boundaries. The search for my voice has become my voice. It has been with me all along.

When I was young I sang church songs to hear my voice. In choir I held out the last note as long as I could so that I was the only one heard. Now I sing the same songs to hear another voice sing to me – the voice of the song. The words, like carefully wrapped parcels, provoke gratitude and open wide like windows and doors. I listen to the touch of my mother's hand on my back, the sound of music my friends create and the taste of the food I share with my family. I learn to sing, I learn to speak, by listening.

ZOLI SUEK KIM HALL

Meditation on Andrew Wyeth's "Christina's World"

Christina is it time to wake up now?
your body rises   one hand moving forward
across an ocean of field
dividing you from the house

would you swim across the grass to get there?
and what would be waiting for you behind the closed door?
would the knife drop to the kitchen floor?
it's silver clang echoing like the stabbing of voices against your chest...
    where is the purple crayon to draw a kite to fly yourself out from here...

I watch the birds ignite into black V's...   freeze in midair
like the shadows of fingers   creased in your pink dress

Christina – tell me is this where the only survivor would go?
        running from the opening of the house's dark mouth

your heart pounding into your back   leaning into the earth
the house becoming a faraway eye
the dragonfly wings of your bangs lifted by the wind
into the honey wheat blades

        with no words left to mind except your own
        in this stopped place
        in the safety of distance
        from the house into the field

which place becomes the chosen place?

if I tapped you on the shoulder   would you turn around to face me...
and when I shed my innocence about you
  my hand then reaches open
  the first exit into the frame of my own life

  a room that unfolds a table of pageantry
  set with alabaster white cake   and *lefse* glittering like snow

  my parent's laughter clinking against the water glasses
  the word alien baptized from my new crisp American name
  and for the snap of a camera's second
  what is caught in the family album

  is the face of a daughter   staring off the edge of a picture
  like a startled black comma,   in a field of blonde hair.

*Norwegian word for a flat potato pancake bread traditionally served with butter and sugar

CAROLYN SUN
Eunice and the Center

My parents like to act like I'm going to day camp even though I am 24-years-old and a bit overripe for any type of camp. I guess it is easier for them to pretend, because they're rather touchy about the truth. My bitch sister has no problem referring to it as "the loony bin." It's not a loony bin. It's a hospital program for women's health issues. For $360 a day, I ought to be able to call it whatever I damn well feel like, although "The Center" suits me fine, since that's what it says on the doorbell, and who am I to argue with that kind of authority.

My father picks his nose while driving and shoves those same fingers inside the bag of shrimp chips sitting between us in the car. I stare at his crude fingers, way too round and wide to be poking around in such small spaces. They belong to the hands of a carpenter or a sheet metal worker. Not an eye surgeon who slices and dices at a tune of $2,500 an eye, cold cash.

"Dad, can you speed up a bit?" I try to counter the irritation in my voice with a hearty fake chuckle, but end up choking on my own saliva, causing him to finally acknowledge my presence by glancing at me and saying, "Careful there, princess."

I used to feel so special when my dad called me princess. Doesn't every Daddy's little girl want to be a princess? One day, back when I still wore Osh Kosh B'Gosh overalls and a bowl haircut, I overheard my dad calling my other sister princess as well, and that plain ruined it for me. I mean, if he's going to be throwing around that pet name to that nasty, old dykeface, then I just don't want it.

"Eunice, hand me a tissue."

I rummage around my purse and hand him a coffee-stained napkin from Starbucks that has bits of tobacco stuck to it. He doesn't seem to notice and gives a mighty honk, which makes me jump. Someday that man is going to blow his brains right through his ears. He hands me back the napkin, and I'm not quite sure what to do with it and end up sticking it inside a map of upstate New York in the side door pocket.

Bored, I reach into the bag of shrimp chips and shove a fistful into my mouth as if my life depended on it. The rhythmic crunch of the chips fills the silent void in the car, and I start to crunch to the beat of Aerosmith's "Dude Looks Like a Lady" spinning inside my head.

"Eh, lay off the chips, Eunice." He grabs my hand before it hits the bag. I am tempted to turn, grab the steering wheel and swerve into a cement-block wall. I am fuming inside and suck my nails for consolation.

We're nearly at The Center anyhow. A few more blocks down Fifth Avenue, a turn onto 36th Street and voila, here we are, Pops, day camp for the mentally disturbed! The car brakes smoothly in front of the nondescript brick building that looks like every other Murray Hill facade, except for the strange shit that goes on inside every day. But this is New York, and strange shit goes on everywhere.

My dad leans over and gives me a tepid peck on the cheek. His kiss feels like a stamp of unspoken disappointment.

"OK dad, see you at five."

He gives me a strange watery-eyed look, and I am afraid for a second that he is about to cry. Then he lets out a gassy belch and drives off, leaving me standing at the curb in a kimchi-and-garlic wake.

I walk over to the entrance of the building and finger the intercom button that reads THE CENTER, 1B. Someone buzzes me in, and I enter a musty-smelling room lit by two cheap halogen lamps standing at the opposite ends. An overly cheery chorus of "Hello, Eunice!" and polite weekend inquiries topple me. I say hello back, ignore the questions and take my place next to the only girl fatter than me, Lisa. Lisa is wearing leather jeans today, which completely takes me off guard. I can't stop staring. Seeing an extremely fat girl in leather jeans is a somewhat rare phenomenon, and I am left wondering how many cows had to die to make that particular pair.

There is a new girl sitting in the room today, which sort of bugs me because I don't like surprises or new people, both of which I equate with unpleasantness I am unprepared for. To make matters 50 times worse, the new girl is strikingly pretty, despite her extremely emaciated form, and I am hell-bent on hating the bitch. This is the kind of girl who waltzed out of the womb all gorgeous and shit and made guys cream since elementary school. I, on the other hand, was the type who had to rely on the short-lived charm of being a chubby kid to get my fill of compliments. We would never have been in the same room, let alone sitting at the same table, had this crazy bitch not let her cheerleader's diet go apeshit. Fury besieges me, and I want to lunge across the table and wrap my hands around her reedlike neck.

"Attention everyone! This is Naomi. Today is her first day, and I thought we could start out the morning by introducing ourselves and saying a little bit about ourselves."

Joan, the program director, makes eye contact with me and gives an encouraging nod. I start to speak.

"Uh, hi. My name is Eunice. I am a compulsive overeater and yo-yo dieter. I am 24 years old and I live in Englewood, New Jersey, with my parents, Jae Sook and Young Heh." I keep my eyes on the tablecloth the whole time, hoping to avoid seeing the expressions of dismay mixed with pity and freak show fascination that midgets and dwarfs must get when they walk down the street in the "big people world." I mean, I already know I'm not anyone's wet dream.

After the introductions are over, the buzzer rings and my stomach growls, anticipating the delivery of our breakfast. We eat breakfast and lunch at The Center, so that we, the patients, can learn how to eat like normal human beings without all the freakish behaviorisms. It's community chow time, then a brief discussion of how we feel during and after the meal, and then off to group therapy.

"One egg-white omelet with feta. Two bagels with peanut butter and jelly—is this your fruit cup? Who ordered the rye toast?" A roll call of the order is shouted out, and my eyes anxiously roam the spread for my pancakes and banana. Someone passes them toward me along with a small carton of 1%.

"Don't forget to drink your protein, Eunice." How can I forget my protein, my darling dipshit? I rip open the foil wrapping and tear into the food like lion does to kill.

SHRIMP CHIPS! PANCAKES! WHERE IS THE GODDAMNED SYRUP??? Pace yourself, girl. After all, I don't want Miss Gorgeous Anorexia Case over there vicariously living through the sight of me stuffing my cheeks. I consciously slow down by chewing my food 20 times per mouthful (which is quite the effort, since you're basically chewing your own tongue by the 15th chew) in an attempt to make my food last as long everyone else's.

Lisa, who is sitting next to me, beings to cry, and the motion of her heaving body causes my milk to splatter the front of my sweater. I shoot her an evil look and proceed to ignore her, just like everyone else at the table except the new girl. We're all used to seeing Lisa cry. She cries at breakfast and during art therapy, movement therapy, child-regression therapy, basically anywhere she has an audience. Better not drip any tears on those jeans, you might shrink them wallet-size.

I am dying for a cup of Dunkin' Donuts coffee–cream–sugar, but the program doesn't allow room for caffeine drinks, which they explained on my first day here. I wasn't paying close enough attention to remember the reason. Random and seemingly nonsensical denials of petty pleasure are standard in any program about mental health.

It's ten minutes to ten and we have to start art therapy soon, so the staff begins to clear the table, at which point I stab the last bite of pancake into my mouth before we start our postbreakfast discussion.

"Since it's your first day, Naomi, why don't you just watch and listen so you can get the hang of things? Lisa? Can you please start off?"

Lisa's pained expression is that of a person who has suffered an open chafing sore on her asshole for her entire life. It makes me wish imminent death and destruction upon her. I impatiently drum my fingers on my knee, knowing that she is about to pull off one of her dominate-the-group-discussion monologues on her woe-begone past.

"I c-c-can't…I c-c-can't! I just can't eat! This food reminds me of…oh the pain…the pain…my life. My childhood. Oh-ho-ho-ho…"

She sounds like a bad after-school-special script and for a girl who claims she can't eat; she seems to do pretty fine in that department. Even Joan seems to be wary and kindly moves onto the next person at the table, me.

"Everything is OK. I feel great." Succinctness is universally appreciated. Next please. We go around the table, sharing our feelings, and Kelly, the art therapist, floats into the room, all wispy and caftans. "Good morning, girls."

Good morning to you, too, Miss Lucky Charms. She is wearing one of her faintly ethnic getups that look like they're hand-sewn by some underpaid native factory worker south of the border. Her unruly blonde hair is pulled back with a banana clip that looks about five thousand years old.

She exhales one of her "cleansing breaths" and looks at us. Someone once told me that she moved from her native Dublin to New York to be with her woman lover, who later returned to her husband and kids after the whole lesbian bit grew old. So Kelly went back to school to get her degree in art therapy at some community college continuing education program and landed a gig teaching here. What a marvelous comfort.

It's time to break out the cheap, grayish paper, Crayolas and pastels. We assemble around the cabinet and compete for the biggest and best box of crayons with the most colors intact. I am not fast enough and get stuck with a crappy box of pastels that have about three nubs of color. Shit.

"Gather around the table, girls. Today we are going to draw our diseased self and our healthy self. Close your eyes for a moment and create a blank canvas in your mind. Draw whatever comes to you, and then we'll talk about it afterward."

I close my eyes but all I see is blackness and some early signs of cataracts.

Then I open my eyes and look around to see that everyone has begun drawing. My diseased self and my healthy self. I like how they call obesity a disease here. It sounds tragic, like I am some hapless victim who just got in the way of too many Oreos.

I pick up the vermilion-hued pastel, because it's the only one long enough for my meaty fingers to grasp, and begin scribbling furiously over the paper. Chalk dust flies all over the room, and a pink dust coats the front of my black sweatshirt. The people next to me glance at me irritably. What, you don't like that? You don't recognize my innate, abstract genius? You're lookin' at the next Joan MotherFucking Miró.

I feel Kelly's New Agey presence looming behind my shoulder and hear her voice, "My, what an interesting drawing you've got there, Eunice. Do you care to share with the group what it means and what feelings were behind this terribly powerful creation you've made?" No, you feel-good, crystal-worshipping jingle bell, I do not care to share either my feelings, or even a cigarette with any of you.

"Yeah, OK. Um, well I used the color pink to express my intense anger. It is such a vivid color, and it also looks so pretty against the paper. This mad scribbling over here, yeah, that one…what?"

Lisa interrupts my explanation to ask me if the angry scribbles represent my overeating, and to make her shut up I agree, "That's pretty perceptive, Lisa, those scribblings do represent the eating disorder and the havoc that it has wreaked upon my life. See this small patch of uncolored paper in the corner? That's me. The healthy part, that wants to come outside."

I speak with the sincerity and clarity that is reserved for my public persona and my peers. The Irishwoman seems pleased with my response, and I get the nod of approval from her before she moves on to the next pupil. My thoughts drift off as someone else starts yapping, and I try to stifle an enormous yawn that threatens to crack my head in two.

My eyes wander around the room and rest on the new girl, Naomi. She hasn't said a word since she has been here, but I bet she'll be on everyone's favorite best-friend list by the end of the day. I watch her as she picks the pills on her sweater and rolls them into a small ball of wool. If she keeps it up, she will have enough wool to knit a sweater for the dog she probably has at home. She seems nervous and even shy. What the hell has she got to be nervous about? I notice that her nails are bitten and ragged like mine, and I feel a surge of affection for her that lasts for a good 10 seconds.

She's nervous, I'm nervous. Maybe we can be friends. But what about the people who snicker and stare and talk behind our backs when they see us walking down the street together and call us Abbott and Costello? Will she be strong enough to withstand the social pressure? Eventually, she will surrender to the embarrassment and pressure, like they always do. One day, she will quit returning my phone calls and act civil when she sees me, but pretend like we never had a friendship in the first place.

My eyes narrow at the injustice that hasn't yet been inflicted upon me by this potentially evil girl, and I shoot the nastiest glare I can muster toward her direction. She returns a confused look and quickly drops her eyes to her lap, where her hands continue to fidget with the ball of wool.

It's nearly break time, and I am dying for a cigarette. At the first indication that therapy is over, I pick up my jacket and dart out the door without helping to clean up. Once outside, I light up my Lucky Strike and start to cross the street. The staff of The Center doesn't like us to smoke outside the building. Apparently they don't want smokers to be synonymous with their clean-bill-of-health image.

While I'm crossing the road, a cab driver gasses up, hell-bent on hitting the "fat girl." Ten points for normal pedestrians, 20 for fatties. I race across and hit the sidewalk, relieved to have my body intact. In the mad scramble, I have somehow lost my cigarette, so I pull out another one and inhale deeply, noting that it tastes like moldy mushrooms but not really caring. At least my migraine is gone.

Maybe I should cut my losses and take the train home early today. I have actually never taken the train to New Jersey before. Is there a train to New Jersey? I wouldn't know, I always get a ride. But Lisa is getting on my tits big time today, and I might be in for attempted manslaughter by the end of the day.

Minutes pass and Joan's figure emerges from the building entrance across the way. "Break's over, Eunice. Come inside." She looks at me expectantly and waits for me to join her. What am I going to do, give her the finger and run away like a lunatic? I stub out my cigarette and slowly move toward her. Story of my life – cowardly. Well, lunch is in an hour anyhow, and today I ordered the baked ziti.

crossing

TINA Y. LEE
My Mom Across America

There once was a mother duck and a daughter duck. Now the daughter duck never listened to the mother duck. In fact, she did everything the opposite of whatever her mother asked. When the mother duck asked her to do her homework, she would go out and play. When the mother duck asked her to come home and eat her dinner, she would throw her food on the ground. When the mother duck was about to die, she thought to herself, "I finally know her game. I am going to ask for the opposite of what I want." The mother duck really wanted to be buried up in the mountain side, but she told her daughter to let her body go down the river. One day, the mother duck died. The daughter duck, looking down on her mother's body, thought to herself, It's time to get serious. I must do as my mother wishes. And so she took her mother's body, and dragged it to the river, and let it go.

—A traditional Korean folk tale

When I was a kid, my two biggest fears in life were dogs and being Korean. Dogs, because I was afraid they'd hunt me down and kill me. Every dog is Cujo to me. When I see a dog, I start running and screaming. Now being Korean—that's harder to explain. I've never actually screamed in terror from being Korean, so what do I mean? Well, for one thing, I panic that Koreans will come up to me and start speaking to me in Korean. I don't speak the language, and when they find that out, they start clucking their tongues and say something like... "*Ay-gu, keun-ill nat-neh!*" which means "Alas, what a shame." I turn beet red and get so stressed about it. It doesn't matter that I'm an adult with an adult lifestyle, adult pursuits. When someone starts speaking to me in Korean, I automatically feel like a little kid. It's just one more thing I'm supposed to do that I don't. I am a fake Korean.

When I was 13 years old, I went to tennis summer camp. I was assigned to room with a girl from Japan. Her name was Hiroko. The camp administrators probably thought she and I would have a great deal in common because we were the only two Asian girls at the camp. Hiroko did not speak a word of English, and I did not speak any Japanese. No one spoke to either of us that summer. No one sat at our lunch table at meal times. At first, I couldn't figure out why, and then I started to think of the way we must've looked to everyone else: different. We did not look like everyone else. That night, Hiroko came to our room, fell on my bed and cried in her thick accent: "I hate America!"

I could've comforted her, but I chose not to.

After that summer, I developed a strategy: If I wanted to be seen as me, I needed to open my big old mouth and talk in my big old New Jersey English. I didn't have any desire to stand out; my goal was to be bland, forgotten, fit in. So I told everybody I was Jewish. I grew up in a predominantly Jewish community. Most of my good friends are Jewish. My junior high school teacher, whom I'm still tight with is Jewish, and so I just started to tell everyone I was Jewish. I loved going to Passover, asking the four questions, singing from my friend's family's tattered songbooks. I used to tell people, "*Ga kaffin often yam*," which means "Go shit in the ocean" in Yiddish. After my first year of college, I came home to visit my junior high school teacher.

"Mrs. Garvin, I'm Asian American," I said.

She turned to me slowly with a stern look. "You are Jewish. I don't want to talk about it. End of discussion."

And then she fed me.

When my mom asked me to go to Seattle and Canada with her and my father, I thought, *Great!* I was in graduate school at the time, getting my MFA in fiction writing. I had to see things, I had to go to new places. Experience would change me, what I thought of the world, and me in it. So travel seemed like a good thing, and I didn't do it that often, because I don't work for Smith Barney. I'm in the arts. And I love my parents. I love being with them. Most of the time. For limited amounts of time. But all in all, we enjoy each other, and so when Mom asked me to go, I said yes.

We fly to Seattle. The plan is to spend one night with my mother's friends, and then go north to Canada. My father, who is possibly the most antisocial person on earth, is always irritated with people, so while Mom bonded with her buds, I had Dad to hang out with. He wears these sunglasses that make him look like he's from *Top Gun*, and he just stands there, not talking to anybody, chewing his Freedent gum, looking grim. But his jacket pockets are always packed with all this stuff he's not allowed to eat (Mom's rules): Kit Kats, Snickers, all kinds of candy he hands out to every little kid we see. If there's a cute face, he's breaking his back to give out that candy. Before we go to meet her friends, Mom insists on checking what we're wearing.

"You gained weight!"

This is a typical greeting from my mother. It's like I say, "Good morning," and she replies, "You gained five pounds!" She's always been critical of what I look like, which she says is in my interests. It's her theory that people treat you with respect when you look nice, pretty. I do have an affection for clothing with holes, but I'm on vacation. I'm here to relax. I could fight back, but I also know that these are my mom's friends and she likes to make a good impression, so I go and change. Dad comes out in this bright orange golf T-shirt and these hideous green pants, the belt pulled up to the middle of his chest. Mom gives him a look. He turns around to go change.

By the time we're ready to leave, I'm in a dress and Dad's in a suit. We go to meet my mother's friends. All three of them bring their husbands, so Dad goes over to yuk it up with the men. It's a bunch of old Korean couples and me. Everyone's talking and laughing, in Korean. Then one of them turns to me and asks me something in Korean.

Now all I know how to say is "*Mi-ahn-hae-yo, han-guk-mal-eun uh-ryu-wo-yo,*" which roughly means "Sorry, Korean is difficult." This is the only thing I remember from a Korean class I once took —that and "*Maek-joo han-byung joo-sae-yo*"—"May I please have a bottle of beer?" Neither of which I can say to my mother's friends without humiliating myself.

"Um, actually?" I start. "I don't really speak Korean."

"*Ay-gu, keun-ill nat-neh!*" says Mom's friend. "That is such a shame."

My mom's friends have planned a "fun" night for us, one of those musical-theater dinner cruises where the wait staff is also the entertainment. Before the buffet dinner, they sing "Rhythm of the Night" by El Debarge and some hits from the '50s like "Leader of the Pack." My mom's friends start to talk about what their kids are doing. One woman's son is a doctor, another woman's daughter is a lawyer, and yet another woman's daughter is a Rhodes scholar who went to England and met another Rhodes scholar. Now they're getting married and having little Rhodes scholar babies. They turn to me, and I can guess where this is headed.

"So, Yunny or Tee-na, what is your job?"

"I'm in graduate school," I say hesitantly. "I'm getting an MFA in fiction writing."

They look at each other. No one says anything; no one's really smiling. They're not rude people; they probably just don't know what that means. They probably don't know anyone who's a writer. Mom grabs my arm,

"I want her to go to law school, but she never listens to me."

My mother has asked me to go to law school, since my first day out of the womb. Though it is clear that I am never going to be a lawyer, she keeps at it. It's like a breakup she never got over. She says it without knowing she's saying it. Once, after a family dinner, we ended up playing Trivial Pursuit.

"Mom? What's the capital of France?" I asked, card in hand.

"Law school!" yells Mom before pausing a moment. "Oh sorry. Did I say it again?

But I also know things would be easier for her if I were a lawyer. People know what that is. It's a real job. It's something her friends can get jealous of. I turn away from the conversation and try to get absorbed in the "entertainment" show, which is a little bit of a mistake, because the band has started playing the macarena, and the wait staff is really into it. They're grinning, singing and dancing around the tables, trying to get people to join in. Now, I really dislike audience participation. It's too much pressure. Once they pick you, that's it; you've got to go. So I turn my chair and stare at my plate, hoping they'll skip me. No such luck. Two baby-faced boy waiters spot me and quickly surround my chair. I can see them out of my peripheral vision, which has always been excellent. I hear them:

"Oh, come on! It'll be fun!"

I'd really rather, at this point, press the butter knife into my temple than dance the macarena, but I don't want to be rude. Maybe if I keep staring down at my plate, they'll think I'm deaf, but then all of sudden, this powerful spotlight shines on our table, and now the pressure is on—on me and the two boys. They start tugging on my arms, and I have to slap my hands onto the table to hold on.

"No, really! I'm fine, thank you!" I smile up at them politely from my death grip on the table, and then Mom butts in.

"Come on, Yunny, you're a good dancer!" I turn to my mother in horror, but she doesn't stop. "She has a good voice too! She was in her high school musical!" she practically screams to her friends. So it's either stay here at the table or get up and dance. I end up dancing the macarena.

Finally, it's time to hit the road. We pull into a parking lot, and I feel enormous relief. Now, I can be myself. I don't have to not know what everyone's saying all the time. We say good-bye to my mother's friends, and it's time for the real vacation to begin. The three of us, driving through the Canadian countryside. No schedule, no homework, no job: I can finally relax.

In the parking lot, there is a bus with the words Arirang Bus Tour written on its side in Korean and English. I see a bunch of Koreans stuffing their suitcases and duffel bags into the bowels of the bus. I stare at them, because...well because, they're Korean, and Koreans stare at each other. And then Mom starts heading toward them with her suitcase.

I turn to Dad. "What is she doing?"

Dad doesn't say anything, just puts a peppermint candy in my hand and follows her. I follow them, not really registering what's going on until I get on board and see a sea of Asian faces. I take in a deep breath. There aren't many seats left, so I follow my parents as they make their way toward the back. Every row is occupied by Asian faces. Senior citizens, parents, kids—and by kids, I mean five years old. I see one girl who's maybe 14 years old, but she is the oldest kid on the bus, except for, of course, me. And all of a sudden, I feel like the 30-year-old seated at the kids' table. That's fine, I tell myself, I can handle this. I just concentrate on Canada, how good it'll be. I keep walking. The seats are all gray, and there are little TVs every five rows. We get to the back by the bathroom. I grab a window seat, and my mother sits next to me. And then the tour guy gets on the mike and starts to speak in Korean.

"*An-nyung ha-sae-yo, an-nyung hae-sae-yo! Yuh-ruh-boon-eui guide Kim il-nam im-ni-da. O-neul-eun, teuk-byul-hee a-reum-da-un yuh-sung-boon-ee man-ah-suh, gi-boon-ee joh-seum-ni-da.*" Something, something in Korean. All in Korean.

People around me all laugh. Apparently, this guy is really funny. And then it hits me, just then, that I am stuck for a week on an all-Korean bus trip across Canada.

British Columbia
We stop in Vancouver for a photo opportunity, then drive through the night until we stop for lunch the next day. Our bus is the only vehicle in the lot, and the restaurant is in the middle of nowhere. We shuffle into the dining area as if we have just been released from a psycho ward—10 hours on a bus will do that to you. Inside, the place seems completely dead, but as soon as we arrive, this two-man band wakes up and starts to loudly play "Arirang," a traditional Korean folk song.

"Welcome, Arirang bus tour!"

The two men are in their 60s. The lead singer is the accordion player, and the drummer just smiles. Both of them seated underneath this sign—this computer printout—that just says K-O-R-E-A.

We line up for the buffet appetizers and watch. When they finish, we clap. It is nice; someone took the time to learn the song of another country. And then they start to play a series of Billy Joel songs, starting with "New York State of Mind," which is not altogether bad on the accordion.

We sit for the main course, a choice of salmon or steak, served to all 40 people from the bus. Dad and I both want to order the steak, but Mom says no.

"No good. Too much fat, cholesterol!"

Dad makes a face and orders the steak anyway.

"You see, Yunny? He doesn't care about his health at all. He eats junk all the time. David Letterman got bypass surgery. He's skinny. He exercises. He still got a heart attack. Same thing could happen to Dad. I want Dad to get bypass surgery."

"Mom, you can't just order surgery. Dad has to get a heart attack first."

"I don't care."

Ahh, I love it when my parents get along. I love when we talk about death before the food arrives. My mother is like Albert Camus trapped in an older Korean woman's body.

"Who?"

"Ca-moo. You know, the French guy who wrote about death. Existentialist. Author of *The Stranger*."

"Oh, Ca-moose."

She brings up death, when it's not even a distant glimmer in the conversation.

"Mom, can you pass the ketchup?"

"We can never catch up. We only live until we die."

We eat. Waitresses come and pick up our plates. The band breaks out into waltzes. "The Skater's Waltz," "The Blue Danube Waltz." There's a din of Korean from all the tables. It hangs like a cloud over my head. These two senior citizens get up to dance. The man must be the oldest person on the bus. His one shoulder is badly sloped down, or missing, and he's doing this one-armed waltz with this woman. They bob up and down, with stoic looks on their faces. There is no sign that they're actually enjoying themselves. Very Korean. I never see Koreans dance. It's an unnatural act.

Everyone is watching. Someone starts clapping, and pretty soon, the whole place starts keeping time as one big unit. Suddenly my mom gets up and starts dancing, and then my father gets up. Parents, kids, everyone is on the dance floor, bouncing around, laughing, having a great time. It's amazing, but I can't join in. Mom comes over to tug my hand, but I tell her I'm tired. I ask the waitress where the bathroom is and go to the back of the room to watch everyone from there. They are all dancing, everyone having a good time. Later, when my mom asks me why I didn't dance, I can't explain it. I feel a lump in my throat.

Alberta

We go to Jasper and stop at this breathtaking lake, the color of turquoise. We are so nestled in the mountains, you cannot hear a thing. After the lake, the bus drives us to a museum. I happen to like wax museums; there's something so creepy about them. They use real human hair for the figures and glass for the eyes. It's like, are they alive or aren't they?

The bus drops us off at the museum. We look around. There's a history/politics room, with past prime ministers and Laura Seacord, Canadian hero and chocolate manufacturer.

Then we go to the Hollywood room. They have John Candy, Michael J. Fox, Harrison Ford, Madonna and Mel Gibson in a Planet Hollywood T-shirt. The figures are all alternately sitting and standing on a platform about a foot from the ground. Behind them, there is mirror paneling from floor to ceiling, so that you can see your own reflection between the celebrities. When I stand on my tiptoes, I can see my own face above a crowd of Asian faces. Sometimes, when I'm at home alone, I look in the mirror, and I get surprised by what I see. It's like, Whoa! I'm Asian! Didn't see that coming! So it's extra-startling when I see my own face among these other Asian faces. I mean, these are my people. I stare at our reflection, trying to take it in. After all, this is the only way I'll get to see Asian faces in Hollywood,

Everyone starts leaving the Hollywood room, so I move up front to get a better look. It's just me and the dummies. Me and Harrison. Me and Madonna. Harrison, Madonna; Harrison, Madonna; Michael J. Fox, Madonna. Suddenly, I feel someone tap me on my shoulder.

"Shhhh," whispers a museum employee. "Hey, where did everyone go? I was going to show you guys this special Hollywood exhibit. Something you might like. Well, do you want to see it?"

He leads me to a door, which opens onto a short flight of stairs. I follow him. It's dusty and dry, but I continue. He leads me to the basement.

"Uh, what is this?"

"This is the special Hollywood exhibit I was telling you about," he whispers. "They say they'll bring it upstairs, but they never get around to it."

The place is packed with wax figures. There's Donnie and Marie Osmond; Gary Coleman; Anna May Wong; Paul Robeson: actor, lawyer, communist, he testified once in front of the House of Unamerican Activities; Michael Jackson, before all the cosmetic surgery, circa the *Off the Wall* album.

"What does this mean?" I ask.

"No idea. I was hoping you could tell me."

Back on the bus, onward to Banff. We have an entire afternoon to wander around on our own. When we get into town, people start to roam the expensive malls, packed with chocolate shops and kitschy gift stores. Mom and I walk past this pricey-looking beauty salon with a sign that says Free Makeover in the window. Mom drags me in.

"Don't you want to look pretty?"

There is something about the makeover option. I have this secret hope that they'll see something in me that no one else has.

"Excuse me, miss?" A handsome modeling agent stops me on the way out of the beauty salon, "But are you a model?"

"What?" I laugh, flipping my hair from my face playfully. "Who, me?

I get sucked in. The salon has these weird, modern computer options. A woman smiles at me and takes my picture with a digital camera. Pretty soon my image comes up on the computer, and the woman starts playing with it, clicking the mouse over my lines and freckles, all my imperfections. Then she starts to apply makeup.

"We can start with just a casual look. Or a more dramatic night look."

Mom chooses dramatic. I sit in this special chair. The woman releases a lever so that I tilt back. I see her and my mom on either side of me. As she applies the makeup, the woman talks over my face, telling my mom what does what.

"Lipstick, blush, eye shadow. Don't be afraid of black," she says, dragging a sharp pencil along my eyes.

"You see how I gently press the brush against the eyebrow? We could pluck these off."

"Yes!" Mom yells. "Let's pluck them off!"

What? The woman whips out a pair of tweezers from her coat.

"Ready for the new you?" says the woman.

"Wait a minute," I try calmly. "Can we talk about this?"

"Hold still, or it'll look *really* bad!" she chirps.

My mother and the makeup lady bend over my face and start plucking. I feel pinch after pinch. It takes me a moment to gather my wits. The makeup lady and my mother seem to hover right above, taking all my air.

"Stop!" I yell from the chair. "Stop right now!"

They back away suddenly as if I've broken a spell.

"Hand over the tweezers. Now."

The makeup lady does. She pushes a lever on the chair so that I am sitting upright and facing my reflection. There are chunks missing from my eyebrows and huge purple circles around my eyes. I look like a deranged raccoon.

We emerge. My father takes one look at me and just shakes his head.

"I know, Dad."

He hands me a Tootsie Roll.

Next, my parents and I take a ski lift up to one of the little mountain tops to take a walk. My mom is trying to tell me my face doesn't look that bad, that my eyebrow will grow back.

"Mom, please, let's just walk."

So we walk. It's silent up here, beautiful. No one's around, and that's when I notice that we're not alone. This boy, this teenager, not from our bus, is following us. He keeps darting in and out of view, like he's doing a relay race. Then he skips weirdly ahead of us; we stop. He tumbles into a handstand, holds it for a second, gets up, makes eye contact with *me*, and then takes off. It's like some weird squirrel mating dance.

"Mom, I think that kid is hitting on me."

"Who, that fat boy?" My mother yells, pointing at the boy as he runs away.

"Mom, can you lower your voice? Some people don't think that's a compliment."

"Yunny, please, when you date, don't have an affair with a married man, and don't go out with a boy with a chip on his shoulder."

"Mom, I'm don't want to date the kid; I'm just pointing it out."

Dad, sensing tension, hands me a Milky Way. Mom does not let up.

"You don't want to get married?"

I keep silent, hoping she'll drop it. We get to an outlook point. Mom is tired, so they both go into a little café. I stay with the view. It's the city of Banff nestled in this valley. It's lovely, this moment of quiet; and then, I hear footsteps. It's the boy. He skips up loudly and stands right next to me. I don't look at him; I just don't think it'd be a good idea for him to see my face up close. Doesn't bother him though; he just climbs on to the bench behind me.

"This view is amazing. Doesn't it make you want to fly? Fly like an eagle? I grew up here in Banff. I'm a musician. I play the drums."

We're silent. But how long can I ignore him without seeming rude? I turn around to give him a polite smile.

"What happened to your face?" His smile has dropped. "You know, you don't need to wear all that makeup. You're pretty enough without it."

And I blush. He's so sweet. He's so young. His face is so young, and him standing so close to me, with that unmistakable look in his eye, that lazy, goofy smile.

"I just wanted to give you this. Something to remember me by." He hands me something and runs away before I can say another word. I look in my hand. It's a key chain. It says Welcome to Canada.

Saskatchewan

We drive all day to Moose Jaw, Saskatchewan, and spend the night. Today, we get to choose our activity for the entire day. The choices are either an all-day yoga retreat or a tour of the Laura Seacord chocolate factory, where we get to sample the chocolates for hours and buy them in the end! Now I am all for sitting on my bum and eating chocolate, but when I wake up, I find that Mom has signed both me and herself up for yoga.

Mom reads me the brochure: "'Yoga works on every individual for his growth and betterment physically, mentally, emotionally and spiritually.' Oh, Yunny, you can lose weight!"

The bus tour has to rent this special van for us because we are the only two people who have chosen the yoga option. When we get there, a woman answers the door and says, "Shhh. You're late! Meditation has started." She leads us to the yoga studio. At the end of a long hallway, she opens a door to a separate room.

Inside, people are sitting on pillows, their backs to us, completely silent. At the front of the room, there's a man beating on an animal skin drum. We sit. After a few minutes, I start to notice that my heartbeat and the drumbeat are synchronized. The man starts to play slower and slower, until I begin to wonder how slow can he play before my heart just stops. And then I think about peace and nirvana, and all those things I think I should be thinking about during meditation. I am filled with a sense of wistfulness and longing for the chocolate factory. My mind is flooded with images of all the bus people happily eating chocolate and my father cramming his jacket pockets for later.

They turn on the overhead lights. It's time for the yoga to begin. We start with sun salutations. There is a bunch of stretching, breathing and posturing. Then the yoga teacher tumbles into a handstand. Now, I can barely do a somersault, so I try but immediately fail. Mom keeps trying; she's kicking up those skinny chicken legs, one after the other. The teacher comes over and picks her legs up. The position is crushing her neck, but before I can say anything, he steps away, and my mother falls. I can see from her face that she's really hurt herself. The teacher, not noticing, prods her to go on. I call the hotel to get picked up.

Mom doesn't say anything. She's never aggressive to strangers, just to me and my dad. During the van ride back, she falls asleep. Later that night, she complains about swelling in her neck, so the tour guide arranges for her to see a doctor.

"Mom," I ask when she gets back. "What did the doctor say?"

"Oh, I'm OK, but doctor said I almost paralyzed myself."

She is officially taking the night off. I go downstairs and get her a sandwich. When I get back, she's completely asleep, in her pajamas on top of the covers of the motel bed.

"Mom?"

Nothing. I put the sandwich on the nightstand and watch her. She's frowning in her sleep. I wonder what she's dreaming about. Her body is skinny, too skinny. She's skeletal. What's going to happen when she's really old or too sick to take care of herself? She's very young-looking, so people don't believe her when she's not feeling well. And her eyebrows look really good. She wakes up.

"Mommy, why do you still have eyebrow makeup on?"

"I can't take it off."

"Why?"

"It's a tattoo," she blurts out. "I didn't want to tell you because you're so sensitive about cosmetic surgery!"

"How long have you had it?"

"A couple of years. Emo recommended it. It saves me a lot of time in the morning."

"OK." I shrug and go to the bathroom to start a bath.

"Oh," Mom calls. "Are you taking a bath?

"No, this is for you."

"Wow, you rock, Yunny."

When I wake up the next day, my parents are already downstairs. On my nightstand, there is a plate with a bagel and a note. In my mother's neat, petite, pretty handwriting, she wrote, "Be a good girl, Yunny! Don't tell family secrets to friends!"

We drive through Manitoba, a land of lakes and wheat fields. We stop in this little neighborhood outside of Toronto. The bus pulls up at this Korean person's house. We all go to the backyard. I wonder if this is even legal. I mean, it's not drugs, but it's weird. This is someone's house, not an official tourist destination. I didn't know there were Koreans in Canada; I mean, other than us. The tour guy tells us that we have one of two options for dinner: *soon-doo-boo-jee-gae*, which is this bizarre primordial broth. It's beige, murky with clouds of tofu, and has mysterious claws poking out going "Help me," while other unidentified masses float by. And then there's *chja-jang-myun*, this kick-ass brown bean sauce noodle dish. It has meat, potatoes and lots of sugar, which I love. Any food that tastes like candy, I'm there. It's not a hardcore Korean meal the way the primordial broth is, so it's more likely to appeal to Americans, the non-Koreans and kids. Well, it's the one I pick—surprise, surprise—and my parents pick the primordial broth.

The tour guide then proceeds to *split us up* according to what we ordered. Excuse me? My stomach is suddenly completely knotted. I mean, I didn't have to talk to anyone as long as I was with my parents, and my secret non-Korean language complex could remain a secret. My parents walk away, arm in arm, totally oblivious to the fate that awaits me. "Mom! Dad!"

Nothing. I watch them get led into the house, while my "group" and I wait outside the house in total silence. My dinner companions are all about, oh, half my size. There's a very cute little 5-year-old boy, Peter, and girls—Elizabeth, age 6, Annie, 10, and Michelle, 14.

We sit at a picnic table, everyone sort of staring out into space. Peter, the 5-year-old, starts getting restless and takes out one of those little Matchbox cars from his pocket and starts zooming it across the table, across his sister's head. Michelle, the 14-year-old, looks bored. She's slim, pretty, showing none of the adolescent awkwardness I had to go through. And then there's Annie, the 10-year-old. She's pudgy, wears glasses and looks uncomfortable. After a while, she pushes up her glasses and turns to me.

"So, what grade are you in?"

Suddenly, it's not cool to say that I'm in graduate school.

"Uh, they don't have grades where I come from."

I pray she won't ask any more questions. No such luck.

"Do you have a job?"

"No, not exactly."

"Then what do you do?"

The woman of the house comes out for our drink orders. She turns to the kids first; the girls all speak impeccable Korean, even the little boy is like "the concept of pi is astonishing"—in Korean, and then she turns to me.

"*Muo-ma-shil-lae-yo?*"

I don't look at her; I pretend the trees are really fascinating. Maybe she'll go away, maybe she'll assume I don't drink beverages. "*Muo-ma-shil-lae-yo!*"

I'm getting redder by the instant. I mean, I understand why she's talking to me in Korean, because why would a non-Korean speaking person take an all-Korean bus tour across Canada. And then there's the pressure of this group thing, the pressure to perform. Can I really stand to get humiliated in front of a bunch of kids?

"*Maek-joo hang-byung joo-sae-yo*? May I please have a bottle of beer?"

She nods and leaves like she's going to get the beer. I'm so excited, I have to give myself a high five.

"What are you doing?" asks Annie.

"Um, high fives?"

"So what do you do?"

"Oh. I'm a writer."

"Like Judy Blume?" she gasps. Eyes widen, and it is the first time that I have ever said these words and received a positive reaction; I mean this girl is on fire with excitement. "Writer" doesn't automatically equal "poor" or "loser" in her eyes. I've never had this experience before in my life.

"Are you famous?"

"No, not really."

"Do you make a lot of money?"

"No, not really."

"Do you write novels?"

"No, I write short stories," which I feel like no one reads except other people who write short stories.

"What do you write about?"

"Actually, I write a lot about death."

"Death?" She asks with a slightly terrified look in her eyes.

"Yeah."

Wait a minute, I probably shouldn't be talking about death to a young girl. I could be causing irrevocable damage to her psyche, sending her to years of therapy, which is very expensive.

"Well, a lot of my characters die, or they lose someone important to them, and then the story is about how they deal with it or not deal with it," I deliver in one breath. I wait, hoping I haven't ruined everything. After a moment, the little girl faces me and grins.

"Wow. It's cool to be a writer."

And she's right. There is something, even when it's the biggest torture, when it's something I'm avoiding at costs. When I get on a writing roll, something else takes over, and I get surprised by what comes out. It's like those love stories where people find love in the most unexpected places.

"Do you write in Korean?" she asks.

"Actually," I say. "I don't really speak much Korean."

She looks at me. She doesn't look disappointed. She still has that look of admiration in her eye.

"Can I tell you something? I want to be a writer, just like you."

"You do?" Oh, this girl is warming my heart, making me feel so good.

"Or a waitress."

We drive for eight hours. To entertain the kids, they show *Mulan* on the bus on those little TVs. It's the fancy Disney cartoon movie with Korean subtitles. The story is about a war, and the father is about to get recruited, but there are all these shots of him hobbling on a cane. He cannot possibly make it through the army. And then Mulan sings about how she's just got to be herself, and she takes her dad's place in the war. She's so pretty.

I look at Mom; she's falling asleep. I look at Annie, who's enjoying the movie, so I try to enjoy it too. They show Mulan returning from war. Her father is all huddled over, but as soon as she approaches, she goes "Poppa," and he's all "Mu-Lan." They embrace, and then something happens to me. I don't know, something about watching the frail old man trembling, watching him hug his heroic daughter—it gets to me, and I start to cry. I'm horrified. I try to calm myself down, but it's overwhelming. Then the movie ends, the lights go up, and people start getting up to stretch.

"Why are you crying?" asks the now-awake Mom.

"I'm not crying," I sniffle.

"Oh yeah, you have tears on your face all the time?"

I don't want to talk about it, so I tell Mom I have allergies. This makes her worry.

We cross the border to Quebec, where 90 percent of Canada's Francophones live. Quebec is the most cosmopolitan territory of all of Canada; it's like Europe. There are tons of wonderful restaurants in Montreal. There's Chinatown, Little Greece, Little Italy—plenty of neat, interesting places to check out. But where do we go? What do we do? We're tourists; we shop.

Dad knows I'm upset, but feels awkward. He's not good with emotional scenes. He puts a Hershey's Kiss in my hand and stands outside the store to practice his golf swing. Mom and I enter the shop.

"Yunny, do you say 'I'm going for shopping' or 'going shopping'?"

"Going shopping."

"Ugh, why don't you correct me?"

"I don't know. You make so many errors, that one didn't seem that bad."

"My English is so bad, I should move back to Korea."

"What are you talking about? Your Korean is lousy too. Remember how Uncle made fun of your grammar? It's changed over there. You can't go back. You might as well stay here."

"Oh, if you made a lot of money, life would be so easy. I could retire. Why you choose writing? Writing is most difficult job. You have to read everything; you have to experience everything; you have to be sensitive about human nature. You have to be better than human! Why you pick most difficult path? Most kids, they start on the straight path, and then they go to sideways, but you—you start sideways. What about law school? You know John Grisham went to law school?"

"Yes, I know, Mom."

"Why don't you write a best-seller? Show me what you write. I want to see if it's any good."

"No."

"Why not?"

"Because you'll think it's weird."

"Oh, it's too sophisticated for me."

"No, that's not what I meant."

"Yunny, get something. I'll buy for you. You live only once. Until you die."

I hold up a white cable-knit turtleneck that says Canada across the front in red yarn.

"What do you think, is it me?"

Mom looks at the price tag. "Seventy-five dollars? Rip-off! If I get this for you, this is your birthday and Christmas present."

"Christmas? As in nine months from now?"

"Yeah."

I pick up this meat cleaver with the Canadian maple leaf sign engraved in the handle.

"What about this wacky knife? This will make a good birthday present."

Mom stops in her tracks.

"No, I will never give you a knife," she whispers intensely. "You sever the relationship when you give a knife."

"OK, don't get me the knife."

"I mean it, Yunny. Don't ever ask me for a knife."

"All right, I won't!"

"Because you sever the relationship when you give a knife! Tell me what's wrong. I saw you crying. It's good to talk. Otherwise, you gonna be like Daddy, and you gonna get a heart attack."

"It's nothing. I just got a little upset at the movie."

"The *cartoon*? You crying about a *cartoon*?"

How do I explain myself? It wasn't Mulan, or her adventures, or her pretty looks or her cheesy voice; it's just that moment when she returns from winning the war. Her parents are literally shaking, and she runs to hug them. They love her, and they miss her. She's perfect; she's the best daughter.

"I'm sorry I'm not a lawyer! I'm sorry I don't make truckloads of money! And God, am I sorry I don't speak beautiful, amazing, perfect Korean. I just can't. This is it! This is what you get. I'm me."

Mom listens a moment before answering.

"It is not your fault that you do not speak Korean. You need only English in this country. You did nothing wrong. That is mine and Daddy's fault. We did a bad job."

"You did a bad job? Good, then can I fire you?"

"You wish! You stuck with me for life! You are my blood!"

Someone once asked me, what is it about mothers and daughters? Why all the commotion? It's just different. Mothers identify with their daughters. They're trying to rewrite their history with you; that's why it's so important that you end up with the right career, the right partner, the right weight, the right hairstyle. Sometimes, I wish I could trade in my title of daughter. Life would be so much easier if I could be demoted to niece, or aunt or even distant cousin. There's too much pressure with the daughter part.

Later that day on the bus, Mom gives me a package; it's from the gift store, but she asks me not to open it till I get back home. In New York, I open it. Inside are a pair of wooden ducks, a traditional Korean wedding gift. People give ducks because they mate for life. There is a note to explain:

There was once was a mother duck and a daughter duck. Now the daughter duck never listened to the mother duck. In fact, she did everything the opposite of whatever her mother asked. When the mother duck asked her to do her homework, she would go out and play. When the mother duck asked her to come home and eat her dinner, she would throw her food on the ground. When the mother duck was about to die, she thought to herself, "I finally know her game. I am going to ask for the opposite of what I want." The mother duck really wanted to be buried up in the mountain side, but she told her daughter to let her body go down the river. One day, the mother duck died. The daughter duck, looking down on her mother's body, thought to herself, It's time to get serious. I must do as my mother wishes." And so she took her mother's body, and dragged it to the river, and let it go.

So Yunny, I give you ducks, because I hope you get married one day. Soon. Time is running out; stop fooling around! But you have me for the rest of your life. You have so much to look forward, so relax. Until you're 40. Then it's downhill.

Love,
Mom

P.S. I didn't mention law school once.

STEPHANIE UYS
Rest Stop

Off the road in Ohio an old man
bent by his wrinkles, his hair a patch
of thin snow, his hands shaking the slim
wood of a bench, feeds the sky words
– something that would listen –
as his tired shoes shuffle dust
across weak roadside bushes.

I stretch one ossified leg at a time,
and leaning on a cigarette
watch as it gathers ash
on his faded American flag T-shirt, an ocean
blue cap that reads Veteran
of the Korean War.

He knows I'm Korean, and as if
I'm South and he's North (or he's South and I'm North)—
we look at each other with suspicion. In this country,
on my way home to a family that purchased
me for almost $600, I wonder what he and I
have to share, if anything.

So what if I'm in his country and he's
been in mine? Anyway, what is mine and what
is his? Does it matter when he
throws a spit my way, gracelessly leans
on the wind which only reminds me of the ex-husband
I loved too much. How two opposite things
move with such force –
cursed to crash clumsily!

I have learned to bring distance with me,
separate this from that, but he goes on
mumbling to a wife that isn't here, to a time
that doesn't equal this moment,
and despite the sun innocently falling
in the west, car lights casting shadows, I move
toward him in the approaching darkness.

KENDRA CHUNG
Neighbors

Yesterday was Tuesday, and so I took the washing down to the river. Besides, I thought the sun had decided to lie on top of my head, and one more *co-co-dack*! from the neighbors' crazy rooster was going to send me marching into their yard with a knife and crown me the peacemaker in this part of town, maybe in all of northeastern China.

I was in the front garden picking a few peppers for the lunch stew, weighing my sleek, purple *gajees* still stuck on the vines in my hand, when a shadow moved across. I looked up and saw a black crow sweeping down toward the valley. A wind passed, my sunflowers began bobbing their heads up and down, my tall corn stalks shifted and sighed. I stood up and turned toward the river, which was dazzling in the sunlight. It was as if its sounds were already in my ear, as if each ripple knew and was calling me *Nancho's Omma! Nancho's Omma!*

I tossed the peppers into a bowl by the water pump and went inside to scoop Nancho up in my arms. She was awake, sitting quietly on the rolled-out *yo* next to *Abayee*, who was snoring, his chin reaching for the ceiling. On his other side lay his two fishing buddies, also asleep, their arms and legs sprawled out across each other. Nancho had kicked her blanket off to *Abayee's* side and was rocking a little to keep her head up. When she saw me, she smiled.

Whites with whites, darks with darks as they say. Nancho strapped to my back, the straw basket of laundry on my head and so we went, leaving the grandfathers to their dreams.

I closed our metal gate behind me and took the shortcut path next to the Zhangs' house, along wooden fences and backs of houses. As I brushed against some bushes, a dog barked nearby and as if in reply, that crazy rooster up on the hill started screeching again.

Who does her washing by the river anymore? Don't think I don't hear snickers from the neighbors, especially from old grandmothers who think they have the right. "A young woman like you?" they say. "Why don't you just throw out the electric rice cooker and cook rice over the wooden fire!" Then, "Ha ha ha ha," showing me their tonsils, which I don't need to see. I just smile and carry on as always. I don't expect them to understand, but I like having this time to myself away from the house. I like sitting by the river and letting the little breezes toss the hair off the back of my neck, watching the water speed over the rocks and listening it go *jol-jol-jol*, as the sound of cars and people come from behind me along the bank.

Across the river, you can see our old homeland Chosun too. Behind a few gray buildings, the mountains there loom like a poor old woman's head full of scabs. A pity, no doubt, but what can they do? Last year's floods had wiped out so much of their farmlands so they started to chop down trees and till the soil to grow food. On what used to be green hills, now they've got tufts of dull colorless stalks which my eyes figure for barley.

Things have been falling apart for several years now. At least that's what people say to Chosun people like us, but who still have family over there and have gone across the border to visit. They come back with stories that spread like wildfires through these parts once the first words catch on like a flame onto a wick. You hear all kinds of stuff now. About people foraging forests for wild roots, digging up soil for a potato even before it's had a chance to become a potato. Even eating the barks of trees! Not that I believe even half of what I hear, mind you. I mean, how can you? The way people talk sometimes; soon, you'd start believing all sorts of nonsense if you aren't careful.

Well, them along the river bank, they're just barely big enough for you to tell whether the shape you're seeing is a boy or a girl, a man or a woman. They're scrubbing their arms or splashing water on themselves, soaking their bodies up to their chests, to cool off like we do here. Or just sitting and looking in our direction, like they've got nothing better to do. And you know they're not planning to go anywhere when you see their border guards walking up and down the bank with rifles tucked under their arms. Sometimes I get an urge to lift my arm and wave or do something crazy like that. But of course I don't. I think it's best if Nancho wants to keep her mother around.

I mean, not that I ever pay much attention to the folks over there. Only I know I've got enough worries of my own. Especially now that Nancho's father has left for the big city and I'm taking care of our baby on my own. I've got Abayee to keep an eye on, too, because Big Brother's family is also gone. I guess at least one in every family's got the itch to wander off to the big city. In my case it's unfortunately two.

The big city with tall buildings, flashing signs and busy streets, the smell and sign of money everywhere. *Ssst!* What is there to draw me? This is the town where I was born and grew up, where I met and married Nancho's father. When he left for the city—to check for himself what was out there, I told him straight I'm not making any promises so he shouldn't go ahead thinking I'd be all agreeable to anything. I'm happy to have what I have here—our small house, my garden patch, even the sound of that crazy rooster in the middle of the night. This river town where *Abayee* eventually settled after leaving Chosun and met my mother, where Nancho's father's *own* father settled after leaving Chosun and met *his* mother. All it took was a look across the river, I'd say, to remind us of where we'd come from, and Nancho would grow up knowing and feeling this, too, just as I had all my life, and "Yah! Yah! Yah!" Nancho's father would pipe up. "Don't get melodramatic on me! The big city is not in Siberia you know. Besides, who says you have to look across the river to remember where we've come from? What's for us here? What are we going to give Nancho besides a view of where her ancestors are buried?"

And that's when I'd know to shush. Because I didn't have an answer for that one yet.

I set Nancho down in a shaded grassy area. "You play nicely by yourself while *Omma* does the washing, *hung*?" I hummed as I washed, slapped the block of soap against Nancho's little shirts, scrubbed and wrung them against a big rock, feeling the cold, soapy water run down my arms to my elbows and drip into the swirling current. I let the constant murmur of the water wash over me.

It's been almost two months since her father's departure, and I wondered when he finally walks through the door, would Nancho look up and think, *Who is this stranger?* When he calls, I hold the phone to her ear so that she can at least hear the sound of his voice. She likes to pat the receiver with her hand, and I'd like to think that this means she knows whose voice is calling out to her from the other end.

But she's growing fast under my eyes and what if she took her first step or said her first word before she saw her father again? I don't complain to him. I mean, you ask me, and Nancho and I are doing fine on our own. Just fine!

Later, when I walked over to her, she was sitting with one leg tucked under her, a hand on her ankle, already like a little grandma. She watched me put down the basket of tight coils of clothes. Then she bounced up and down and grumbled in her own language that I should pick her up. "You missed your *Omma*, you little rascal?" I said, rubbing her belly. "You miss your *Abba* too?"

I stood holding her in my arms, looking across the river. I saw those ravaged mountains and below them, pale, concrete buildings that looked crumbling and hollow. *What would be there once this little girl grew up? What would become of our people, of our homeland then?*

As soon as I caught myself having these thoughts, I shook my head. Like I said, people here, we've got enough troubles of our own. But I felt something swelling up inside of me, the kind of feeling that sometimes overtakes me in the middle of the night, when I'd wake up to the darkness and feel Nancho's small body breathing on one side, and on the other, the cold empty space where her father used to lie.

I pulled our daughter closer to me and held her like that until she started whimpering and struggling, so I laughed and bent down to plant a kiss on her melon-shaped head. Then I noticed two women. They looked like women across the river on the bank. They were sitting with their hands around their knees and looking in my direction. Did they see me too? I wondered what they saw. If compared to their buildings, ours seemed bright and busy to them. If, on days when the wind blew a certain way, they could catch sounds coming from the center of our town, the lively outdoor music coming from vendors' tables, what would they think?

It wasn't until I had gotten back and started preparing lunch that the three Chosun boys came to the house. I was in the kitchen, chopping up *gajees*, when one showed up at the front door. The kid he looked about 12 years old must have crept up like a mouse. I didn't hear him come up the path, and before I knew it, someone was standing at the doorstep behind the beaded curtain and calling me in a clear, young voice. "Excuse me."

I pulled the curtain aside, and there he was. The front gate was opened, he said, and he had just crossed the river. Could he please have some food?

He didn't need to open his mouth. You could tell just by looking at him. He wore a thin navy jacket and, underneath it, a dirty white tank top that was so stretched out the collar hung down to the middle of his chest. His pants were rolled up to his knees and still wet around the cuffs. His hair was cut short—rough as if he had done it himself with a pair of shears—and sticking out all over the place.

I stared at the boy. Sure, I'd heard about people crossing over for a day or two, to beg from the Chosun and Han Chinese alike. There were also those who fled for good and hid in the mountains behind our town and, at night, came down to beg or steal. Some tried to escape further inland on foot, but they had to go around steep mountain cliffs to get to the cities or wherever they were trying to go to, and many died along the way.

Maybe I'd even seen a few of them in town and didn't know it. It was possible. Just last week even, *Abayee* had run into a man from over there. This was when the leftover monsoon rains were still coming down on us from time to time, and on one of these nights, *Abayee* saw a strange young man sitting on a dark street, in front of a fire coming out of a small garbage pail. The man was burning garbage to keep himself warm.

"I asked him if he needed anything, but all he asked for was a cigarette," *Abayee* had said, shrugging.

A cigarette! Ssst! I'd thought. *He must've not been that hungry then!*

This boy, the boy now standing before me, he was looking past my shoulder toward the kitchen. I thought maybe his eyes would light up or do something at the sight of food back there, but his broad face remained as stoic and stubborn as a young boy's could be, and it occurred to me then that this here was a tough little kid.

I fumbled with the money pouch inside my skirt pocket. Maybe I'd give him a few yuans and send him away. A kid like that would surely find a way to eat, even if I didn't feed him. Like I said, he looked strong and cunning. He looked like a survivor. In fact, he looked like he'd be one of those boys who went around school stealing other kids' candy. Like those boys I knew from grade school who used to torment me by lifting up my skirt and running away, snickering. Just as I was about to pull out some money from my pocket, Nacho, who was strapped to my back, reached toward the boy with her hands and went "oowa oowa," and I saw his face break into a tiny smile, his lower lip slowly peeling off his teeth.

I pushed the curtain aside. "Come on in," I said. Then the boy asked if he could have food in a plastic bag. He had two friends waiting outside the front gate, and they were hungry too.

My eyes turned toward the gate. Two more? I couldn't see anyone. Where were they? Hiding in the bushes? Maybe he and his friends had just eaten at the house next door. Well, how was I to know for sure that they didn't?

We stood in the doorway, this boy and me. Wind stirred the beaded strings of my curtain they tapped gently against the doorframe, as if reminding me that I had to do something. Three supposedly hungry boys. Three supposedly hungry, *Chosun* boys...

"Well, what are they waiting for," I said finally. "We don't want guards to see them hanging around my gate, do we. Tell them to come on in and make it quick," and he ran back down the path to get his friends—too shy or scared to come up to the house with him.

This little one who came to the door—the smart one, as we later called him—he was in charge as far as anyone could see. There was another who was bigger and looked older than the other two, but he was quiet and let the smart one talk. Later, sitting on my floor all silent and dumb although I could tell he wasn't so dumb, just a little careful—as though he was afraid of making a mistake and getting them all kicked out of my house. He and the other one wearing pink pants looked at the smart one doing all the talking, as if he got a hold of their tongues but they were in no hurry for him to give them back.

They all came up to the doorway and stood quietly, lips dry and split, pants rolled up and wet around the cuffs, beads of water still clinging to their thin legs. The tall one and the pink one stood behind the smart one in the corner, like scared pigs, but the smart one stood straight and proud like he was a guest of the house.

I went back to scrubbing the rice—it was a good thing I hadn't put the rice cooker on yet, there were now three more mouths to feed.

I drained the milky water from the bowl. "Where you from?" I asked.

"Dosan," the smart one said. The city across the bridge.

"All three of you from there?" I said, turning to the two mute ones.

They looked at me for less than a second, then down again at their dirty canvas shoes. The pink one got a sudden itch on the back of his neck and scratched.

"Yes," the smart one said. And I left it at that.

They watched me throw *gajees* and peppers and garlic into the big black pot. It made a sharp sizzling sound that stirred the grandfathers awake. I could hear them moaning and groaning, tossing back and forth on the floor, mumbling "*Aiguda, aiguda*" or "Ay, my back, my old bones" and "Yah, I was a little cold and no wonder! You took all the blanket!"

I could hear *Abayee* saying, "Oh you crazy old bastards, get up now! We slept all morning! My daughter's preparing lunch, and we should be eating soon!"

The grandfathers were probably still hung over from the night before, I knew. How could I not?

I was trying to go back to sleep in the middle of the night, when they returned from their fishing trip and raised a racket with their loud voices and bickering. Nancho and I were in the back room. And while Nancho, who takes after her father and doesn't open her eyes until light breaks, no matter how crazy the rooster next door is getting, no matter if an earthquake were to jiggle her across the floor, slept soundly, I lay in the dark, blinking at the ceiling. I listened to them getting more rice wine from the chest, then singing old songs from their youth. I couldn't help but wonder about Nancho's father all alone in the big city. Wondered what he had done that day and if he missed our home. Wondered what was going to happen to the whole lot of us.

I set a small table in the kitchen and one in the bedroom for the grandfathers. They had all gotten up now and gone outside to the water pump to wash up. I placed three stools around the table for the boys and a plate of *gajees* and peppers, bowls of rice and soup, *kim* and kimchi. We didn't have much, but at least we got by. Nancho's father did OK driving a truck before he quit and left us for his dream of more money, and Big Brother was helping out since I was the one taking care of *Abayee* now.

I turned to the boys and told them to stop standing about like that and sit down, they were making me nervous. I thought I'd get a tiny smile out of maybe one of them, but they all kept staring at the table as if they hadn't heard me.

When the grandfathers came back in, they finally saw that we had strangers inside the house.

"Wait a minute, wait a minute, who are these boys?"

"Huh? What have we got here?"

I said, "Go and eat and leave them alone. They say they're from Dosan."

Steam was rising from the plates and bowls. The boys looked sheepishly at the grandfathers crowding in on them. I shooed the grandfathers away. "*Abayee, Abayee*, let them eat first," I whined.

And yah, did the boys eat. They ate. They ate and ate. It was like watching someone swim underwater and seeing him come up for breath once every mile up the river. What could I say? Standing by the water jar, feeling the plastic scoop go strangely heavy in my hand. Hey kids, eat a little slowly there, you think someone is going to snatch food out of your mouths, *hung*?

Which happens, or so people say, over there. People, kids who have the strength left in them, going around like bandits. Even a piece of sticky rice cake that falls on the ground. Not even time to wipe the dirt away. Someone always there to slap you on the back so the *ttuk* will fall out of your mouth before you have time to swallow. A piece of *ttuk* isn't yours, they say, even if it's in your mouth. It's yours if you get it down your tube.

When each bowl had been scraped clean, the boys sat silently at the table.

"You want more?" I asked. I was still standing by the water jar, pretending to put things away.

The smart one looked up. "No, we ate plenty and are done," he said. Then he got up and started stacking the dishes, which prompted the mutes to do the same.

"Oh, leave them," I said, swatting them away. "Just leave them there."

Abayee heard this from the other room and ordered the boys to come and sit inside. The boys, the mute ones especially, felt more comfortable around *Abayee*, who bossed them around. "Why are you sitting there? No, sit here! You, sit closer to us!"

In the room I wiped the table and lay dozing Nancho on the floor, on her blue blanket next to *Abayee*. Then I went back into the kitchen to clean up and put the dishes away, slowly, making sure not to slam the cabinet doors so that I could hear every word.

Two of them were 14 and one was 15. Fourteen and fifteen! Who would have thought! It wasn't just that they were skinny, but they were short, really short— even the tall one hardly came up to my nose, and I'm a short woman, they tell me. They said it was their third time crossing the river. One time, two of them got caught on our side and had to spend a night in the Chinese detention hall on the island near the bridge. There, the smart one befriended a guard who gave them corn kernel rice and sent them back the next day. The second time, Chosun guards caught them and went through their things but let them go. "When kids get caught, we just tell them the truth, that we went to China to look for food, and they let us go," the smart one said.

I went to the door and stepped outside, listened for any sound. I knew *Abayee* had seen the TV announcement, too—that the Chinese authorities were going to begin fining people who took Chosun refugees into their homes. We'd even talked about it. "50,000 yuans!" we'd said. Why, that was twice the price of this house! Outside, I heard only the rustle of trees—wind rolling through the tops—and the sky looked clear and blue as on any other summer day. Once I went back inside and shut the door, though, I could hear a buzzing in my ears like a ceiling light. The sound quickly flickered out, and I was back in my kitchen again, standing on the concrete floors in my old plastic slippers. I had three Chosun boys in my home and *Abayee* was talking to them.

When I brought tea into the room, Nancho was asleep and the smart one was talking. He was saying he had a younger brother who disappeared a while ago. He was now living with his mother, who had somehow hurt her leg and couldn't go outside to search for food. The tall one was alone. He was originally from a town south of Dosan, but he didn't get along with his stepfather, and because there were too many mouths to feed anyhow and he was the oldest, his mother said maybe he should be on his way. The one in the pink pants was living with his mother and two sisters.

"Where are your fathers?" demanded *Abayee*.

The boys kept their eyes cast down.

"*Hung*?" *Abayee* said. "Speak up, now!"

"My father is dead, sir!" the smart one replied.

The grandfathers hung their heads.

"And you two?" *Abayee* said more gently this time.

"Have your fathers passed on too?"

The tall one was quiet. Then his voice cracked. "Yes."

The pink one sat hugging his knees.

The grandfathers nodded their heads. They cried, "*Aigu! Aigu!* What are we going to do? Our poor people. What is happening to our poor people?"

The tea was getting cold, but no one touched the cups I had laid out. I listened to the clock hand move forward, one tick at a time. No one has a father, no father. What did this mean? Just then we heard a dog bark. Then a clanking at the gate.

"Anyone home?" A male voice cried out in Chinese. I looked at *Abayee*. Something cold and wet spread over my face. Everything in the room turned dark and still. The thin gauzy drapes over the windows. The clock ticking in its painfully slow rhythm. The metal door rattled again. "Hello? Anyone?"

I never saw these grandfathers get up so quickly in my life. Like they suddenly got tired of sitting all day long and getting served. Now they sprung to their feet as if fierce heat from the *ondol* floor shot up their backs.

The boys and I also followed. I grabbed Nancho who felt heavy and warm and good—so good—against my pounding chest..

Out the back door, the boys went. We slipped out, and I led them to the only place that came to mind. On the way, I heard *Abayee's* voice. "Who's there? I'm coming! I'm coming! Stop shaking the door or you're going to wake up my granddaughter here, and she's got a voice louder than you!"

When I finally started walking to the front door, I saw the green color of their uniforms peeking from behind the grandfathers, shoulders. *Abayee* and his friends were nodding.

"What is it?" I asked. "What's all this noise, *Abayee*?"

He was talking in our language to one man who must have been one of our own. "Yes, yes, of course, of course," he was saying, "But around here, no one comes. You know that hill coming up here and so we hardly ever see any of them." He sounded bored and tired, as if he had just been roused from a nap.

It was the other one, the tall Han Chinese one, who looked vaguely up and down at me, then behind my shoulder toward the house. In a state, I say, use what you've got, so I took the skin of my daughter's soft warm leg and pinched it as hard as a mother could, and out came a torrent of wails.

I lifted her up and shook her gently. "That's right, that's right. What's wrong with our Nancho? Want to go to sleep, is that it? Shush, shush, my child. These men are here to see you're all right and safe."

That sent them away.

We waited a couple of hours before getting the boys out of the privy. I wasn't sure they'd still be there when I opened the door—maybe they'd snuck away and were already halfway across the border—but there they were, squinting at the bright light suddenly flooding in and trying to shield their eyes with their arms.

I was afraid that they'd ask to stay, but the smart one stepped forward. We were ready to go down the hole if we heard them coming up to the house, we really were," he said. Up close, in the direct sunlight, his face seemed different, older, as if he had aged since a few hours ago.

In the kitchen, I packed some white rice into three plastic bags. I told the boys I wished I could give more, but that was all I could afford to give, and the smart one said, "Oh no, thank you very much," and bowed his head.

Abayee grilled the boys in preparation for their departure. What are you going to say if you get caught going back? You're not going to tell them anything about this house, are you? You know you can't say anything about us here, you know that, don't you? Or we'd all be in trouble. People here, we're in a tough situation, too, you know. What if they ask you which house gave you food? What are you going to say then?

The smart one piped up as if he were in class and asked to stand up and recite an answer. "We'll just say that we were sitting on the side of the road and a woman came and asked if we were from across the river and she told us to wait and came back with food. We'll say we never went anywhere, but sat on the side of the road so we didn't see anything, so we don't know anything!"

One of the grandfathers nodded and chuckled. "This one's smart," he said.

Abayee took out a few small bills from his pocket, maybe enough to buy a few more kilograms of white rice, and handed the money to the smart one. "You're going to guard it well now, right?" Without a word, the boy bent down, rolled down his sock, shoved the money inside, then straightened up—all in the time it would have taken me to cross my arms. Right then—and don't ask me to explain—I felt I knew what I'd done wrong in my life, that I'd lived too carefully, with too much fear, and I wished I could be like this boy, who now stood before me with his arms stiff at his side, nearly shouting a determined "Yes!" like a little soldier.

When the boys left, I was standing in the doorway with Nancho quiet again in my arms. I watched them walk down the path, toward the garden where my beautiful *gajees* grow bigger everyday, and lettuce heads line the rows, and sunflowers sway under the slightest breeze. Down below, the gardens of my neighbors stretched on and on and beyond the river flowed. The smart one turned around—I saw him lift his hand and tears streaming down his face. I felt something inside of me kick. Come again, I wanted to cry. Come another day. But my mouth hung open and inside my head, the word that circled around and around was run. Run.

IKHYUN KIM
Pan-America

From here motion seems
ever outward

amidst power lines
and lights strung
willy-nilly, everywhere voltage
high enough to kill.
On wind up off the lake,
from a demonstration tent,
the acrid smell of
burning elephant flesh.

On October 29, 1901, at Auburn Prison,
120 miles east of Buffalo, a signal
was given and 1,700 volts of electricity
passed through Leon Czolgosz's body
for one minute. A prison official said,
Give him another poke. 1,700 volts of
electricity passed through Leon Czolgosz's body
for one minute.

The only acknowledged
political assassination in our
history happened here. September 6, 1901.
The Pan-American Exposition.
Buffalo, New York.
A festival of all things electric.

In *The Temple of Music*, amongst
woodwinds and strings,
animal skin drums whisper
warm water rhythms: artillery tossed
stem to stern for one hundred days. It is a
Morse code report from Cuba: Take the
Philippines, Guam, Puerto Rico, Hawaii!

Shot twice, one
across the chest, the other
into the gut, off center,
left to suffer eight days
burbling breath, in a fine home
in a fine city, on fine sheets
spun by hand. William McKinley, Jr.,
from rural Ohio pig-iron, seventh
of nine children, to railroad Buffalo
steel, the twenty-fifth president,
dead of infection.

More than one hundred
years before you, Washington
crossed the Delaware in little more
than a wooden crate. His Delaware
was not a roadway lined with millionaires
but water, wet and frostbitten. No
crowds to watch his brown box
click clack toward its destination, forever
soil bound, never to sail again, from
this inverted delta, this city of parallel lines.

And you, legislator, author of
Hunting Trips of a Ranch Man and
The Winning of the West, Police
Commissioner, Assistant
Secretary of the Navy,
Rough Rider, Governor,
Vice President, you went
deep inland,
hiked the Adirondacks,

emerged a different man, decided to
rewrite the crowning, to make the greatest
canal of all history, to map mighty *Beau Fleuve* onto
the northern territories of Colombia, the
sinew of the Americas, above its gentle knee,
swollen with cash, and carve yourself
into the earth

(A grand attempt, a
narrative worthy of repetition: hard
hitting Teddy, the great weakling
turned ass kicker who lost an
eye to a pro boxer while
sparring in the White House,
taunted him, said
go ahead,
take the other)

400 years earlier, through the still heat of
September, Balboa and 1200 others
swung machetes through prickly jungle,
westward across isthmus,
the first Europeans
to find see name it *Mar del Sur*.

Tired of French failure and American
expansion, Colombia resisted.
We need that ribbon
of ditch! said Roosevelt. Spanish
blood-scented gunships
pitched idly off shore. The people
of the sinew led into revolt,
protected and irreversible,
claimed independence, and tabled up
uneasy to the woolen cowboys.

"In exchange…independence…
Panamanians…accept…treaty…
no Panamanian…signed…

It took ten years to dig fifty miles.
Thousands died of malaria and
yellow fever. Thousands more brought.
Mosquitoes multiply, dance, stand
atop water and wait.

Teddy, the first
President to travel,
determined to craft
a most beautiful scar,
went to visit Panama,
hiked himself in,
left dry land for mud,
straddled two oceans, two continents,
and whispered,
Where the French
have failed, we shall not,
no new world conquistador
shall ever turn back!

EUGENIA SUNHEE KIM
The Fire Tower

My father, a minister and community leader, was among the first to hear that Korean teens and youths were invited to a free camp in the Blue Ridge Mountains of southern Pennsylvania. My sister and I were jobless that summer in the '60s and we stayed up nights reading, then slept late into the afternoons, oblivious to my mother's yells or the crash of the vacuum cleaner being dropped in the middle of our messy bedroom. Because it was a Peace Corps camp, my father thought it was safe. That his two youngest daughters would be cloistered for six weeks with other Korean kids was only an added advantage. We were to be guinea pigs for Peace Corps volunteers who would receive training for service in rural South Korea.

I didn't consider myself a "Korean kid" because I didn't speak Korean. I thought I was as American as the trainees would be, except perhaps for my looks. So I worried that I wasn't Korean enough and that Korean pigeonholing was likely to occur at Blue Knob, but I was happy to get away from home.

I packed flannel nightgowns; my favorite tan jeans, whose legs I had decorated in yellow and red flowers with green magic marker vines around the ankles and running up the stovepipe legs; sneakers; hooded sweatshirt; a couple of shirts; my guitar; and my three spiral binders filled with words and chords to songs made popular by Seeger, Peter Paul & Mary, Baez, Cohen and Dylan. What I didn't have in vocal talent I made up for with earnestness, and folk music gave me the illusion that I was connected to something in those confusing, ambiguous years. I rejected my family's history and tried instead to adopt early America as my history with songs from the Wild West and before Emancipation, railroad ballads and traditional hymns. I garnered glimpses of societal belonging through protest songs, and an elusive, dangerous yearning for a boyfriend was touched upon through love songs.

The two-hour drive to Blue Knob was typical of our family car trips. My mother talked about church events or gossiped, and my father responded with one or two syllables. Vicky and I stared silently out the windows in the back. Vicky, 15, was a year older than I, so we were close, but with different temperaments. She was serious, studious and calm. I was energetic, social and edgy. If her hand drifted into my personal space on the back seat, I'd push it back.

"Stop it."

"You stop it."

"You started it!"

"You did!"

"*Gobble-ji mah!*" Stop fussing! said Mom.

After we left the suburbs, the hills became more rolling and the roads narrowed and emptied. We passed small cow farms nestled in the pockets of valleys, and fields of corn and hay. Anxious about what people would think of me in this new setting, I imagined two scenarios: country-bumpkin Korean kids who couldn't speak English who would snub me for my lack of native language, or show-off rich Korean American kids who wouldn't bother stooping to speak to me. I couldn't imagine what the trainees—college graduates from all over the country—would be like. But it was interesting to be going to a ski resort in the middle of the summer, and I pictured myself in pale blue stretch pants, matching ear muffs and fuzzy *après*-ski booties around a bonfire with my new friends, all of us tow-headed and blue-eyed.

We passed Altoona, and Dad drove the steep hills for half an hour more, our ears popping. Mom gave last-minute remonstrations. "Yah," she lectured in Korean. "Because you're the minister's daughters, you have to set a higher example. People are going to judge you, so don't forget your manners. Think about others first. God first. Others second. Yourself last. Don't be selfish. Remember that you're Korean girls, so speak Korean as nicely as you can. It's a shame you can't speak better. There's another daughter of a minister coming, so see if you can be friends with her—Reverend Chang's only girl, from New York."

Yeah yeah, I said to myself, eyes turned outward to the hazy blue-green of the hilly woodlands, hair leaping like black wings out the window. I could glimpse ski slopes between breaks in the trees, verdant and flowing with lush summer grass.

Finally, the tires crunched on gravel roadways, and we approached the main building at Blue Knob resort. It was exciting and scary to see that the few people hanging around the check-in office seemed to be hippies. Exciting because I thought hippies were "groovy;" scary because I felt woefully inadequate in their realm. One guy standing behind the desk had a light brown Fu Manchu mustache and aviator sunglasses, and his blue jeans were tucked at the knees into fringed, beaded deerskin boots. He looked so cool and relaxed, and I immediately wanted to be just like him, or at least, have his suede fringed boots.

"Aigu, he's so dirty!" my mother whispered. Diane, the woman he spoke to, was the coordinator of the camp program, and I was relieved for my parents' sake that she looked like a teacher. Later, when I learned that the hippie man in the fringe boots was a Peace Corps veteran whose exemplary service landed him this plum job as a trainer at Blue Knob, I liked him even more, because my mother would understand this contrast even less.

Our little group toured the dormitory rooms of double-deckers where we would stay. The resort was Tyrolean-themed, and each cabin was labeled with a wooden carved sign. Ours was Yodeler Lodge. We also toured the cabins that housed the trainees. All their furniture had been removed, replaced by crates and sleeping bags on bare linoleum, so its occupants would become accustomed to sleeping and working on the floor. My mother was impressed with this kind of advance preparation for Korean living, but I was glad to take a top bunk above Vicky in the Yodeler Lodge, up from the bugs.

Simple wood-slat barracks, each cabin had two stories of 12 rooms paired across a long center hallway brightly lit with naked bulbs. The boys had the second floor. Community bathrooms held rows of showers, toilet stalls and porcelain sinks with drains ringed with rust stains. All of it was strange and exciting, and when we ran into other Korean kids, we shared shy hellos. I could tell who were recent immigrants by their heavy accent, black-framed eyeglasses, stiff posture and the fact that they bowed and kept their eyes low when they were introduced to my folks. Dad visited with the other parents, and Mom was underfoot as Vicky and I unpacked and made our beds. We hung one of the resort's multicolored plaid woolen blankets on the heavily painted cinder block wall in a feeble attempt at decoration and impatiently shoved clothes into drawers, until finally our parents left.

Our neighbors, Miran and MeeSook were very Korean. Miran hardly spoke any English; she was the recently arrived daughter of the minister from Queens that my mother had told us about. I was prepared not to like he, based on Mom's recommendation, but she had lovely round eyes and was sweetly tentative, and I was disarmed by her gracefulness. They spoke Korean until we told them that we understood, but couldn't speak.

Miran smiled. "Good, you can help me with my English!" she said in Korean.

MeeSook, perky and short with a bowl cut that swung with each bouncy pronunciation, said she was Miran's designated interpreter and we could be of help because her own English wasn't that great. "I come here one years ago, but Miran is here only one month."

I was relieved that our inability to speak Korean wasn't frowned at or remarked upon as it typically was in my parents' church community. At dinner in the central building, the Meisterhaus, we sat at long tables with the other campers who had arrived that day. Some of the trainees stopped by the table to welcome us. They seemed so old, worldly and casual that I was intimidated and could barely say my name. The trainees would mingle with the campers on scheduled shifts so eventually we would all get to know each other. Within the first few days, everyone was so friendly that I finally began to feel less anxious. A few of the other campers also didn't speak Korean, so some of that tension was diffused. I met Peggy Kim, a Korean American half-and-half who had heavy brunette curls that were frosted and extraordinarily long-lashed eyes with dramatic slanted double-creases. She had a Brooklyn accent, as did Lucille Wallenberg, Peggy's roommate, who was the skinniest girl I had ever met. Long hair that swept the back of her knees and tiny bones gave her an ethereal, delicate presence, but she laughed like a donkey, loud and often.

At our first camp meeting, we were asked to choose a camp name. Lee, an older boy recently from Korea suggested *Ko-San*, a derivation of *Chosan*—ancient Korea—and "Korea mountain." He drew the Chinese character and the discussion concluded with the decision to make a flag for Camp Ko-San. Vicky volunteered to sew a design of the Chinese character appliquéd over the blue-red yin-yang symbol from the Korean national flag. Miran had raised her hand to vote, but was otherwise nearly invisible during the meeting. Even the way she raised her hand was shy—her elbow close to her body and just her hand barely raised, fingers slightly waving. I couldn't decide if she was going to be a pain in the ass or if I was feeling protective of her.

We took regular trips on a school bus to the little town at the base of the mountain, and purchased poplin, thread and needles at the Five & Ten. This became Vicky's main activity. After supper and between activities, she snipped and sewed while I played guitar. Miran and MeeSook often joined us, lolling on the empty bunks across the room. MeeSook sang along to songs that she knew, like "Hey, Jude" and "Bridge Over Troubled Water," and sometimes Miran hummed the melody. Eventually, she taught me a Korean tune that was popular in Seoul then, and I figured out the chords to play along while we sang. MeeSook told us jokes, dramatically translating punch lines with such mistaken flair that many nights we'd collapse in giggles and silliness. I began to enjoy MeeSook's frolicking as well as appreciate a noticeably peaceful warmth that emanated from Miran's fine square shoulders and fluid body movement. There was an immediate, affirming familiarity with Miran, MeeSook and other the campers that I hadn't felt with my American friends at home. It was a culmination of slight details: the shape of MeeSook's fingernails, the plane of Miran's cheeks, the way her hands lay still in her lap when she listened, the lilt and timbre of her voice. This affinity with my new friends made it safe to be open to other possibilities.

One evening, a blond-haired trainee, Dick Christensen, poked his head in our doorway and asked if he could join us. Vicky and I had talked about him. I had confessed one night that I thought he was awfully cute. Vicky said he was bow-legged and straight-looking, which was true, but he was cute all the same. We sang songs from my spiral notebooks, which he was fascinated by. He asked me about a song I didn't know how to play and, taking my guitar, showed me that he was an accomplished guitarist, classical and folk.

Curiosity overcame my shyness. "Can you teach me how to play like that?"

"Only if you teach me all the songs in your notebooks." He smiled.

Dick taught me a simple Bach piece for the guitar, and I taught him Leonard Cohen. He came over nearly every evening, often with his own guitar. Other trainees and campers also dropped in, and our room became like a Victorian parlor filled with singing, teasing and growing friendships, while Vicky sat on her bunk or on a blanket spread on the floor, sewing the flag. The trainees practiced Korean with us, and while I was glad that I knew enough to be able to correct pronunciation, I was relieved that MeeSook and Miran were usually nearby to do the job right.

Miran had the Korean habit of holding hands with her friends while walking, and soon she and I were hand in hand when we went from one place to another.

"So what're your parents like?" I said one day.

"They good. Busy with church all time."

"Mine too. We have to go every Sunday. Sometimes, though, Dad takes us to American church, but we still have to go to Korean church in the afternoon."

"I do Saturday and Sunday."

"Do you have many friends at home?"

"Nobody like this," she said and smiled at me. "My father, he– " and she indicated in Korean that he was very strict. As we became better friends, I learned that she was terribly lonely at home and missed her friends in Korea. We went for walks on the empty ski slopes, the unmowed grass tickling our knees. There was a fire tower not far from the resort gates. The trap door to the wood cabin on top was padlocked, but to climb to the top of the stairs until the floor of the cabin brushed our hair was a sight of the stars that was unforgettable. With no city lights to blur the view, the Milky Way shimmered like a river, falling stars like minnows flitting in sparkling water. Miran and I climbed the stairs and talked late into the nights. She was so quiet at first, but I asked her lots of questions. Her English increased rapidly, and soon we could share our fears and dreams.

I told her how it felt funny to look Korean on the outside and feel so not-Korean on the inside. She said she was nervous to go to high school in the fall. We talked about the trainees we liked. Miran had quickly became their favorite. She listened with great seriousness, partly due to her deciphering of English, but more because of her thoughtful nature. It was a joy to make her laugh. Each time she laughed, she raised her hand, touching her nose with a knuckle and covering her mouth, and her shoulders and bangs would shake. Soon, she'd be slapping her thighs, but always with one hand covering her mouth.

Rick was particularly fond of Miran. He liked all the campers and was close to Lucille and some others in particular, but he treated Miran with an obvious and special respect. Tall with dark red hair and the square features and tight mustache of an Englishman, Rick was intense in his gaze and his demeanor. He played hard and spoke loudly. When we teamed up for Capture the Flag one beautiful afternoon on the slopes, Rick was passionate and excited, very into the game. I saw him leaping in and out of the trees and across the tall grass, a bandana tied around his head, his arms taut, wide, as if he wanted to forever capture the glory of that perfect summer day.

The oldest girl among us, Mimi from Manhattan, was sophisticated and very feminine—she wore makeup and low-cut red ruffled blouses, and her hair was fringed and layered. I thought she was going to be stuck up, but she was extremely outgoing and made friends with us quickly. Mimi fell in love with Rick. By the end of the summer, she was crying over him. He frightened me. If he said something to me, he'd look right into my eyes, staring almost as if his pupils were whirling, and it was unnerving. I felt silly and insignificant with Rick, but he was consistently warm and kind and seemed to prefer hanging out with the campers, including Mimi, who became his close friend, and Miran in particular. When we went to the town's public pool, Rick lent his jacket to Lucille, who, skinny as she was, was always chilled. Lucille tucked her legs beneath her and zipped his jacket closed around her knees and chest, looking like a penguin. Rick held her hair up in funny angles and teased her until we all were laughing. If it wasn't one of the two little camper kids, it was Lucille riding Rick's shoulders. I wondered about Rick's obvious attachment to us campers, but I was glad that Miran liked his attention to her and how his warmth made her shine.

Dick Christensen was my guy. He was from Wawautosa, and I marveled at meeting someone from Wisconsin. I mooned over how his eyebrows flew up and made his blue eyes even rounder and bigger when he sang and played guitar. I thought he had a terrific voice and loved that he wrote poetry, even if I couldn't entirely understand it. Even his handwriting was cool, and his loafers without socks and madras short-sleeve shirts. Deep attachments grew slowly—we had the time and the days for lingering, yet there was enough structure with camp events and classes for the trainees.

I was glad to have Miran as my friend because while I was close to the rest of the campers just from being with them every day, I still felt reticent and unnatural. The others would be roughhousing at the pool, building human pyramids and tossing the little ones to and fro with group-banded arms. They played water games like Marco Polo, or with campers sitting on the shoulders of the trainees, trying to make the others fall in. Neither Miran, Vicky or I could swim, and we hung back from the sports. Vicky seemed content. Joe Pretti, a squat and handsome Indian-American man, sat beside her at every opportunity, and they talked quietly while she sewed the Camp Ko-San flag. I yearned to be as free as the others seemed to be with athletics and all that raging physicality, but I couldn't break away from self-consciousness about my body and being touched.

At home, we didn't hug and rarely shared physical affection, so I felt squeamish about it and thought not touching was a Korean thing. But faced with a dozen Korean kids whose arms and legs were tangled in collapsed human pyramids, I had to ask myself, *What was Korean? What was I? And what was so difficult about hugs?*

The informal songfests in Yodeler Lodge brought other amateur musicians. There'd be singing, playing, and I readily lent out my guitar for someone to try a new riff. It gave me a sense that I possibly had something to offer. Some nights there was a steady stream of trainees wandering in and out of different dorm rooms, saying hello or sharing a box of home-baked cookies received in the mail. We teased the trainees that they came to Yodeler Lodge because our rooms were heated, we had chairs and soft beds they could sit on, and because Mimi had a turntable in her room and plenty of LPs. They stayed until curfew, ten o'clock, drinking sodas and chips purchased from the vending machines in the Meisterhaus. The surface of my bureau was littered with cans filled with cigarette butts, candy wrappers, scraps of paper scrawled with verses of song, stray jackets of 45s, bits of fabric still waiting to be sewn into the Camp Ko-San flag and white ring stains from wet cups and glasses. I took a picture of the mess to preserve what it represented—a camaraderie that I had never experienced before. I was more spontaneous and peaceful than I could ever remember being. I was happy. It was scary.

As the weeks went by and the Peace Corps trainings elevated in intensity, the volunteers became more serious. The week that psychological testing was administered, our friends rarely visited and Miran and I spent our evenings on the top steps of the fire tower, talking about Dick and Rick. I told her how odd it was that I felt so close to the people at Blue Knob and so alienated at home. She wondered why Rick was so nice to her.

"What do you think about Mimi?" I asked.

"I think she is love with Rick. He like her too so why he so nice to me all the time?" She frowned.

"He thinks you're beautiful."

She laughed, embarrassed, covering her mouth, her bent finger lightly touching the rounded tip of her nose.

"No really," I said. "He says that all the time."

"Mimi is pretty one."

"He likes her because she's sophisticated and outgoing." Then I had to explain what that meant, and she taught me the same phrasing in Korean, agreeing that Mimi was very *dok-dok*. "Anyway," I said, "you hear him all the time how he says you're so beautiful, don't you?"

She flushed and laughed again.

"I mean, he'll be looking right at you in our room, or like yesterday on the bus to the pool, don't you remember? He said right there in the middle of a conversation, 'God, you're beautiful.' Remember?"

Smiling, she was quiet and then she said, "I think I could be loving him."

I thought it was brave of her to admit that—I knew that I really liked my guitar-playing Dick an awful lot, but also knew that I had no idea what love might be about—certainly I could never say that I might be in love with somebody! I could however say how much I loved the way that Dick's brow would wrinkle completely up when he sang, raising all his facial features, his chin tilted as well. I'd linger on visualizing his wrinkled forehead, long blond lashes, bow legs in tight tan jeans, bare feet shoved into dusty loafers.

A few days later, there was a tense buzz during lunch. It was much later in the afternoon when we learned from Mimi, who came to our room crying, that the psychological test results were in, and two of the trainees were disqualified from the program. Rick was one of them.

"He's devastated," Mimi said. "They're calling it a 'medical discharge.' He can't believe it. I've never seen him so upset." She leaned against the wall, sobbing with her face buried in her arms. " Oh, Rick!" she cried. I rubbed her shoulders and gave her tissue, surprised by the depth of her reaction. I didn't know what to say. We all understood that it meant Rick would be leaving Blue Knob and that he would probably get drafted. I wondered if Miran was as equally upset as Mimi, who cried for hours that night. But it was one of those things that Miran and I never got around to talking about.

The next day, we had an afternoon on the slopes. The ski lift was turned on, and we went for rides. Rick and Miran ended up in a chair together, and I could see his dark red curls tower above her small-boned profile far ahead as they rode the wavering creaky chairs. I was glad for her, and the ride was long and pleasant. Shortly after that day, I found Rick on a terrace behind our lodge overlooking the slopes, lying on his stomach in the grass reading *Grapes of Wrath*.

"Hey, Genie." He sat up, calling me over.

"Hey." I sat nearby and started to pull up blades of grass, looking for the perfect one to blow like a reed between my thumbs.

"So did you hear?" He said, rolling onto his back, gazing at the high spotty clouds.

"Yeah." I didn't know what to say. Sorry? That wasn't right. Would he leave the Peace Corps forever or something else? "What does it mean?"

He laughed loudly and held his hands in his head. "It means they think I'm fucking crazy!"

"I didn't mean that!"

"It's true though. Crazy!"

"But you're not a mental case or anything."

"Ha!" He turned over and looked at me suddenly, his eyes like bores. "Do you know what they said, Genie?"

I was squirming because he used my name so pointedly and he was worked up. "What?"

"That I'm too intense! Can you believe it? They said I was too intense and that made me unpredictable! Bullshit!"

"Wow," was all I could come up with. Then, "They're nuts!"

"Yeah! Ha!" His body sagged in the rough grass.

I blew grass stalks and showed him how to hold the splintery blades. His thumbs were too curled to work properly so he couldn't make the grass scream like I could. I asked again, "What does it mean?" wanting to know how long he'd be around.

"It means I'm going to fucking Vietnam." He sat up again, staring at me. "This has been an unbelievable summer. I meet all you guys—you and Mimi and Miran. You've got to take care of her for me, OK? Miran."

He was too intense. I thought his mention of me as part of his "unbelievable summer" was gratuitous, and I didn't know what he wanted from me or what to do with the situation. "Miran's my friend," I said to agree. "She's great."

"She's one of the most beautiful women I've ever met."

"She is beautiful." Because of his angst and the reverence he had used to say her name, Miran in my mind seemed to glow from the inside with a purity and simple beauty that reminded me of the chant I once heard the single time I'd been in a Catholic church: "Lamb of God who takes away the sins of the world." For Rick's sake, I wished I was her. Tongue-tied again, I said something stupid like "Well, good luck."

"Take care of Miran, OK, Genie?" was the last thing I heard him say. He skipped dinner that night and by morning, he had left Blue Knob.

After Rick left, there was a winding down of Camp Ko-San. It was late August and the Blue Ridge nights were cool, the midnight sky moonless, cloudless and streaked with indigo beneath its layers of stars. The trainees who needed glasses were issued round wire-rim spectacles like the kind my mother wore in postwar pictures. That's how I found out that Dick wore contact lenses. I knew one of the first things I'd do when I got home was to beg my father for wire-rim frames.

Vicky finished the flag to perfection, and we hung it in our room. Skinny Lucille, Peggy, MeeSook and two others slept beneath five blankets together in a double bed for warmth. Mimi had Rick's address and had already written him a letter. I took dozens of pictures with my Instamatic, sensing that there was something I needed to preserve from there: the image of the wide span of Dick's guitar-callused fingers; the tips of grass bending to the tunnel of wind down the mountain; the rusty smell of scrounged quarters for Zero bars in the candy machine; the curve of Miran's slender waist draped in a favorite red sweater on our chilly nights at the top of the fire tower; the crackle beneath our sneakers when we crossed the gravel roadways hand in hand, her bangs bouncing, my hair trailing in the breeze.

The trainees, who would stay at Blue Knob another few weeks, made our last night in the Yodeler Lodge a party. They brought candlelight, pretzels and soda, and there was music and dancing. When I saw her dancing in hallway, I thought about how shy Miran had been when I first met her. I moved my clod feet to the beat, and across from me it seemed that Dick's metal-rimmed eyeglasses sparkled like a chandelier in the candlelight. The trainees would be in classes the next day when we departed. Dick asked me at the end of that night, as did some others, "Can I write to you?" and I was overwhelmed by the flattery of it. In a month's time, the trainees' addresses would be somewhere in Korea, so I gave them mine, half not believing and incredulous that anyone would want to write to me.

The next day, Vicky and I folded the flag and the plaid blanket we'd hung on the wall. We cleaned the top of the bureau of its debris and stripped the bunk beds down to the ticking. Our parents arrived, and as I began to transfer my clothes from the drawers to my suitcase, I felt such a profound sense of loss that I began to cry. By the time I dragged my suitcase to the car, I was crying uncontrollably, my nose running, chest heaving, glasses cloudy with tears. I wasn't sure then what it was about, but it was so deeply painful that it makes me now feel sadness for how blind and unprepared I was for the rawness that was my kernel of discovery of self. My mother, embarrassed, kept telling me to stop and said to the other Korean parents who were there to pick up their children, "I don't know what's wrong with her!" My father said to try and pull myself together and handed me a box of tissues he always had in the car.

In my misery I barely realized that I was hugging my friends tightly, new friends that I had learned to love, who had taught me what it was to love. I hugged Miran, and we agreed that we'd soon see each other because her parents and mine were acquainted in that small-world way when both fathers are Korean Protestant ministers. "I come to Washington to visit you sometime," she said, "or maybe I can be spending next summer in your family." She had her red sweater on and in my tear-streaked blindness, I missed seeing her face and captured instead the image of the red knit cuffs of her sweater snug against her willowy wrists as she pressed the car door closed. "Don't be sad," she said.

Within a week of being home, I received a letter from Dick, full of poetry that made me cry, telling me what he had seen that was special in me and Miran. It was rambling and disconnected, but enough of a gem that I could hold onto it later for strength. He sent me portraits he'd taken with his 35mm Canon of the regular visitors to the Yodeler Lodge. Miran's was a close-up of her face, pensive with a smile just emerging on the edges of her lips, slightly pouting, her complexion smooth, her demeanor exuding peace.

School began, and Miran and I exchanged a few letters. In her first letter, she wrote, "I think about how you always like to go up high places, you always like to reaching up. It gives good hope." In a letter in November, she mentioned that they had moved to a new apartment in Brooklyn, and that she had seen MeeSook and was feeling—as she misspelled it in a strange foreshadowing—"quiet close."

On a Saturday soon after that, when a cold snap chilled a bright fall day, I came home from an outing and saw both my parents shadowed in the family room, silhouettes against the back patio glass doors awash in sunset. At that moment, my father, who is exactly five feet, appeared in a trick of light to be a towering, looming man in robes. "Genie, I have some bad news. Miran Chang committed suicide. She hung herself in her closet."

Now, 32 years later, I can finally cry for Miran. I remember nothing of what I might have felt, perhaps so taken aback by the news that I didn't know how to react. I'm sure I must have asked what is always asked and no one can answer— why? I remember that my mother said she suspected that Miran was pregnant or had boy trouble and, as the daughter of a minister, couldn't face the shame. I was angry that my mother would think that and, when I recall this now, horrified by her immersion into the culture of saving face and by her lack of compassion at the time. At dinner that evening, I asked if I could go to the funeral.

"No, we're not going," my mother said, "and besides she's already been buried." Neither my mother nor my father said anything more about it.

I looked repeatedly at the picture of Miran that Dick had shot and couldn't understand that she was gone. What was it that made her take such a drastic way out? I didn't have any facts—I didn't even know what day it had happened, so there was a nebulous quality to her death, as if the entire event had never occurred, that she had simply been blotted out.

As things went in my family, even Vicky and I didn't talk about it, until recently when I told her I was writing about Miran.

"Yeah," Vicky said, "That was so strange. She hung herself at home, didn't she?"

"You can't help but wonder what she used, what she was thinking." I still had the same gruesome image of her in her closet that had struck me when my father told me years ago.

"I don't remember too much about it."

"That's because Mom and Dad didn't say anything! What's even more weird is that nowadays, you wouldn't think of not talking about it. I mean, there's counselors coming into the schools and suicide watches and prevention education!"

Vicky suggested that I ask Mom if she remembered any details, but I doubted she would, since at 90, my mother's memory was spotty. A few weeks later, my husband, Brian, and I raked leaves at Mom's house. Afterwards, we sat for pizza, tea and persimmons. It was still on my mind, so as she peeled the soft orange fruit, I said, "Mom, do you remember Chang Mok-sah? Reverend Chang in New York? I think Brooklyn."

"Chang, Chang…"

"His daughter, my friend Miran, she committed suicide in their apartment."

"Uhnn! Chang Moksah, k'rae. His daughter killed herself. Nobody knows why."

"Whatever happened to them? That family?"

"He's not so reputable now. He divorced his wife, has another wife and runs a big church. Makes a lot of money and talks big."

I translated my mother's Korean for Brian and asked, "Still in Brooklyn?"

"Yah, I don't remember, somewhere in New York."

"Do you know what happened to her?"

"That girl? She had boy trouble, must have been pregnant. Only that kind of problem could have brought her to suicide and all their troubles."

"No. I can't believe that. You shouldn't say that if you don't know! Is that what they said?"

"They? They didn't say anything!" My mother was annoyed that I had talked back to her. "They never said anything again. It was as if they never had a daughter. They buried her quickly, so fast it was almost in secret."

"But why?"

"People were talking."

"God."

"Yes. Even back then, I thought it was strange to bury her so fast then act as if nothing happened."

I wondered aloud about contacting Rev. Chang to ask him about Miran, but Brian said if a guy couldn't admit that he ever had a daughter, he sure wasn't going to appreciate some stranger asking him about her now. "It would be cruel," he said.

I remembered how reluctantly Miran had talked about her father—her eyes turned down, her shoulder-length hair parting at the back of her stiffly held neck, her arms firmly crossed against the front of her red sweater—and the image that I had of him: stern, severe, dark, angry. So I agreed with Brian.

But if the spirit lives on in the memory of the people left behind, it was a great sadness that her own family was so stuck in something as stupid as shame to never speak her name again. I had already revived Miran several times over. The protagonist in many stories I wrote was named Miran. I named all my female lead characters Miran until I remembered that I'd used her name before. She was the first native Korean I knew who didn't question or judge my level of Koreanness. She was the person with whom I came to understand sisterhood, who completely accepted me without a thought to the Asian-American equation. I think of her next to me on the top stair of the fire tower, her profile outlined darkly against the cloudy light of the stars, her chin lifted, her lips calm. She was indeed beautiful, and showed me that I was, too.

JENNIFER KWON DOBBS
Cure for the Swedish Fever

When i tell Mother i'm not from Sweden, but Korea   static
holds the line carefully lest it hangs up

       the only opportunity for clarity   she opens up
the absurd can of cola   the banal tuna

       packed with wafers and relish   she spreads together   she breathes
through a body too large with its own

devices that shut down   as if a camp torn down   hundreds of lanterns snuffed

packed for campaign   due east Mother moves the receiver
           bites into thick

says: *it's-good-for-lunches-have-you-tried-with-little-crumb-cakes*   pushes the line

o what will stop her   mouth

         .   .   .

i am Korea   passing through Mother's throat:
sulfur lit epiglottaltunnel of two-lane traffic   i come on

       like an illness that wants to end   i go in hard
       as a capsule of yellow
truck that can't stop   its confused hurl toward

the gut   someone had to open up

America's gateway to the West   burgh belly/three arteries
once good with cargo now junked

                                       with cancerous
                                              not-thought-out-geography

building cruelly and beautifully
to the hills   to the rivers   a downtown of crooked teeth
                                                      poised for bite down:

pausing from lemon pie i baked by her recipe, Mother says:
        just like your Swedish grandma's.

i stare at the proof: floured hands i'll scrub to the true

                        .   .   .

Sweden's ancestors loomed in the hallway all pale
sepia tones that moaned   cracked open rows of portals for sea air
cracked open   reached through a hand   cracked open nuts for dust

pulled from shells now from frames
                        a dust no less futile

though i cooked St. Lucia's feast with its candlelit garlands
sang Noel across crowns of flames
offered shellacked fruit   as if for a gold Buddha
brought to America in a crate   i ached with an orphan's hunger
so dulled Mother didn't need to strap me down

                                        to a high chair

she did with her Christmas indifference
she threw out beef as if the poorest food
she tore bread with the might of the privileged
she declared the cabbage i seasoned unfit for her tongue

                                        that'd canker from spice

                        .   .   .

static as the Statue of Liberty

                        raising a fiery sword before Eden's harbor

                                        Mother taught me to brave a way toward
to dwell needy   as a penis in womb

to rock back and forth in rapture
                        like "a boat girl"   i am

ambitious in the engagement picture   daring a dragon red dress

                                                against his pale face

(his mother in blue rayon and pearls)   with best intentions my teacher kept asking for this poem,

                    "Only in America" unwinds

                           not anaphora

                                   but helixes of DNA

that bind for a bride

               price in white

                    bandages that break skin and bones into naturalized code

                                   for my own good

he desired me thick   boot's tongue laced to the honeymoon bed

my words drowned in honey   my breasts   two brown does alert

his back cedar for God's temple   his hands Moses and Moses parting

                          my cove my alarm

while prodded as the boat people delivered to Ellis

                    while stern gate-lady   looks on and on

                       . . .

when Sweden adopted Korea it taught the small wrinkly country how to iron

                              out the epithantic eyefold

to hang difference in closets of the mind
it called this epistemology and gave out foil stars   if i could spell
Freedom

i'd be the Disney movie

                    girl standing on the toilet to piss   not yet trained to sit

                                        but i'd learn

how to win the Elks Lodge scholarship

write "the good citizen" essay

touch the Liberty Bell

                  when guards turned their backs

sneak under

          constitutional reqs for president   an immigrant can't meet   minor points:

though i sold poppies for the American Legion

bleached my hair blonde though it chose orange

cut out my clothes from patterns

as strange as when i'm alone   i put my head on my desk and dream a paisley

field in Korea   it's enough

when omoni recognizes me   for her sorrows   muttering i can't

understand

         but still want to hear

JAMES KANG
Hotel Normandie

The Tin Can was nearly empty. It usually is around the time I arrive. Most nights three girls work behind the bar, masterfully dividing their attention among their customers. I didn't see Katie, the half-Korean girl. The longhaired music selector who doubles as a busser was still letting Led Zeppelin play on. After nine he plays the eighties ballads mixed in with contemporary Korean pop. I heard him argue with Katie one night. He claimed that Journey could be categorized under Korean ballads because Steve Perry was one-quarter Korean. I sat where I usually sit, near the TV, and watched ESPN highlights while the double album *Song Remains the Same* was somewhere deep in the solo drum sets.

On the far side of the bar, on the stool below the television set that I have stared into for many idle hours, there was a man who looked to me as though he possessed absolutely zero interest in the environment that surrounded him. Naturally, the bar was dimly lit, and there wasn't much of an environment in the Tin Can where one can come to lose oneself. The girls behind the bar were always eager to chat with you when they were not busy. Whereas I stared blankly into a television screen, he periodically swiveled on his stool as if to rotate his perspective on something of an intricate inner matter. A plate of grapes, honeydew, watermelon and strawberries was in front of him, barely touched. Another full plate of dried fish and squid was also uneaten. He lit up cigarettes, one after another, puffing on them in a rhythm with sips from his drink. Pretending to be looking at the television screen, I glanced at him from time to time. Since the time I had come in, which was nearly an hour ago, I had not noticed a single change of expression on his face. I gauged that he was 35-years-old, at most. His shave was at least a week old, his hair still short but uncombed. He had the robust jowls of a young Marlon Brando. In contrast, his lips were elegantly curved. His eyes were black, black enough to appear starkly in the light of a dimly lit bar. He wore a dark suit jacket with no necktie. In the stock of characters I had imagined for my films, he would be a leading man. He possessed a look capable of projecting depth on the screen. I had not created a scenario in my mind for the man. Nor had I gone so far as to begin to speculate on the ball of thoughts around which his solitary mind was revolving. I too, was at least half-engaged with my own persistent worries.

It happened like I was in middle of daydreaming. I saw his figure rise out of his seat and take swift, determined steps toward me, not looking up once to glance at me, but assuredly coming my way. Before I had time to conceal the look of a voyeur's embarrassment, I felt his hand firmly rest on my shoulder. The man I was turning into one of my stock characters stepped right into my daydream and started speaking to me. I had no time to settle the question of whether he was violating my sense of reality, or whether he might have gotten helplessly caught in my daydream. Regardless of my concerns about what it meant to begin speaking to someone who was a character in my imagination an instant ago, all in the supernatural order of things, it was with such ease, how he pushed aside the world that I was viewing from my usual seat in my favorite bar. "Would you mind my company to drink with? It's terrible to have to drink alone, don't you agree?"

"I won't mind. I am not waiting for anyone," I replied, with some earnest. I could smell his cologne, a dominance of lavender with hints of citrus and amber. However refined, the smell of his cologne seemed to state that I was unmistakably in the presence of a man. I am not often around men who wear cologne.

He caught the attention of the bartender, pointed to what I was drinking and signaled for one more. "Do you know what I read in the Korean newspaper this morning? Can things ever get so bad that a man can destroy his own child's chances of ever living a normal life?"

"What did you read?" I asked, explaining that I hadn't been keeping up with a lot of current events.

Lots of people are hurting economically in Korea right now as we know it. Fathers are running out on their wives and kids because they can't cope with the shame of losing their jobs and watching their kids go hungry. There are literally thousands of men loitering and sleeping around the Seoul Central Station. They've become beggars. Companies are laying off tens of thousands workers. The country has not faced an economic situation this bad since the postwar years. But back then you would never hear of a father chopping off his own son's right thumb to pull off an insurance fraud. Ten thousand dollars. I read it in today's Korean newspaper. The man believed his son's thumb to be worth ten thousand dollars. Any other finger would pay off less, he must have figured. The kid was only nine years old. It took human beings more than a million years of evolution to develop a thumb that enabled us to use our hands like no other animal on the planet, and the father lopped off the two inches of his son's flesh like it was chicken fat. The little boy was so traumatized that when the insurance company came to investigate the accident, he could not recite the story his father had fabricated about an accidental injury. The investigator suspected something was wrong, because the boy started sobbing with his whole body shaking whenever the father came near. Eventually, the boy's aunt was able to get the truth out of the boy, and she went to the police to make charges against the father. The father is going to get ten years in prison, and you know his son isn't going to miss him very much." He shook his head and then took a swallow from his glass of whiskey.

"That kid who lost his thumb is going to have a tough life ahead of him, but what I think is worse is how much he is going to hate the world and how difficult it is going to be for him to trust anybody. If he doesn't find a meaningful life, Korean society will pay the price." He looked at his fingers, as if to make sure they were all there.

"I agree," I replied dumbly. "And there's been a lot of crazy, screwed up things like that happening in Korea. A whole country thrown into some new kind of madness, all kinds of unheard of violence. It makes Los Angeles seem like a paradise I don't ever want to leave." Then I recalled what had happened to Katie, brawling it out with the bar owner's girlfriend and all that.

We talked for a long time. He had his views on many different social issues, politics and world economy. He managed to keep our conversation from becoming personal. The moment where it seems appropriate to ask what the other person does for a living never passed. I had to go piss three times, and he didn't have to get up once. It made me nervous to think he must have an iron bladder. That is what I was thinking after I came back from my third trip. We were both silent. He then turned to me to begin to unravel something that was carefully thought out.

"I'll say that this will sound strange, but I have a proposition to make. I didn't think I would find an appropriate person until now. I have a hunch it would interest you. You'll have to at least listen to what may seem crazy at first. It's really not, and what I want to ask you to do is quite simple."

"As long as I don't have to cut off two little thumbs, I'm interested. What is it?" I shifted on my seat.

"There is a woman staying at the Normandie Hotel, room 411. It's that hotel down the street from here? Do you know which one I am referring to?"

I nodded.

"I need someone to look after her and let me know that she is doing all right. Contact me every couple of days and tell me how she is doing. Yes, the difficult part is that you'll have to stay at the Normandie Hotel too."

He must have known that I was unemployed and had plenty of time on my hands. I was thinking about how much money he was going to offer. "How long are you talking about?" I asked.

"Unfortunately, that cannot be determined. A week, two weeks, a month possibly. I'll need a commitment of up to a month."

"A month! That's a serious relationship you're talking about. Who is this woman? You want someone to stalk a woman for a whole month or even longer? There is a hazard of developing an incurable habit of stalking after that much of a time commitment. I guess already that I am not supposed to know who this woman is I am to stalk, right?"

"No, not followed around or stalked really. Just whether she is doing fine. For five thousand dollars. Hotel paid for. A bonus if everything works out."

"What do you mean if everything works out? Do you have something in mind?"

"No. Not exactly. But I'll let you know. I mean, if you're interested in the offer."

I had always wanted to stay at a hotel as a resident. There were no particulars that he asked me to conduct. After we agreed to some arrangements, I drove back to my uncle's place in Glendale where I had been living for more than a year.

He is my father's younger brother. I have a car on loan from him. I told him I'd pay my own insurance fee, but I let my insurance expire last month. If I got into a terrible accident I could just leave Los Angeles. My uncle resented my father for being the progenitor. My father inherited most of our grandfather's wealth, even if it wasn't much. My uncle came out here on scholarship, studied aerospace engineering and now lives comfortably in Glendale. I've begun to feel creepy staying up all hours of the night watching strange cable television. The people on infomercials use polite English, the way I've learned in my ESL classes. Very cheerful and polite. That's why I've watched it. I've called 800-numbers to order products and hung up when they asked me for my credit card number. It was a terrific way to practice English. I knew Uncle's wife was becoming fed up with me and started to worry about me being a presence around her children. I overheard her say to my uncle, "He has no direction in his life. He's 27-years-old and he has no interest in pursuing a career. He stays up very late and watches sex TV. Don't you hear the nasty sounds at night? I'm afraid the kids can hear it too. I don't think that he has been a very positive influence on our kids like you said he was going to be. You said he was going to become a filmmaker. Is that the kind of movie he's going to make? Screaming naked-girl movie? It was a mistake to let him stay with us. Why did his father send him here?" I heard my uncle mutter something in response, but I wasn't able to make out what he said. It was time for me to find my own place in Los Angeles.

I haven't heard back from the film schools I've applied to. I've no idea how I am going to pay for film school, but that's what I've come here to learn. A month after I get here, the IMF gives my country a temporary third world status. I think that was a punishment for being a part of the world that started epidemics. First it was the Asian bird flu and then the Asian economic crisis. I got confused over what an epidemic meant because both were called epidemics. Doctors must have been working together with businessmen to figure out ways to sedate the rabid tigers and dragons. My country especially is not very popular with the world at large. We've been on the cover of *Newsweek* and *Time* magazines as the nation of conspicuous consumers. The "IMF Crisis" put my entire clan out of business.

When I was in Seoul, I had always wanted to live in a hotel, a big first-class international hotel. I believed hotels must be the least homogeneous places in Korea. I stayed at the Intercontinental once in my college years with a rich girl I seduced. I ate ramen for the next two weeks straight to rebound financially, but she was well worth the MSG shock. I wonder if she would have stayed with me longer if we had conducted all of our rendezvous at first-class hotels. Twice in a fleabag sex hotel and then she didn't return anymore of my pages.

This place isn't what I imagined my hotel existence to be like, but it's probably the closest I'll ever get. The bright blue-and-white awning over the hotel's main door seemed like a cheerfulness out of place, a New England beach resort smile on a hump of red bricks on Normandie Avenue. The buildings and houses that fall into the pedestrian perspective at the intersection of Sixth and Normandie Streets have the power to remain incomprehensible.

The entire lobby was empty after the two people had left. It did not bustle with goings-on, with people checking in and checking out. People stayed here months at a time. The place held a secret for me. I felt certain there was some knowledge to be coaxed out of it. The air was moldy and still. The floor of the hotel was made of hard stone. I think marble, with deep grooves and skid marks from wheelchairs. There were dining tables and chairs spread out over the one half of the lobby floor. Tablecloths covered all the tables, but none of the tables were set. They hadn't been set, in actuality, in more than twenty years. But the tables have yet to be removed. They were there to remind the visitor of a rambunctious past. The glory of the hotel's past hung from the high ceiling, frozen in the crystals of the chandelier medusa. It loomed, mocking the solitude of transiency. The residents eat in a small cafeteria in the rear of the hotel adjoining the kitchen. I don't eat the food here. It's food for the elderly. Lots of porridge, mornings and evenings. I only eat the porridge or the soup when I want to expel a hangover.

The hotel is partly run as a retirement home, receiving subsidies from the government to stay afloat. A hotel must be the loneliest place to die in. Fortunately, in the time that I've been here, no one's croaked. Those who die must go straight to heaven because I've no doubt this is purgatory for those poor, neglected retired folks. There's no such thing as a retirement home in Korea. It would create a national hysteria, if not an uprising of dead ancestors. We're much too fearful of the dead and the close-to-dead to keep them cooped up in prefuneral homes.

I was told by the male student who lives on the floor above me that the proprietors of the hotel, the two ladies who alternately work inside the reception booth, bought out the hotel with the insurance money they collected after their restaurant business had burnt down during the Los Angeles uprising in 1992. They had to wait two years before their insurance company begrudgingly paid up half a million. Before they saw any of the money, the two women joined the Buddhist sect that chants *namyohorengekyo* to stay off the streets. They are friendly and accommodating. Their chanting can be heard morning and evening, but the women are so kind that most of the residents have learned to live with the strange and punctual vibrato. The sound of their chanting traveled out of the two women's room on the lobby level. Lying in my bed, I would feel connected to their sounds as thoughts are to the groveling murmur in the pit of the stomach. I'd imagine that my stomach was an enormous cave on top of a mountain in which hundreds and thousands of people gathered, huddled in prayer.

I want this hotel to be the location for my first feature film. I wanted a train station for a series of shots where my lead characters carry on their clandestine rendezvous, but this city lacks trains. I thought all great cities of the world had trains. This hotel will do just fine I think.

I heard the clattering of a computer keyboard. A middle-aged woman turned around to greet me. "How can I assist you?" she asked in a soothing voice. She squinted slightly behind her ebony-framed eyeglasses. I thought she had an unusually long face with a nose that looked like the beak of a toucan bird. Her calm demeanor made you forget her stark features.

"I am looking for a room," I said.

"How long do you wish to stay?"

"Two or maybe three weeks. I am a student and I am waiting for my school admission to finalize. I'll need a place to stay until then." I made up an excuse.

"Many international students stay here. I figured you were a student too. The rate is $250 per week or $750 for a month. You can have breakfast and dinner on weekdays for $50 per week."

"Do you have a room on the top floor, the fourth floor? The higher the better, for the views."

"A young man moved out two days ago from 403. I think 403 is available."
She glanced at the board where the room keys hung to make sure.

"Then I'll pay for a month."

After I checked for pubic hair on the sheets, I turned on the television. I was
equipped with a VHS player and cable. I could watch some porn, I thought. The
bathroom had no leaking faucets. That and pubic hairs on bed sheets could be the
worst things about a cheap hotel. The air conditioner was noisy, but it worked
fine, just in case I needed it. The room overlooked a mini mall on Sixth Street. It
was late in the afternoon, and I felt a little drowsy. I tried to conjure up in my
mind the image of the woman named Seulgi who stays in room 411. I got a combination of a lot of girls I had adored in the past. I felt myself grow hard. It had
been a while since I slept with a woman and since I masturbated. I ejaculated
watching her on top of me smiling, her black hair tousling over her breasts. A
hotel room is not only an erotic place to have sex with a woman, it also gives lone-
some masturbation an anonymously erotic sensation.

It was near six when I awoke from my nap. Her room was four doors down
the hall. The walls and doors of the fourth floor were painted in lime green. The
third floor was pink. The second floor was baby blue, and the lobby level was
ivory. The carpeting on my floor was tan. I wondered how old it was because of
the slight moldy smell. The hallway floor creaked a tiny bit as I approached her
door. I slowed down my pace and paused for a second to hear if there was any one
inside. I heard nothing.

I turned on the television. The newscasters were talking about a 7.6 earthquake that had struck a South American country just two weeks after another one
of equal scale had completely demolished a city in the Middle East. They said the
United States had its own series of natural disasters to worry about. A powerful
hurricane was about to reach the Florida coast within the next 24 hours. I flipped
through the channels to find a sports station. I found one where teenaged kids
were doing fantastic stunts on skateboards. Boldly, they invited self-destruction

and then skillfully, they evaded it. The skateboarders swooping back and forth started to make me feel anxious.

I looked into my leather satchel. I saw the envelope that contained five thousand dollars. There was six thousand, and I had taken out a thousand to pay for the hotel. For the first time, I tried to figure out the relationship between the man I met at the Tin Can and Seulgi. He could not be a father or an uncle, unless Seulgi was a lot younger than I had imagined. Estranged lovers or husband and wife was the most reasonable conclusion I could make. What began to worry me was that his face was fading from my memory. He was around thirty. If I tried, I couldn't describe his eyes, nose, hair or any of the particular traits of the man I spoke with no more than two days prior. At the same time something nearly the opposite seemed to be occurring. I can almost feel his persona as if it were a fabric. It was the kind of feeling one would have about someone you knew for a very long time. It is just a feeling of knowing that the person was there in the same place. Someone you've known for a long time—you don't have to recognize the shapes of their nose or eyes or ears to tell you that it was the same person you had known for many years. In fact the longer you know a person, you see deeper beneath a person's qualities until you feel things that you cannot see. I had that same feeling about the man from the Tin Can.

He should have contacted me by now. Shouldn't he be concerned whether or not I had begun carrying through with my end of the deal? Was he in a completely drunken state and can't recall our meeting? Or was it possible that he had his way of tracking what I do? The thought made me look out my window. There were very few cars in the mini mall across from the hotel's view and a couple of cars parked in the street. No one lurking about anywhere in the vicinity.

I went downstairs to the reception desk. Jeanie, the long-faced, bird-nose woman was reading a Korean daily. "Is everything fine with your room? Speak to me anytime if you have any requests," she said in an earnest voice.

"I like the room. And this hotel has plenty of character. I came down to ask if anyone has called for me today."

"No…I'm positive not. Will your school contact you here?"

"Oh, no. I was wondering if a friend might have called."

"It's good you like the place. Some residents have been here for almost twenty years," she remarked, squinting one eye to gesture her own disbelief.

"They must be students," I chuckled.

"Students are all foreign. Like you, international students. Senior citizens. The government pays half. Mrs. Cha made a deal with the government. This is a government building. Hee hee!"

The first time I saw her I recorded in my mind a perfect shot of a woman entering a hotel. A hundred suggestions in a single frame. A momentary play of light and shadow from the opening door produced an effect of disturbance within the frame, and she passed through it, eyes downcast, emanating a slight hint that she was aware of being watched, or filmed for that matter. She wore white knickers and a beige top. When she approached the reception desk, where I stood talking to Jeanie, she looked startled and shuffled her steps. She said good evening to Jeanie, and Jeanie called her over. "I have a message for you Seulgi. Kyung Mi wants you to wait to have dinner with her. She says she is going to down to Irvine and wants you to come with her. She is coming back at eight."

I had begun to notice the rhythm and pace of her daily routine. In the evenings she left the hotel at random times and sometimes returned after midnight. Once she came back after I had already fallen asleep, which must have been later than three in the morning.

At two o'clock she leaves the academy where she studies English and walks to a café on Wilshire Boulevard. She takes her iced coffee and reads there for an hour or so. She walks back to the hotel taking Fifth Street instead of the busier Sixth Street. Sometimes she stops in at the 7-Eleven store to grab a bottle of water and cigarettes. Between three thirty and four she is back in her room. She is often very quiet in her room until around six o'clock, taking a nap probably.

More than a week went by, and the man at the Tin Can still had not contacted me. I was becoming weary of my own routines. I looked out the window onto Sixth Street a thousand times and heard a hundred wretched souls scream out profanities against their girlfriends, against their boyfriends, against their mothers and their fathers, against 2 A.M. drunk demons. I heard half dozen screeches of car accidents. I was getting tired of doughnuts and sick of the smell of vomit rising into my hotel room. I even stopped following Seulgi around. Instead, I would watch other random people.

Sometimes I would see a face I had seen before. Then suddenly Koreatown became a much smaller place, inhabited by a number of people no greater than the population of an average village in Korea, a thousand at most. I could almost get a complete picture of a person. I'd know what kind of work they did. I'd see them having lunch with a group of people who are probably coworkers, and then a few days gone by I might spot the same individual again with a whole family. I saw a girl who I recognized as a bartender in one of the bars I drank at a few times. She got out of a nice-looking car driven by a man at least ten years older and then drove off in her own car. I happened to be parked on a quiet street looking through a newspaper to get the time of a movie I wanted to catch. She drove off in a hurry with only a quick glance behind at the man who had just dropped her off. I couldn't help feeling that there was an element of danger involved in the way that the woman and the man had parted. Two weeks later, I saw her again getting out of her car at the Chapman Market, this time with a little toddler girl and her grandmother. She had sunglasses on, which made it difficult for me tell whether she recognized me. I was almost certain that she did, but she walked past the table where I was seated in the patio section of a restaurant without making eye contact with me. That didn't bother me. Rather, I felt an odd comfort in seeing other people in Koreatown whose lives were not normal, like a young woman with a child living together with her own mother. There was beauty in the three of them walking together into a store on a sunny day. The men were lost at war, at war with themselves, against themselves. Three generations of women without a man and they were complete. I was overcome by a sudden loathing toward myself that forced me to flee from the enclosure of the plaza.

descent

AMY KRAUSE
Bastard

I don't remember when I started to hate my father. This is the topic of conversation as Park and I sit on the edge of the porch and drink beer. We're both out of work early on a Friday night and haven't a place to go, and his front porch is as good as any other. Park is not only my best friend, but also my favorite drinking partner, because not only does he never judge me, but by the time I start getting into anything deep, after two or three beers, he's usually too drunk to process anything. He's the perfect sounding board.

"How can you hate your father?" he asks, polishing off his fourth.

"I don't know. He's not really my real father anyway," I say. "I never knew my biological father. He left my mother before I was born. And then my mother left me. Guess if I left it would complete the cycle, eh?"

"Hate is a pretty strong word, you know."

"Well, it fits." I toss the bottle into the recycling bin.

Somehow these Friday nights always end up the same, both of us getting too drunk and me having a bitching session with Park, with the topic nine times out of ten being my dysfunctional family, namely my relationship with my father.

There is a dream that I have from childhood. The room is darkened except for some faint light creeping in through a window, and I can feel the presence of someone in my bedroom. I see the shadow and I may even talk to it; I don't know. I think that it is a friend of mine. I can feel some breathing down my neck and hands pressing down on my shoulders. I'm afraid at first to think about what is happening here, but since it appears to be my friend Sam, I let it happen. He kisses me, and I can feel his hands starting to lift up my dress. I'm kind of in a daze and don't know exactly what to do. I finally realize what this is going to lead to and at the last minute, as I feel him pressing himself into me, I push him away. I spout something at him about my boyfriend finding out. He gets up, murmurs something unintelligible and leaves the room.

It is about this time I wake up and see my father closing the door behind him, the light from the hallway slowly disappearing into blackness.

It wasn't until years later that something made me think back to that dream and wonder what, if anything, had happened that night. It's not that I can claim to be physically abused or anything. My father rarely laid a hand on us. What he lacked in physical abuse, he made up for with verbal and emotional abuse.

I was eight years old when the explosion happened. I don't remember what I had done; just that he was upset and I was in trouble. I walked out of my bedroom to find him waiting for me. His face was crimson, and I could feel his spit spray on my face as he screamed. My father was lunging at me, screaming obscenities and degrading remarks until I stood there, after it was all over, scared shitless, in a pool of my own urine.

My mother is in her bedroom, working on a crossword puzzle and eating a bag of potato chips. The sound of the TV is off, and the picture is showing snow. I stand in the doorway and just watch her; she doesn't know I'm standing there. The family dog, Kramer, is sprawled out at the foot of the bed, either sleeping or entranced by the snow on the screen. My mom is in her trademark sweats, chewing the end of her pencil, in deep thought as the steam from her cup of hot tea snakes into the air.

My mother has been keeping pretty busy lately, between her bookkeeping for my sister's basketball, just helping out at the church with the monthly fundraiser, or just doing yard work. Our lawn has never looked so good.

I have a head full of questions for my mother someday, when the time is right. Is she happy with her life? Does she hate my father for spending more time at work and at the bar than at home with her? Does she think he has been unfaithful to her over the years, on the many nights that he never comes home? Or is she glad that he stays away, so that she can avoid one of his "moods" that he so regularly brings home with him, destroying everything in his path.

Does she still love him?

I am about seven years old in the dream. We are still living in our old house on Chicago Street. I see a beautiful white horse, large and powerful-looking. He is radiant–almost glowing–and I see the horse running down the street. It looks so majestic, so strong, and so good, that I stand on the edge of the driveway by the mailbox and just stare at it. It comes up in my driveway and stops to look at me. We stare at each other, and I am trans-fixed, unable to move, until all of a sudden he turns and gallops away. I look down the street and see a large crowd of people headed in my direc-tion. The people are lined up in perfect little rows, almost militaristic, marching in perfect time as they follow the horse. Some of the people come up to the horse to pet it. As they come up to him, he stands back on his hind legs and comes straight down on them, stomping them to death. Flat. Their bodies disappear into the driveway and their blood runs off in thick red pools, until it dissolves into the grass enclosed by the driveway.

I'm frightened by this display and run back to my house, to my garage. Usually our car is parked in there, but this time there are empty cardboard boxes in its place. The boxes are piled high, almost to the ceiling, filling the entire garage, and I am careful not to knock them over as I make my way through the cardboard maze. I run to the door that leads to the kitchen, looking for my mother, and yell to her through the door. I have to stand on the garage steps and can't enter the kitchen, because if I do, I will track mud into the house and my father will be upset. I finally see her and notice she is baking a cake in the oven, entertaining a roomful of guests, all people that I do not know or recognize. My mother is fat and her belly sticks out, pos-

sibly pregnant with my little sister, but I don't know for sure. I tell her about the horse and the dead people and the pools of blood on the driveway and she smiles at me. That's nice, she says, and goes back to her cake. But look, I say, pointing at the horse, who is claiming even more victims in our front yard. She smiles and keeps on with her baking, giving me that look that so many adults give when they are saying, "OK, I'll humor you this time, just because you don't know any better."

I'm still scared and hurry to take off my shoes so that I can go inside the house, even though I know that I still will not be safe from the horse. I remember feeling that if the horse comes in and kills my entire family and all the other people in it, it will be my fault. I couldn't stop it.

My mother notices I'm standing there and tosses the crossword puzzle at me. "Try to finish this one," she says. "I'm stuck on thirteen across." I take the pen and scrawl the word adulterer. I don't know if it is the right word, but it seems to fit. My mother has known that my father has been having an affair for years. I don't mean that he is having your typical affair with another woman outside of the marriage. I'm not sure that's going on, though in the past it has definitely crossed not only my mind, but my mother's as well. But ever since I have been old enough to understand, he has had an affair with his job, with his drinking buddies, with his work. Sometimes I think that an affair with another woman would be a lot easier for my mother to take than the love affair he has with his job. And I can see it in her eyes, in the way she has let herself go over the years. My mother is an attractive, smart woman, who like so many her age, traded in her individuality and future plans for a wedding ring. It's not something we talk about, but I know it's true.

I see her alone, eating those chips, and I hate him even more.

Park's now flicking bottle caps onto driveway and trying to land them in a square on the cement. It's been so long since someone has said anything that I think he was starting to doze off from all the alcohol. "Did you know that my mom had two miscarriages before they adopted me?" I ask.

"No."

"They adopted me after that, and then a few years later, they got my brother. Then out of the blue, my mom got pregnant with my sister, and then my youngest sister followed later.

I am walking through a poor neighborhood. I think that I must be downtown. All of the signs are in Chinese characters, and though the storefronts look vaguely familiar, I cannot interpret the language. There are fires burning in the streets, and judging from the amount of smoke and ash, it seems that the entire city was bombed. I turn around and see my grandmother chasing after me. She has on a robe and is holding a staff. She reminds me of an Old Testament prophet and is spewing scripture verses at me, screaming and ranting till she foams at the mouth. I take my fingers and form them into the shape of an inverted cross, and she slowly starts to shrink, just like the wicked witch in the Wizard of Oz. *My brother and mother walk up to me, and my mother hands me a paper bag, wrinkled and worn. I open the sack and pull out a bright red tomato. Placing it in the sack again, I tell my brother that we must burn all of it. He starts a small fire, upon which we place the sack. I pick up a stick and start to peel away at the bark. Under the bark I uncover a tail of a rat instead of wood, and I throw it on the fire in disgust.*

The photo is recent. It's of my parents and my two younger sisters on a vacation in the Caribbean. The resemblance of my sisters to my parents is quite remarkable. They both have the perfect balance of each of my parents' genes, to look like they belong together. Sandy brown hair, brown eyes, perfect skin. You'd think they were the perfect, complete All-American family, just the four of them.

The second photo is older, at little bent at the edges and faded. *Florida, 1987.* My father is holding my younger sister, and my brother and I are standing on the other side of my mother. My brother and I are severely contrasted to them with our dark skin and hair and small, slanted eyes.

My father came home from work one night when I was about ten and told my mother that someone had started rumors that he had been fooling around with an Asian woman before they were married, resulting in the births of my brother and me. I was too young to understand, but will never forget the resentment in his voice.

"Funny," I say, as I reminisce to Park, who's peeling another label off of a beer. "I guess I knew more than I thought back then." Park's giving me that look, the one that says, "don't say that," but he can't disagree, either.

"I guess that since he was never around when I was young, and even to this day, well, I kind of got used to being self-contained, and not wanting to share a lot of things with him."

"Don't you believe in second chances," Park says.

"Yes. But I've run out of those for him."

It's getting late and this conversation has begun to wear on us both. Park and I start picking up orphan bottle caps and match them to their respective owners. The evening has left us—as it usually does—up too late, a little too drunk and no wiser, throwing meaningless words into the air, where they spin, sometimes dance for awhile and fall to the ground again, the same place where they started.

I can hear my father's steps outside my door. I know that he has been out there for the last 10 minutes, just waiting for the perfect time to invade my territory. He finally came in and asked what I was doing. I told him I was working on some writing, but when I don't let him see it, he says, "You're just a pile of bullshit, that's what you are."

Both of Park's parents are dead. He tells me it is better to have an absent father than to not have one at all. I've gone through life both ways, first time with no father, and the second time with one who was never around when I needed him and thinks I'm a pile of bullshit.

I think I'd choose the first route had I the choice to make again.

SUNG RNO

Corrosive Influence

When our mothers called, there had to be trouble. We could have
looked beyond the situation and seen through the painted window.
The sense of things gone astray, of unbalance. Bombs and waste
dumps, test-tube families. Terrible things happen and walls were
built up. They separated us, we got used to it, and we liked it that
way. Each day a challenge rubbing in our hands, dissolving into
time and history.

"How could you know that the sky would do that, right then, right
there?" It just happened, as when a house burns down, a baby cries,
or an old man trips down the stairs and breaks his hip. Things will
be altered, permanently.

An hourglass with a hole in the bottom. Most things are irreversible, and putting black onto white doesn't help matters any
more than the people who made a house of glass, just to see who
would throw the first stone. A man trapped himself inside, couldn't
tell which was which. He tried to tell his friends about being inside
a frame where there was no border, but they weren't interested if
there wasn't any plot.

"Maybe this time the picture will work, it will succeed." The car
caught on fire, willfully. The kids in the neighborhood all laughed,
they thought it was the funniest thing, better than ice cream or
God. The police car cruised the streets hoping to catch someone in
the act, and in the meantime our friends got together without us.

JANE PARK
Falling

While the pages burn, I sit by the fire, surprised by my calmness. I have waited 20 years, and now I watch as the fire consumes the paper and transforms my father's scribbled words into ash. I know every page. It has taken me 20 years to learn his language, to read these words. And in 10 minutes, nothing will remain, but a pile of ash.

I will say these words from memory while I sleep, or so my husband says, though he does not know Korean. Sometimes when I wake on these mornings, I will panic. To stop the panic, I will say a prayer and then make coffee, feed Charlie and get ready for work.

Make coffee, feed Charlie and get ready for work. A few months ago, an old man came into the clinic and sat in the reception area eating a pear. The way he chewed his food reminded me of my father. I didn't cry at his funeral, so I was surprised when I had to excuse myself. "My contact lens," I said, blinking ferociously, hating myself for crying now.

My father chewed his food slowly, whittled twigs and wore a brown wool worsted cardigan. This is how I remember him. He used to find twigs or branches near his "office" and carve imaginary princes, princesses and monsters—toys for Thomas and me. Now, I realize that he made these toys because he could not afford to buy them. But with the twigs he would transform our living room into far-off villages, battlefields, heaven and hell.

His office was in the woods, a 15-minute walk from our store and house. For a desk, he placed a plank of wood between two branches, and used milk cartons for his seat. He went to work before the break of dawn, before the store would open. Sometimes he would write well into the day, and my mother would shout from the back of the store, or the front of our house, "Elly, get dad, the dairy order is here and I have customers."

I would run to his office and find him writing, forgetting that today was the day the dairy order arrived. I hated interrupting him. Sometimes I would quietly walk up behind him, hoping that he would see or sense me first.

"Elly, is that you?" he would ask without turning his head.

"Yeah, Dad. It's milk day today."

He would turn off his portable radio, gather his papers and his pens, and pack everything into the milk crate he used for his seat.

Come rain, come shine, come snow, come sun, he would go off into the woods with his milk crate to his office. It wasn't really so much in the woods as at the base of a forested mountain. It was less a mountain than the last whimper of the great Rocky Mountain Range.

We lived in Pincher Creek, a town just off Highway 21 that used to be a booming mining community. When the coal disappeared, so did the men, and we relied on the highway to bring in a lonely truck driver, a wandering tourist. We lived in a house attached to the store at the back, so the front of the house faced the woods. Before us had lived the Kroshinskis—three generations of Ukrainian grocers—until the great-great grandson Bill Kroshinski died an aged bachelor, a notorious profligate. Our store was still called Kroshinski's General Store, although on our store sign somebody had painted a *t* over the *n*: *Kro-shit-ski*.

Thomas and I attended school in the next town. A school bus would pick us up from the store every day and take us to Crow's Feet Elementary School. If we ever complained about the 40-minute bus ride, the bullies who called us the Kro-SHIT-ski kids or the teachers with their stale saliva breath, our parents would remind us that they had never received a formal education, and neither had our grandparents.

My parents revered education like religion. They had grown up poor and could not afford to go to school and, ironically, only when my father immigrated did he begin to formally learn Korean to place structure into his speech. He was constantly practicing his reading and writing.

Before every parent-teacher interview, my mother would wear a smart dress ordered from the Sears catalogue and my father would wear his only suit. They would close the store early—for that night only—to visit my school and my teachers. Afterward, they would come home with their eyes sparkling as they reported to us what our teachers said about our progress and our potential.

I can imagine them in front of our teachers, nodding their heads, saying nothing, doing nothing, because they were so cautious about unknown codes they might violate. Once, during our Christmas concert, I was playing a piano solo. My parents closed the store early to attend the concert. My mother wore a fuchsia dress to match the poinsettia pinned onto her lapel, and my father wore—for the second time that year—his suit. They entered the school the way the Ukrainians in that town entered a Cathedral: silently, solemnly, and with their hands hanging awkwardly. They walked down the halls, not knowing if they should be walking straight or holding plastic punch cups or speaking with somebody, anybody.

Mr. Stevenson approached us.

"It was good of you to come."

"Yes."

"I did not know you lived in Pincher Creek."

"We do."

"How are you doing?"

Miss Shell, another teacher, interrupted us to flirt with Mr. Stevenson—my parents not knowing whether to be relieved or offended. I always enjoyed watching Miss Shell, with her drawn-out laughter and her hot pink fingernails, which she ran through her teased hair, her words making Mr. Stevenson blush. I have often wondered if my mother was ever like her, brash and sexy.

My father told us that he married my mother because of her rice cakes. In Korea, during the *chusok* Thanksgiving festival, he tasted "the most delicious rice cakes in the world." Later on in the evening, he met their creator and was stunned that a beautiful 15-year-old girl had enough "wisdom," as he called it, to make these rice cakes. He was 19 at the time. They married three weeks later. There is a photo of my mother in a short skirt and with long hair, holding my father's hand the evening after their wedding, though I cannot imagine them in love. I imagine my father recited his poetry into her unschooled ears. My mother was easily impressed by anyone who knew anything. They came to Canada immediately after their wedding.

I was born prematurely eight months later, in Crow's Feet General Hospital. Two years after that, my mother sponsored her eldest brother and his wife. They bought a busy supermarket in Crow's Feet that enabled them to afford a son, a daughter, three dogs and a trip to Disneyland for the entire family—including the dogs—every summer vacation.

We called my mother's brother Uncle Sam, though he did not have an official English name. Later, when I was learning American history, Thomas and I chuckled as the angular Uncle Sam pointed to us from my textbook and said I WANT YOU.

"I WANT YOU!" and I placed my father's white calligraphy brush against my chin.

"I WANT YOU!" and Thomas put on my father's straw fedora.

My Uncle Sam sat solemn and stoic like an Indian Big Chief. My father laughed and tried to explain to him what the hilarity was all about. My father loved stories like that. He loved whittling his twigs. He loved calling me the Princess of the Orient. He loved telling Thomas that snow fell because the gods were eating porridge for breakfast that day.

He loved winter best, with the snow falling down gracefully, whitening the world. He would disappear then, both in his office and at the store. At the store, he would sit behind the counter beside the glass window and watch the sun stream, the snow fall and the wind blow. Some customers commented that he was "a dreamy old man." Others got impatient and banged their cola cans or tapped their fingers on the counter to get his attention.

He read his books, his English books, which were carelessly tossed and forgotten around the store. Sometimes he would place his book on top of a counter, a shelf, a barrel of loose beans, and forget about it until a passing customer would pick up *War and Peace*. "Does Tolstoy make the beans heartier?" a customer once asked, impressed.

As in Korean, my father was self-taught in English. He began by reading my schoolbooks. I was angry that he would take my books when I had a book report due the next day. Books were constantly disappearing from my schoolbag. In the winter, the snow discouraged me from venturing into my father's office. So the next day, when I could not submit my book report, I would lie: "not enough time" or "lost my book." Mr. Stevenson wouldn't understand, and I was ashamed.

Soon my father graduated to the classics. Monthly, a hardbound classic novel would arrive in our mailbox: Simpson Publishers World Masterpiece Series. Because the postal office was in Crow's Feet, I was the mail deliverer. Every day after school before the school bus came, I collected our mail from the post office. At the beginning of every month, as I came home from school, my father would ask me casually, as if it were a passing thought rather than an obsession, "So, did anything arrive in the mail?" When the book finally arrived, my father would disappear for a day or two into his Reading Room—a spare room where he lay on the bed and read. Later, he would emerge and act as if he'd just remembered he had a wife at the store and children to feed. Though he never apologized, he was always embarrassed. My mother was also embarrassed for him and asked him how he could selfishly sit and read all day while there were milk jugs arriving, customers buying, tomatoes rotting, and only my mother to "work like a dog," as she would phrase it in perfect English.

I tried to help. After school, whenever the Reading Room was locked or my father's milk crate was gone from the closet, I would go immediately to the store. My mother would often place me behind the counter so she could check food inventory, spray vegetables, dust shelves. My cheeks would burn if someone I knew came in: my friends, boys in my class, Mr. Stevenson.

"Oh, hello there, Elizabeth."

"Hello, Mr. Stevenson."

"I didn't know you lived in Pincher Creek."

"I do."

"How are you doing?"

"Fine, and yourself?"

"Fine, just fine."

And we would talk about the snow, or the sun, or the school, as he walked down the aisles, filling his basket. I hated having to take his money, pack his groceries, and say "have a nice day" when I secretly wanted to dishevel my hair in the hopes that he would pack me into his basket, in his Buick, and drive me away from Pincher Creek.

There were many times when I wanted to run away. Once, after a particularly cruel fight between my parents, I slammed the door and ran as fast as I could, as far as I could, which was about half a mile, before the snow began freezing my toes, my nose.

When I turned around, I saw my father walking toward me.

"Why do you make Mom work like a dog?" I yelled, crying. "Why can't you be like Uncle Sam so me and Thomas can go to Disneyland?" and I started asking him many more questions that all began with "*Why do you?*" or "*Why can't you?*"

It's funny the way my father was so obsessed with words, and yet he could never use them when they were most necessary. He was silent, stunned, and stood in front of me as I threw these darts at him.

The next week, I saw a book lying on the bed in the Reading Room entitled *Fatherhood: The Journey*. The week after that, it was replaced by *How to Love Your Wife*. Soon my father cleared a shelf and devoted it to the literature of self-improvement. Books like *I'm OK, You're OK* or *Making Your Millions Begins with Your Mind* were arriving in the mail.

During this time, my father insisted that Thomas and I eat dinner with him. Usually at dinnertime, my mother and I would stay at the storefront so that my father and Thomas could eat first. However, my father arranged it so my mother tended the cash register while he ate with us. During dinner, he would straighten his posture, rest his index finger on his knife, and ask, "So, Tom, Elly, tell me how your day went."

"Fine."

"Good."

"Anything happen at school?"

"Nope."

"Nah."

"Any funny stories you want to tell Daddy?"

Silence.

I dreaded these dinners because I dreaded the silence that I could not break and the words I could not say. My father would ask the same questions over and over, and Thomas and I could not answer them. We felt as if answering his questions would be a sort of betrayal of the way things really were.

Soon these dinners stopped. The book collecting also stopped. I noticed that more than half his self-improvement books still had their spines uncracked, their glossy dust covers still shining.

The fights between my parents continued, although they weren't really fights, because my father was a passive man, and he would just listen as my mother shouted her complaints. Once a man came into our store drunk. He asked my mother for some pussy, and when she didn't understand what he wanted, he began fondling his groin. "Pussy," he said over and over, and she did not know what to do except scream. My father, who was stocking shelves at the time, ran to her, saw the man and stood there shocked.

My mother, acting on instinct, jumped over the counter and began pushing the drunk man out of the store. He thought these were embraces and held my mother fast and kissed her neck with his moist lips. Still my father stood there shocked. It was only when my mother began yelling at my father that he pushed her away from the drunk man, who was almost double my father's size. "Go home," my father said in a tone which may have sounded mild but was quite violent coming from him. Throughout all of this, my mother continued yelling at my father, how could you let this man disgrace your wife? How could you just stand there? And only because the drunk man felt humored did he leave the store, slapping my father on the back and telling him, "Your wife needs to get laid."

I felt bad that my mother felt bad because my father was a coward. Thomas, when he heard this story, punched the wall and said that if he'd been there, the man would have had his fuckin' balls punched out.

My father would not make eye contact with me or anyone else that night, or on the nights following. It was as if he was a child and we were the judging parents: It was that type of fear. And I hated hating my father for not being able to punch out that man's balls.

This incident happened at the beginning of the coldest winter ever recorded in Crow's Feet County. I remember in late November the insides of my nostrils froze as I collected the icicles hanging beneath our van. Inside the house, we listened to the radio as the announcer announced, "CLOSED, Crow's Feet Elementary and High School. CLOSED, major banks, stores and the hospital. CLOSED, Highway 21 and 14, until emergency crews can clear the roads. Please stay home. Please stand by."

The snow continued to fall for two weeks as the school and the store remained shut and even the icicles disappeared, for nothing melted. The snow only collected and grew. My mother could do nothing except drink tea at our kitchen table and worry about the fruit, vegetables, milk and meat rotting in our store. The bananas rotted first. Even in the cold, fruit flies managed to breed. The first day there were no flies. The day after, and the succeeding days, they bred and multiplied and soon danced their way into the other aisles and then into our home.

One night my mother sat staring at the wall.

"Look Mom," and I began trying to kill the fruit flies, clapping and dancing and leaping like the flies, at the flies.

"Elly, don't do that."

So I sat across from her, putting on a solemn face.

"We will be with Uncle Sam next week."

"Uncle Sam's visiting?"

"No, we will move in with Uncle Sam and work for him."

"But we have our store."

"No. Not anymore."

I remember the cold, which you could not escape. It frosted your fingertips, chilled the windows and entered your mind, numbing it from sense. Despite the record-breaking cold, my father still woke early every morning, filled his mug with hot tea, layered his body with wool, cotton and down, and collected his milk crate to go to work.

He would not stay long. He would arrive back in the house an hour later and use his icy fingers to shock Thomas and me into waking up before he disappeared into the Reading Room for the day. Then again, late at night, he would refill his mug, put on his clothes and walk out the back door with one arm clutching his milk crate.

The night my father was to leave for Uncle Sam's supermarket, he visited me before going back to his office. As he cracked open the door and crept into my room, I pretended to be asleep. The hinges squeaked and the floors tweaked. I tried to compose a sleeping face, even though my muscles twitched.

He slid my head gently into his lap and caressed my hair and he whispered words in Korean. I do not know what he said, only that it was difficult for me to pretend that I was sleeping. He probably knew, I thought, that I was faking my sleep though I could not open my eyes.

I wish I had opened my eyes. I wish I knew what he said. He used a strong quiet voice and hushed out words as rivers pour forth water, meandering everywhere, seeping into the soil, the soul.

I fell asleep while pretending to be asleep.

I wish I had opened my eyes.

My father died 20 years ago. The next morning my mother was packing at the store and my brother was still sleeping, so I was the one who answered the *knock knock knock*. I went with my mother to identify the body.

A dead man looks asleep, only his skin glows flesh green. My father was still frozen when I came to him. There were red and black blotches melting in his skin. They found him a quarter of a mile away from his office. The avalanche, they said, fell on him and rolled him down the slope.

I didn't cry at his funeral. I do not know if this was right or wrong. All I remember were the cabbage rolls brought by the Ukrainian Orthodox Church for consolation. It was my first time eating cabbage rolls, and I felt guilty for eating three quarters of the pan while Thomas and my mother were properly mourning.

I do not know how people are supposed to grieve. My auntie cooked a dinner for a hundred people the night before my father's funeral. My mother prayed alone in her locked room for many nights afterward. And my brother wept aloud, making others weep with him when he kissed my father's closed coffin and proclaimed "I love you, Daddy" to the entire congregation.

A few days after the funeral, my mother collected my father's clothes, books, twigs, anything flammable, and burned them behind our store in an empty oil drum. She told us that our ancestors burned the possessions of the dead to purify their souls so that their spirits could journey on.

The smoke rose and created a screen that tinted the moon a dark yellow. I remember my mother's face as she watched the clothes, books and twigs turn into ash. Without telling her, I had stolen a pile of pages from my father's Reading

Room in the hopes that I would one day read its contents. I do not enjoy lying or hiding, but I did not want to tell my mother that there were still possessions of my father lingering on. Nor did I tell her or Thomas about the dream, or the reality, of my father visiting me before his death, for I was ashamed of pretending to be asleep.

The ash blew and mixed with the falling snow.

Sometimes my mother will visit me at the clinic, unannounced. The receptionist will interrupt a session and politely whisper, "Mrs. Lee is waiting for you," and I will excuse myself and see my mother waiting on a chair, swinging her legs like a little girl.

These are never emergencies. They are silly visits to ask me if I need more kimchee prepared or if the reverend's wife received the lemon-loaf recipe. My mother enjoys periodically dropping by the clinic—as opposed to my house—to ask about these nonemergencies. She is getting old and looks hurt when I ask her to wait until I finish with my patient. But she waits and may even mention to those waiting in the reception area that I am her daughter, how are you, why are you here, and make other small conversation.

Her period of mourning is over. The photos of my father lie with the dust in the attic. She is currently dating a Korean widower. She is old and should no longer be living alone. She is nearing blindness, though she watches television to pass her days. Last Christmas, Thomas took a vacation from his accounting firm and came home. We discussed my mother's living situation.

"How is she doing?"

"Fine, Thomas, fine."

"Does she still receive those checks?"

"Yes. I'm paying half of her rent, but don't tell her. She doesn't need to know."

"You don't need to Elly, she receives *a lot* from the insurance company."

"How much?"

"*A lot*. When dad died, he was in their premium plan."

"He was?"

"Those checks saved us from being dead poor."

"I did not know that."

Later, much later, in fact, only two weeks ago, Charlie invited a linguistics professor over for dinner. Although Charlie teaches in the physics department, he knew how badly I wanted another person to read my father's manuscript, so he befriended Dr. MacLennan, who was also married to a Korean woman. After tea, I casually asked Dr. MacLennan if he would read over some Korean work. He agreed, and his eyes quickly scrolled down the pages.

"Elizabeth, are you learning Korean?" he asked.

"Yes, yes, how did you know?"

"Funny, I used these exact exercises when I began learning Korean."

He then told us about his fascination with *hangul* and the phonetic nuances of the Korean language, and then about his current project, which was to record the oral languages of aboriginal North Americans, for their languages would be lost forever since, in many cases, this was the last, literate, legitimate generation. I kept silent throughout the night as the revelation slowly unfolded: This was not my father's work, but his exercises, copied and memorized to learn and perfect. They were stories about cats and dogs and children playing on the riverbanks and nothing more.

The only work of my father's that I have ever really known was a poem about the falling snow. He read it to me eagerly one night because, I believe, he needed to air his creation, and I was the only one home when he returned from his office. As he held the page his hands shook, and his voice fell like the snow outside. Afterward he translated the words into English.

The poem was about the comfort of falling snow, which falls carelessly and covers the earth and makes people forget the dead grass underneath. And the snow symbolized words because just as no two snowflakes are alike. Neither are the words we say, which also fall and melt into oblivion.

At the time, I could not appreciate the meaning of the poem, so I kept silent after his explanation.

Some nights I wonder how it was, the last moments of my father's life. I wonder if he died first from being so cold or from the lack of air or from the shock. Afterward, I think about why he died, and then my mind becomes blank, as blank as the color of snow, and I try falling asleep, even though my eyes will not close.

SASHA HOM
Classification of Bones

movement:
Movements of bones occur at joints. Terms of
movement are therefore applicable to joints, not
bones. Flexion of the humerus is to break it! If a
penny were placed between bones it would grind away to
copper dust within seven years.

If you were to dig deep with fingertips in soil damp
as morning moss, you would touch: stones, and worms,
and roots, and then, bones. Bones as hard as rotted
teeth pulled out by the core of a wooden apple.

Ranges of motion are limited by the bony architecture
of a joint, related ligaments, and the muscles
crossing that joint. It is from the anatomical
position that specific directions of movement can be
clearly delineated and ranges of motion measured.

The ocean covers 70% of the earth's surface. South
Korea is roughly 70% mountainous. It is said that the
continents were once joined by tissue and ligaments,
like an ear torn off then superglued back onto the
head. The earth's surface was watery, and smelled
like sea salt imbedded in the skin's creases.
    And if I wanted to return home? Would I simply
engage one repetitive motion, originating at the hip

bone, rotating at the pelvis while foot is placed in front of foot until, Return.

Or do I need the flight of dreams and mind and wings unfolded to touch a land still separated by water?

rotation:
Rotation of a joint is to turn the moving bone about its axis. Rotation toward the body is internal or medial rotation; rotation away from the body is external or lateral rotation.

My eyes look back and forth, and rest gazing backwards. They bore through the facial structure of skin and cartilage and veins; through the brain which thinks only thoughts about a bird's fancy; through the skull which when rapped upon sounds like the echoing of the word "good-bye." Behind my bones I see only more bones lined up on the shore waving farewell as my body dissipates into evaporating Heaven. I think only of motion and flexibility. I still cannot touch the tip of my nose with my big toe, and so I wonder if I'll ever learn to walk.

GRACE ELAINE SUH
How to Live. What to Do.

The grey February morning haunting the narrow window couldn't decide between sun or gloom. It gave no warmth and little light. Stumbling into his room from his first all-night shift as a Terrific Temp, Joe Park, 24-years-old, recent law-school dropout, flipped on the buzzing green fluorescent ceiling light, winced, then just as quickly killed it.

He shed the clothes he had worn since the morning before and dragged on sweatpants and a T-shirt. He lined up his dress shoes on the floor of his closet and hung up the shirt, tie and suit—his only of each. His movements were sluggish and frenetic at the same time.

If he was going to make it to the christening, he was going to need a nap. Lowering himself gingerly onto his unslept-in bed, Joe was only grateful that Lulu couldn't see him now.

Really, when he thought about it, the downward spiral of his life had all started with her, was all due, in fact, to those damned shoulder pads, to Wallace Stevens, the illiterate clerk at Barnes & Noble, his mother's addiction to AOL.

When Joe landed at SUNY Binghamton six years ago, the last thing he had expected was to fall immediately in love with a stunning Korean woman who had grown up milking goats on her adoptive parents' organic cheese farm near Woodstock. Joe and Lulu were together all four years of college, and although their relationship never took on any semblance of ease, rhythm or stability, there was always strong feeling, Joe was sure of it, on both sides. In fact, he attributed their turbulence to the depth of that strong feeling.

Lulu Eun Me Chandler was tiny, beautiful, brilliant, insecure, unhumorous and unhappy. To exercise some measure of control over the fears, neuroses and inner turmoil that kept her up nearly every night, she ran her life by fierce discipline and a strict schedule. Every afternoon, she left the library at 3:50 and took a high impact step-'n'-sculpt class from 4:00 to 5:15, showered, ate a fat-free yogurt, and studied from 5:45 until 9:15, when Joe arrived. They had sex from 9:20 to 9:45. Then Lulu jumped up, showered, donned color-coordinated leotards, tights, leg warmers and sweater and rushed to the evening yoga and meditation session that was supposed to help her sleep. Joe adored her.

While Joe spent his college years dressed nearly exclusively in long underwear, flannel shirt and baggy corduroys, Lulu wore power suits, button earrings, pantyhose and pumps, even in the snowy dead of upstate New York winter. She presented such a formidable front that Joe's friends were afraid of her. If there had been a Least Likely Couple contest at Binghamton, Joe and Lulu would surely have won. And yet it was obvious to Joe that Lulu was just a bundle of nerves, a sweet girl hiding her sweetness behind a veneer of perfection.

Senior year Joe watched her getting ready for an investment-bank job interview, stuffing shoulder pads under her silk blouse, one set over another, plus the ones that were sewn into her suit jacket.

"What are you doing?" he'd demanded, looking at his 100-pound girlfriend with the outsized deltoids of a linebacker.

"I need them," she said, precisely applying a somber, professional shade of dark red lipstick. "Otherwise, I look *cute*."

Joe noticed afterward that she piled on the shoulder pads any time she was particularly nervous: exams, parental visits, meetings of the student council, of which she was treasurer. His heart nearly broke to think how frightened she must be beneath all the foam.

Lulu got the job as an analyst in the Chicago branch of a major investment bank. Right after graduation, they drove out with their stuff crammed into the back of Joe's ancient Nissan hatchback and found a cute apartment in a nice neighborhood near Lincoln Park. They got a bread maker and an orange kitten they named Tang. Except for the fact that Lulu worked weekends and late most evenings, Joe was perfectly happy.

Then she started in on him. What was he doing with his life? What was he making of himself? What kind of man was he? Didn't he mind that he was selling himself short, serving *chai* at the Café Ennui?

"But I'm working on my 'Stanley' collection," Joe told her. "And I like the Café Ennui." He was working quite diligently in fact, compiling and editing the comic strip he'd begun in high school and continued through college. And he was developing several new series that he planned to shop to *The Chicago Reader* and other local alternative papers. Actually, with Lulu hardly ever home, he was getting a lot done.

In August, Lulu's department closed a $350 million merger (her first), and she moved in with a 32-year old lawyer with whom she'd worked closely on the deal. "I can't be with someone who isn't interested in making something out of himself," she told Joe by way of explanation. She had never understood the point of "Stanley," or of why Joe dedicated so many hours to comics. To Joe's mind, what had begun as a series of sight gags and in-jokes had developed into the epic drama of an Everyman who was not born to greatness but who struggled nobly, against the constraints and limits of his kind, to attain it. But Lulu didn't see it that way.

Lulu took the cat (even though it was Joe who had cleaned the litter box and fed Tang and played with him and was teaching him to fetch), and left Joe the bread maker, which made horrible, spongy bread.

Joe moved into a dismal studio way up in Rogers Park and fell into a serious depression. Time and time again, he headed for the freezing lakefront to watch the wind-whipped waves pounding the concrete embankments. Just a mile or two down the coast, Lulu was watching these same waves from the warmth of a glass-wrapped Gold Coast high-rise luxury apartment, in the hairy arms of a corporate lawyer named Roland Ryman who was "going somewhere" fast enough and high enough to suit Lulu. And the worst of it was, Joe still worried about her.

In October, Joe heard or read or dreamed (things were a muddle to him) that

Wallace Stevens had written something called, "How to Live. What to Do." He didn't know that he'd ever heard a better title. The hope it gave him broke the paralysis long enough for him to get to the giant chain bookstore on Wabash.

"Help," Joe bleated at a clerk, "I'm looking for 'How to Live. What to Do' by Wallace Stevens."

The young man was zippy and eager. He said, "Upstairs, How To."

He propelled Joe up several escalators, down a catwalk, and into a huge annex housing The Self Help Café. Joe was pretty sure the author in question was Wallace Stevens the poet and not a self-help guru, but his confidence and spirit had eroded to the point that it was easier to be taken in hand like this, the inert led by the ignorant, than to protest. Joe appreciated the clerk's energy. He thought it must be nice to be so young, so vigorous.

Joe waited patiently while the clerk fingered spines, and there, amid the colorful stacks, between *How to Feed a Bedouin: My Adventures as Private Chef to Sheik Fayad* and *How to Live Like a Millionaire on Only $250,000 a Year*, Joe saw the fateful book: *How to Get into Law School in Four Easy Steps*. He bought the book (Step 1), took the LSAT three weeks later (Step 2), did phenomenally well (Step 3) and applied to four schools (Step 4).

He then plunged back into numbness and forgot all about his brief spurt of activity. In March, he was utterly shocked to receive letters admitting him to two of the four schools. But at the time, he'd seen the 50 percent failure rate as just something else to feel bad about.

Now, on the twin bed with the lumpy mattress that had come with the dorm room at Columbia, one of the two schools that had admitted him, Joe repositioned his head on the pillow and shifted his body. He was getting no shut-eye whatsoever. He looked at the clock. If he remembered right from three years ago, christenings took hardly any time at all, and it wouldn't do to be late.

He only hoped Myung didn't plan on singing again, the way he had for the firstborn, Enrico Caruso Jung-won Park. That was horrible. The way he broke down in the middle, crying. And started that rambling, melodramatic speech about how he had never expected to be *here*, at St. Joseph's Korean Catholic Chapel of Corona. Had his uncle forgotten already, Joe had thought, about the wedding to Soo Mee only 15 months earlier? Was he regretting the conversion from Presbyterianism to Catholicism that had been necessary to marry her? It was only later that he'd realized that what Myung had meant was to be standing before them a happy husband and father.

It was hard for Joe to believe too. All it had taken was a blind date arranged by Mrs. Choi, Joe's mother's friend from church, with the former Buddhist nun-turned devout Catholic school teacher who lived downstairs in the Choi's Elmhurst apartment building. And now his perennial bachelor uncle was father of two. *Que milagro.*

Joe rubbed at his face. He was wiped. He should have (if only) minded his mother's e-mail of yesterday morning: "Joe don't forget come early if you can I can make pancakes. It is very cold today but I think it will not rain. Your father has cavity he think. See you tomorrow study hard not too hard. Be sure get good sleep. Love you love Mom."

Instead he had been up all night at his new temp job, the first day of his post-law school career.

His mother loved to send e-mail. And she always mentioned the weather, as if he weren't just right across town. Maybe she thought he didn't get a glimpse of it, stuck in the library as he surely was all day. His housemates at Binghamton used to love her e-mails. They'd begged him to read them aloud and had written her back more often than he did.

It was one of the daily e-mails from his mother last spring that took his whole law-school lark to the new, catastrophic level that had ended thus.

"What are you doing there in such a cold place why not getting job or doing something good that I know you can do it," she had e-mailed. "Here it is not so cold for winter, not much snow. I will be happy when you have plans for doing something good soon."

In response, in desperation, in guilt, to fend her off, he'd mentioned the law-school acceptances, trying to make it sound as though they were just one of the many promising irons he had in the fire.

"Joe I am so very much excited and proud for you," she'd immediately cyber-responded. It was the most hopeful she'd sounded in ages. "I always knew you would make something good from your life, I always believe in you. I tell your father, every great man has time when he is maybe only waiter for coffee shop, then becomes something great. And of course you should come Columbia, not Northwestern. I saw on CNN Chicago got another bad storm. Better to get away from there. I don't think is good there for you." Her tacit way of sympathizing over the whole Lulu episode.

Eleven months later, in his dorm room at Columbia, Joe sighed and gave up on sleep. He smoothed his bed and took a brisk shower. He gave the white shirt a brisk shake and slid it on. It was a bit rumpled from the day before, but would have to do. His slumbering fingers were thick on the buttons. Come on come on, he cheered himself. Redon the raiment. Get on the get-up. Resume the position.

He tossed on the tie his father had selected to match the suit, then the pants. Even after having been worn all the day and night before, the fabric felt great—smooth rich wool, cool to the touch. It was a very good suit. It cost $600 on sale, much more than any suit his father had.

From their friends whose children were lawyers, his parents knew the law-school drill almost better than he did. You had to get into a good school and make top marks the first year to get a summer associateship at a prestige firm. Then, if you didn't screw up somehow, they asked you back for the next summer, and that was it, you were home free, the job was yours.

So, a good suit was important, to make a good interview impression. His father (with his immigrant faith in self-improvement and businessman belief in best-sellers) had read a book that said you should always dress like the person whose job you want.

"Brooks Brothers, you look like young guy, just starting out," he advised Joe. "We got to take you to Barney's, where the partners go." From his long years of experience in the best-dressed zip code in New York, Joe's father was an expert on fine corporate attire. Once he had even given a speech to the Korean-American Small Business Association of New York entitled "Secrets of a Dry Cleaner to the Stars."

Not that he actually gave away a thing in that speech. Joe's father took pride in his professional discretion. A number of well-known people came to the store, but he would only hint at their identities, even to Joe: "I will tell you that one of our best customers, very loyal, was important member of the city government," he'd said to Joe once, apropos of nothing. "Been customer very long time. He is always in news, very important man, always brought his shirts himself, very picky about every detail," he continued, shaking his head happily.

"Dad, you mean Andrew Stein?" Joe asked him.

His father looked suddenly stern. His face gave away nothing.

"Did your mother tell you that?"

"She didn't tell me anything. I just remember him from summers I worked for you. Was that who you're talking about?"

His father sipped his coffee, eyes wary above the rim. He said, "Some day, Joe, I tell you. Not now. When you are older, maybe."

At the store, Joe's father drank his coffee out of a Columbia University mug, and when people asked which, to his gratification, they often did, he told them, as nonchalantly and as modestly as he could manage, "Oh my son, Joe, you remember? He goes now to the Columbia Law School." Joe knew this because his mother told him in an e-mail. His father only told him things like, "Life is something you plan, one step at a time, like a general. An unplanned life is a life planned for failure." He didn't do email.

The week after Christmas, Joe and his father went to the Barney's Warehouse

Sale. His father picked out the suit: charcoal grey wool crepe, single-breasted, three-buttoned, luxuriously sober. It fit perfectly. Instead of risking getting it hemmed at Barney's, they took it back to the store, for Istvan, who as always did a beautiful job. The cuffs were perfect, the break elegant, the drape relaxed but stalwart.

That made Joe slow down completely, shirt sleeve in hand. This being Saturday morning, the fourth day of February, meant it was 20 days ago that Istvan died, as near as had been able to be determined. The coroner's report estimated that he had been dead a day or two before Joe's father and the manager of the hotel where Istvan lived found him lying on his bed as if sleeping.

Joe had been sitting at his desk, drawing, when his mother phoned. Sorry to bother his studying, but could he come over right away? "It's emergency," she said. "Or I would not bother to you."

Classes had begun a week earlier. Some of Joe's suitemates had done half the semester's reading already. Shelley accused Hollis of having finished all of his over Christmas break. Hollis denied it, but no one believed him. Joe, on the other hand, hadn't bought any books. He hadn't attended any classes. He hadn't even registered for any.

Joe's mother was alone in the store when he got there. She was sitting on the window seat, her back to the street. Without preamble, she plunged in.

"Monday Istvan didn't show up to work. Nor Tuesday. They didn't think too much of it; this had happened several times before over the years ("I didn't know that," Joe said. "Oh Joe," his mother said, impatient. "Why do we bother to you?"). They had no number for Istvan; it turned out Istvan had no phone.

This morning Joe's father had gone up Second Avenue to Zabàn, the Hungarian restaurant where Istvan ate his lunch every day. A waiter gave him an address, the same one Joe's father had from nearly 17 years before, when Istvan first came to work for them. The address was to a dilapidated, small building on 95th Street all the way east, where the streets slope down to the river. It was tenanted mostly by elderly men from Germany, Hungary, Poland, widowers and bachelors. The narrow halls were lined with single rooms, bathrooms at the ends. Joe's father was there now, taking care of arrangements.

"It's so sad!" Joe cried out, suddenly, overwhelmed with feeling. "All those years of work and saving, and he never made it back to Budapest!"

"Joe-ya!" his mother said, with a sharp intake of breath. She looked over at the wall of colored spools and shook her head. Her voice quiet. "Istvan wasn't going anywhere."

"He *was*!" Joe said. He paced back and forth. "You didn't know. It was a secret. I wasn't supposed to tell you. He was saving money, he was going back to Buda to live."

His mother looked out the window for a while before she went on.

"Your father describe it to me on the phone, like a movie," she said. "He say never did he saw anything like this in his life."

Istvan's room was tiny, with one window. The bed was a narrow metal one like in an ancient hospital. Under the bed and against the walls, covering the floor and piled in the little closet and lined up on the window sill, were hundreds of empty flat liquor bottles.

"We knew," Joe's mother said, "he was drinker man. But he was good worker, come always on the time and almost always come. So we never bother to him."

Joe imagined the bottles, blunt-shaped like Istvan, a crystalline forest, holding the green afternoon light off the river. He pictured Istvan lying on the narrow bed in his plaid suit, hands crossed on his stomach, toes pointing out. Absorbed in this vision, it took him a minute to take in what his mother had said.

"But you *should* have! You should have said something to him! You could have staged an intervention!"

His mother's blank face prodded him on. "That's when everyone in the person's life gets together and tells the person to stop drinking, or doing drugs, or whatever. Because you care."

His mother looked troubled. "But Joe," she said. "I don't think..." She bit her lip. "I'm sure Istvan was not doing the drugs."

Now she stood up briskly. "Anyway. That does not seem good. How can we tell him, a man elder to us, what to do in his life? It is not right."

Joe wanted to keep going, he wanted to explain better, protest, against something, but suddenly he was winding down, sagging into grief, beginning to comprehend what his mother was telling him, that Istvan was dead. A month ago, while Joe stood on that stool in the corner, twirling slowly like a chicken on a rotisserie, Istvan had pinned expertly around his ankles, humming to himself in his happy, mournful way. His old friend.

His mother was talking, shaking her head. "I don't know, Joe. I don't know what. But if he want go back, he made enough money. He could be gone long time before."

The desk in Joe's dorm room was nearly bare. He flicked the reading lamp on and off, on and off. Old friend—what had he ever known about Istvan, really known? The one thing he'd thought he'd known, the secret between them, now turned out to be untrue.

The only other things on the desk were a pencil cup and a book. The pencil cup held six Uni-Ball pens (two each in black, blue and red) and three highlighters (in yellow, pink and green), the law student's arsenal, ready to annotate another semester of case studies. The book was *Let's Go Hungary*, the one book Joe had bought this year. He'd spied it on a sale table in front of the Barnard Bookforum. He'd read it front to back like a novel and heavily highlighted its pages: yellow for the places Istvan had spoken of so wistfully, like Margaret Island and the ancient streets of Buda; pink for major tourist sites, like the Royal Palace and Màtyàs Church; green for smaller landmarks that had caught Joe's eye, like the Lukàcs Baths.

The rest of the room was as neat as the desk, as neat as the room of an obsessively neat person as neat as he, Joe. He pulled out the chair and pulled on the grey socks he found himself holding. The floor was spotless, the bed, as always, impeccably made, the green comforter without a wrinkle. On the dresser, two packages, the same size, side by side. They were meticulously wrapped, one in pale blue tissue and one in glossy Kansas City Chiefs paper. He'd gotten the latter at Weber's Closeout for a dollar the roll. He had had to go to three stores to find the ribbon that picked out perfectly the brick red of the logo. The pale blue package was wound a dozen times around with curling opalescent strands and topped with a pair of crocheted white baby booties. Rather elaborately wrapped, he saw that now. Any fool could see he was feeling a need to compensate. Or that he had an awful lot of spare time.

The presents were miniature Columbia Law School sweatshirts, size 3T for Rico, baby-doll size for the new one, Franco Corelli Jung-hyo Park. The sweatshirts were his mother's idea. "I will take pictures," she'd e-mailed, "and maybe, if they become Columbia lawyer, like you, then will be funny pictures for future!"

Yesterday morning, at Terrific Temps, Incorporated, Trudy Rosenstein, Placement Counselor, read through his résumé. Joe was wearing the charcoal grey suit for the first time ever, unzipped that morning from the Barneys garment bag in the corner of his closet. "SUNY Binghamton, history with honors, very impressive. Columbia University Law School, one semester." Trudy looked up.

"So Joe, what gives? You're leaving?"

Joe felt like a flying rubber band. "Yes," he said, nodding, his fingertips bumping hard against one another. "Yes, I'm leaving." This was the first time he'd admitted it to anyone, said it out loud. It was an incredible relief. The follicles on his scalp itched, his arm pits were soaked, two swamps. The sharp spicy musk of his deodorant hit his nose.

Trudy cast him a sharp glance, her keen green eyes rendered even shrewder by a mesmerizingly complicated application of eye shadows. She patted Joe's knee in a soothing way. He stared down at her exquisitely lacquered nails.

"Joe," Trudy crooned, her voice as liquid and cool as her charmeuse blouse,

"Why?"

Joe was not taken in by the sham intimacy. He took a minute to think. He was being called upon to justify himself before the tribunal of man, before the universal jury, and he'd be damned if he wasn't going to acquit himself well. He could think of nothing.

All he remembered was the sensation of displacement, the conviction that for all the study of the law suited him, he might as well be studying aeronautics. Or aerobics. The leaving of himself he experienced every time he walked into the ugly, dark, low-ceilinged law school building, the total inability to wrap his mind around the thousands of pages of case history he dutifully read the first half of first semester.

By November, he'd stopped taking notes in class, started doodling in the margins of his torts notebook, comic strips of classic cases: The professional runner who slipped on ice in front of the five-star restaurant and broke both legs. The doctor who left a clamp in the patient's abdomen and charged for the operation to take it out. The woman whose dog barked at the old man so excitedly that the man had a heart attack and fell senseless to the sidewalk, then licked the man back to consciousness and saved his life, only to be sued by the old man.

The first frame of each strip always featured a stick figure of the unfortunate plaintiff at the exact unfortunate moment, a big "Oops!" bubble above the head.

The nightmares began around the same time, every night the same: his natural law professor, a kindly, tweedy, white-haired old man who had had the class to his grand apartment on Riverside Drive for tea, wielding a bloody gavel, chasing him down the twisting dark halls of The Toaster, screaming, "Right of Law! Right of Law!"

Joe had tried to confide in Hollis. "Do you ever wonder," he'd ventured one night, "just why we're here? Doing this?"

"Oh sure," Hollis said, "it's simple," and the hope of an answer at last buoyed Joe's sinking heart. "We're here for one reason and one reason only," Hollis grandly declared: "Because we didn't get into Yale." Then Hollis chuckled at length at his own terrific joke.

Last week Joe sneaked a long, sober look at Shelley's syllabi. It was clear that even if he somehow bought his books and registered now, it'd be no good. There was no way he could catch up with the past three weeks and get up to speed on the rest.

Meanwhile, every time he spoke to his parents, it was epistemological quicksand. He was sinking himself.

His mother: "I called yesterday. Must've been maybe you were in library studying."

Her son: "I was in front of the computer all day." (Playing DOOM in the SEAS computer lab).

His father, who had read Scott Turow's *1L* twice, and had great respect for what he believed to be his son's heroic scholastic endeavors: "Is true second semester is worse than first?"

His son: "The work load is heavier, and the classes go faster, but after this, second year will feel like a breeze." Quoting what he had heard Shelley and Hollis say. Not to mention that even as he lied, he was continuing to live off their money. And so here, to Trudy, who awaited a reply.

"I suffered ambivalence," Joe said, "about the law."

"That's too bad," Trudy said briskly, riffling her papers, and he saw that the question that had demanded such painful on-the-spot soul-searching had been only a formality, a professional niceness. She wasn't the one who needed to know.

"I give you money later," his mother had e-mailed. "Buy big one for Rico can grow into it too."

He'd bought the sweatshirts. How could he not? It was outrageous how much they'd cost, things that small. He felt light-headed from exhaustion. He should go. It was nearly nine, service began at eleven. The M4 was unreliable, and he should be at his parents' by quarter to ten. His father liked to get everywhere early and regularly allowed additional time for traffic and other unforeseen delays besides.

He knotted his shoes ($255 Church's) and smoothed his tie ($90 Zegna). He wanted to tell his father the suit had worked. Trudy had remarked favorably on his professional appearance.

Overcoat. Keys. Wallet.

For this and all the other above referenced reasons, your honor, I wish not to go to this family function. At which I shall again have to lie to my parents, to their faces, in the house of God (albeit the Catholic One). At which, for my mother's tireless Instamatic camera, I shall be forced to pose again and again with my uncle's young children, in their new sweatshirts—three Columbia lawyers we.

Gloves. Gifts.

Joe headed out—his father's son—early.

AMY KASHIWABARA

This poem grows smaller the more I write it.

Grandmother practices
the slow art of dying.

Waking each morning,
she takes three
slow breaths.
In, out.

She has prepared
for many years,
growing smaller.
My height
measuring her loss.

She sorts
her belongings
into six children
piles, twelve
grandchildren piles.

In; Out.

Her blood flows
a little shorter
of her, each day.
The sensitive fingertips,

the calloused toes
losing touch.

On another coast,
I am an extremity
to which her circulation
begins to fail.

In.

flight

N. RAIN NOE
Untitled

After dinner at Empire Korea, Gina hops on a bus back to the Bronx, while I head for my car. More specifically, the third car of the N train. In front of the turnstile, I'm fishing around for my Metrocard when I get a hollow feeling in my stomach and pause, realizing I've lost something: my Sense of Self.

I slap my front and back pockets frantically, but hear only the jingle of change and keys, and the leathery slap of my empty wallet. Panicked, I tear my shoulder bag off and rifle through it; today's Times twisted into subway origami, my big-ass pre-'90s walkman and some loose tapes, no Sense of Self.

Shit. I know I had it when I came to K-town two hours earlier; I must have dropped it in the restaurant or somewhere between 5th and Broadway. I close my bag and let out a my-life-sucks type of sigh. This isn't like losing a dog, where I could just put up fliers with a sketch. "Have you seen my Sense of Self? It looks like this." As simple and undeveloped as it was, it would take me forever to draw that damn thing accurately.

Wait a sec, maybe Gina had picked it up? Worth a shot. I run back up the subway steps to street level, break out the Motorola and speed-dial her. She picks up on the first ring.

"Gina," I say. "I'm Self-less."

"Why you cocky son of a bitch," she says.

"No no, that's not what I meant. I lost my Self, my Sense of Self. Maybe in the restaurant. Did I leave it with you?"

"No," she says. "And even if you had, I sure wouldn't know what it looks like. I told you, I don't really know who you are. You won't open up to me. You never *share*–"

"We're breakin' up, babe," I say. "The connection, I mean. Can't quite hear you. Lemme call you back." I click the phone shut. I know I'll probably get slapped for that later, but that's what you get for dating roughneck girls from 718.

I take a second to mentally backtrack. Where had I gone tonight? I had gotten off the train, killed some time at the Han Ah Reum grocery, met Gina at Empire Korea. That was it. Had to be at one of the two places or somewhere on the way. Han Ah Reum was closest so I headed there first.

On the way I sweep the crowded sidewalk with my eyes, peering around the spandex-clad getaway sticks of the hair-salon aunties and the tree-trunkish cargo pants of the little bad-ass Korean rave brats. My Sense of Self is smaller than a newspaper but bigger than a chewing gum blemish, so if I've dropped it on the street it shouldn't be too hard to spot.

But on the sidewalk, it's nowhere to be found. I pick up the pace—I'm doing that idiotic-looking half-walking, half-running thing now—and enter the Han Ah Reum grocery store.

Inside I blow past the refrigerators and head for aisle 3, Japanese Snacks. That's where I remember standing earlier when I saw a guy who kind of looked like me, but was speaking fluent Korean to his beautiful Korean girlfriend, causing me to engage in a moment of sullen reflection. Maybe I lost it then.

Rounding the corner to aisle 3, I see that this is my lucky day—there it is! I spot my Sense of Self all crumpled up and sitting between the boxes of Pocky and New Men's Pocky. I grab it and put it on, hurriedly, gratefully.

Then I do a double take; it smells a little too much of kimchee, which I don't eat that much of, and then I realize—*Christ, this is someone else's Sense of Self!* Wearing it, I feel a firm belief in the Korean-Confucian social hierarchy and the knowledge that I can still cheat on my beautiful girlfriend on my frequent business trips to Seoul. *Jesus.* I pull it off in a hurry, fold it neatly and stick it back on top of the Pocky.

I breeze out of the store like a novice shoplifter and set a course for Empire Korea. I'm getting a little nervous—this is more troublesome than the time I lost my soul (Amsterdam) or when I lost my Innocence (at my best friend's girlfriend's house in high school). I could live without that crap; I mean some of it, like the Innocence, looked absolutely ridiculous on me, and I'd only put it on if I was having dinner with my parents. But without a Sense of Self, what would happen to me?

I walk maybe twenty paces when I pass a gleaming, silver, tricked-out BMW I'd seen before. When I was heading over to meet Gina, some Armani-clad punk had eased it up to the curb, and I remember staring at it in a mixture of horror and awe. The driver couldn't have been older than twenty, but the car looked like it cost more than my education.

As I pass the car this time, I notice something dark and flat under the rear bumper on the passenger side. I backstep into the street and kneel down to inspect it.

The streetlight cuts a hard shadow on the asphalt beneath me, and as my eyes adjust, I realize I'm looking at a crumpled garbage bag, not my Sense of Self. *Shit.* I'm about to stand when I see two more shadows, standing, slip into place around mine, which is squatting.

I stay low and turn my head, slowly.

Two Korean men, one younger, one older, stand flanking me, arms clasped in front of their crotches like soccer players lining up in front of a goal kick.

"Are you looking for something?" asks the younger.

I'm a little startled. "Yeah, I am." Is my lack of Self showing already?

"You're looking for Jesus," says the older one, confidently.

"Uh - actually, I'm not," I reply. For chrissakes, I'm squatting next to a car and looking under the bumper—what the hell would Jesus be doing hanging out under a BMW? Like he's down there fixing the suspension.

"Jesus loves you, " says the younger.

"Listen," I say. "I don't know what he told you, but we're just friends—I was drunk and confused. And it's pronounced *Jésus.*"

"Do you know that you have a soul?" asks the older one.

"Yeah—I mean, no," I say. "I mean I did, but it's in Amsterdam now. Long story." I place my hand on the bumper and stand up.

"Jesus will show you the way," says the older, sensing I'm about to leave.

Then a bright light hits me square in the eyes. Nothing divine, just the headlights from a crosstown bus that's turned onto 32nd and drones toward us.

"Riiiight. Listen, whaddaya say we talk redemption a little later? I'm kind of in the middle of something."

"You're in the middle of the street," intones the younger one. A real semantics expert.

"OK, ciao," I say, crossing the street in front of the oncoming bus. I make it to the other side just in time, and the bus runs my shadow over like a freight train, cutting the two men off from me. I wanted to do it like in a spy movie, where after the bus passes I just disappear, but I'm a little too slow and they see me jogging down the sidewalk.

"You can't run from Jesus," one of the men cries from across the street. Maybe that's true. You could probably make a clever Nike commercial out of that.

I look at my watch. It's now four past midnight. I jog down the block until I reach the pink-and-green neon sign of Empire Korea, which is thankfully open.

I go through both sets of double doors, and the hostess steps out to greet me. "I left something here," I say, gesturing toward the table I'd been sitting at, which is in the back.

"Ah," says the hostess. "Was it this?" She pulls an expensive-looking silk scarf out from behind the hostess stand.

I eye it for a long second, then feel ashamed for actually considering substituting an Italian silk scarf for my Sense of Self. "No, it was…" I let the sentence trail off and head to the table where I'd been with Gina.

Luckily the restaurant has slowed down by now, and my table is empty. I check the seat, nothing. Peer under the table, nothing. I get down on my hands and knees and check under the booth. Nothing.

Christ. Where the hell is it? I open my bag again, to see if it had magically materialized. But the only thing in my bag that's changed is the newspaper, which is technically no longer today's, but yesterday's.

Where else had I gone tonight? I'd used the bathroom...

Then it dawns on me. I think I know where I'd lost it. How could I have forgotten this? It was only a two-second incident, but that must have been it.

While having dinner with Gina, I'd gotten up to use the bathroom. Empire Korea is huge, and I always forget where the bathroom was. In my search, I'd accidentally opened the door to one of the banquet rooms.

Inside was what looked like some sort of cult meeting or presentation. There were rows and rows of chairs, filled with twenty-something Koreans of both sexes, maybe 50 people total. But they were different from what I was used to seeing; in various states of dress, and they all had their own individual style. Dressed in everything from blue jeans and vintage fly-collar shirts to business attire, but there was something about them—something in their facial expressions, their haircuts and their demeanors—that set them apart from the cloned Korean clans I normally saw roaming this area.

I had accidentally made eye contact with a young woman sitting in the front row. She, too, had a very distinct and confusing air about her; though she wore a grey business jacket and skirt, and appeared to be anywhere from 25 to 35 years of age, she wore hair in braided pigtails.

The whole room had been an odd sight, made even odder because everyone in it was staring at me because I had swung the door open. There was a young man standing in front of the group, obviously about to give a speech or make an address, and I'd interrupted him. I had apologized and shut the door hurriedly.

That must have been when I'd lost my Sense of Self. Has to be there. I head for the banquet room.

Entering the appropriate hallway, I spy the right door—and even better, I see my Sense of Self, sticking out from under it! I knew it. I stoop down to grab it, but it's stuck under the door. I grab the gilded knob, edge the door open slightly, and yank my Sense of Self free.

I'm about to close the door when I happen to glance into the room and experience a moment of shock. The identity I'm holding slips from my fingers and hits the soft carpet. I push the door open all the way and step into the room, amazed.

The room is void of people and hasn't yet been bussed; all the chairs are still in place, and the lights are still on. And scattered all around the room…are Senses of Selves.

They're all over the place. On the floor, draped across chairs, sticking out of empty glasses. There's even one hanging from the rotating ceiling fan. Some appear to be men's, some appear to be women's, and about one in ten are shaped like pink triangles.

I pick a few up and smell them, but though each odor is distinct, I can't seem to remember what mine smelled like. At first I figure the one by the door has to be mine, because I didn't actually enter the room before, but now I'm not so sure.

I let out a life-is-strange type of sigh, and slowly take a seat on one of the chairs. What the hell am I gonna do with this?

I'm still grappling with the situation when I hear footsteps in the hall, and then the woman with the braided pigtails strides briskly into the room. She's got a coat on and has clearly just returned to the restaurant from outside.

She takes three steps into the room and stops short. Her mouth pops open as she scans the place. Eventually her eyes hit mine.

"Lose something?" I ask.

JUNSE KIM
Son of Kings

I am the first son of the first son of the first son and so on. The sixty-second generation of the royal Kim line traced all the way back to the founding of the Shilla dynasty in 668 A.D. My father has shown me that this is fact. It's documented. I've seen our lineage book, which has records of 17 kings and one of the kingless queens of Korea, and, though I can't read it, mine is the last entry.

My father named me Jae-Hyun. *Jae* is the name-prefix for males of a sixty-second generation and means *to be.* As for *Hyun,* when I was born, Dad flew back to Korea and visited a Confucian scholar to choose the most auspicious suffix. The word he came up with was *wisdom.* I know this naming process sounds extravagant, but it's necessary. It's ritual. One-thousand three-hundred twenty-eight years of my heritage call on me to continue this same tradition, even though I'm known to most people by my middle name, Nolan—the word for *champion* in my mother's mother tongue, Irish. When transliterated into Korean, it means *frightened.*

Even though it's my duty to propagate a son to continue this lineage, I know my father is the one who feels responsible. By marrying outside the culture and having me, he didn't exactly cut the family line, but irreparably frayed it. After Mother died, he made it his duty to see that I fulfill my destiny. He shouldn't worry, though, because I know my role and I don't take it lightly. I know what I have to do to purify the bloodline. It's for the family.

After graduating from Harvard, I told Dad I wanted to live abroad, maybe join the Peace Corps. He didn't like the idea of his only child going somewhere other than the land of our ancestors, especially because I had never been there. Plus, he said, I had a responsibility to the family. I replied that I wanted some worldly life experience, to gain some wisdom, before I went to Seoul, learned our language, found a wife, had a son, and brought Dad back to his homeland vindicated. He couldn't argue with that. He gave his approval and a warning: Don't stray from the path; remember the family. He'd be watching.

The Peace Corps assigned me to Tunisia as a community developer. I was placed in Wled Malik, an isolated village in the center of the country, just north of Sbeitla, a second-rate tourist town. My job was to help nurture development plans created by the community, a tribe of Berbers who changed their ancient nomadic lifestyle to a sedentary agricultural one. Unlike some of the other volunteers, I made sure the projects I took on were completed. Fulfilling responsibilities, it's in my blood.

Sometimes I'd collaborate with other development organizations. That's how I met Fiona, from Dublin, Ireland. She was serving as a midwife in Sbeitla. During my first month, we created a plan to reduce infant mortality in my village. I met her once a week to chart the project's progress and to take in her handsome face—amazingly like Mom's in an old photo. As the weeks passed, I came to admire the ease with which she lived. Nothing weighed her down. She experienced life fully and freely, taking only her work with absolute seriousness.

Eventually we slept with each other. At first it was something to kill time with during a break in our meetings. Then it evolved. It became a respite from time. Then, after a year together, the simple act of sex splintered into something past the physical limitations of pleasure; it began to root me to a contentment that I knew could never last. That's when I told her how my family's past had determined my fate. I tried to make sure she had no illusions about our relationship; I couldn't allow it to become something meaningful. Neither my honesty nor my resolution, however, seemed to sit well with her. I think that's why her humor became increasingly crass. Whenever we undressed, for example, she'd put on a thick Irish brogue and say something like, "Show us yer willie, Nolan. C'mon, let's have a look. Hurry up, me tits'r out fer ya, me tits'r out fer ya. Now have a go." And other stuff as over-the-top as that, the exact opposite of her grand public face, the calm dignity of a Trinity graduate. Alone behind closed doors, though, it would be back to "Shag me! Shag me!" I don't know, maybe by being so crude, she reminded herself of exactly what we were doing. Or maybe she was trying to remind me.

When I had only a couple of months left of my two-year service, I started to work at a youth club. I organized educational activities for teenagers; after all, they were the future of Wled Malik. Abdel-quessem, Kamel, Neji, Anis and Mohammed-Hedi were all bright kids, but they didn't know much about their country's rich history. I told it to them like Dad did to me: in order to build a future you need to know your past. So I decided to take them on a weekend field trip to the ruins of Carthage. We would learn how great civilizations followed one another down a historical line in that ancient city. The founding Phoenicians begat the Romans begat the Vandals begat the Byzantines begat the Arabs.

The tour guide began by explaining the importance of preserving the ruins; he requested everyone not to touch them. I thought this reverence was a bit misplaced because most of the original city was torn down and developed into commuter housing. Our guide then told us some of the myths of Carthage. The kids especially loved the story of Aeneas and Dido. After the destruction of Troy, Aeneas had been commanded by the gods to create a new empire in Italy, but somehow his ships blew off course and he ended up in Carthage. He became Dido's consort. Finally, Mercury was sent down to remind him of his destiny, and Aeneas had to choose between that and his love for Dido.

Abdel-quessem kept on talking about it at the hostel that night. "This has always been a beautiful and holy country," he said in Arabic. "Why else would a man forsake his gods, unless he fell in love with one of the homes to Allah."

I chose not to remind him that all this happened long before Mohammed was born; and that Aeneas had fallen for Dido, not the city; and that, in the end, he had left her and founded Rome. Everyone takes what they need from their history, so who was I to tell him what to believe.

The weather was beautiful and unseasonably mild for July when we headed back Sunday afternoon. The silky blue sky stayed with us as we drove past orchards rich with apricots and figs. Then the land turned arid brown and salty white, and the hot southern wind known as the Shaheelee began to swirl and pushed against us.

It was unusual for the Shaheelee to blow with such force during the summer. The kids thought it an omen and began to guess its meaning. We arrived in Wled Malik at dusk.

I walked to my house from the youth club and saw the front door open. Fiona had probably let herself in, I figured. Slowly, I entered my bedroom and started talking dirty in Arabic, "*Kul zibi kul zibi kul zibi, kul kulshay.*" From the darkness, I heard someone say, "Are you home?" in Korean.

"Dad?" I turned on the light and saw my father lying on my bed. "What are you doing here?"

He got up, stiff and regal, and patted me on the shoulder.

"*J'al iss-uh?*"

"Yeah, I'm fine, but how did you get here? What are you doing here?"

"I was thinking about you," he said with his upside-down smile. "So I decided to give you a surprise."

"When did you get here? Yesterday? You should have written me. I could have picked you up in Tunis."

"I just arrived this afternoon. I didn't hear from you for a long time, so I was worried."

"Dad, I'm fine. There was no need. You should've told me."

Dad stopped smiling. "Anyway, it's good to see you."

"It's good to see you, too."

He looked at my grit-covered body and laughed, "You look like a peasant."

"Well, this is what I turn into when I don't bathe for a few days. I wish you would've told me you were coming."

He sat back down on the bed and leaned against the concrete wall. "If it's a burden for your father to visit, you don't have to worry. I am going back on Tuesday. I just wanted to see you."

"I wish you could stay longer. I'm glad you're here."

Then the front door opened and shut and Fiona started singing: "Tits out fer th' lads, girls, tits out fer th' lads." And she walked into the bedroom with her shirt and bra pulled up, fingers cupping her breasts and thumbs covering her nipples. She saw my father, yanked down her shirt, and screamed, "Jaysus! What the hell is going on, Nolan?"

Dad looked at Fiona calmly, then at me. "Is this why you wanted to join the Peace Corps, Jae-Hyun?"

Dad had met my mother when he lived in Dublin in the early seventies. He was there to work on his company's design entry for the new home of the Irish Historical Society. She was one of the locals on his team. They didn't win the contract, but they did create me. They married four months before I was born. They chose to have me in San Francisco and raise me as an American. Where else could a halfie be accepted? But my father's royal blood was potent and completely dominated my genetic makeup. The only signs of the other side are my creased eyelids and aquiline nose.

Mom died when I was three. A Muni bus ran a red light. I don't remember much about her, but I do remember someone holding me, stroking my head, and making me feel secure. I'm sure it was Mom. And I'm sure it was her loving nature that Dad had fallen in love with. He never told me that he loved her, but I can tell it in the wedding photo I saved, the one in which Fiona sort of looks like Mom.

It's a close-up of Mom kissing Dad's cheek, her arms wrapped around his neck; Dad is facing the camera, unable to hide a smile in his otherwise stoic face.

He was devastated when she died, not just from the grief of losing her, but the fact that he couldn't go back to Seoul—his family wouldn't have anything to do with him or his illegitimate, halfie son, lineage carrier or not. That's when he came up with the plan for me to marry a Korean. He hoped this might make it possible for him—for us—to be accepted back into the lives of his parents and sisters. It pained him that he, the only son, couldn't take care of the people who suffered so much to raise him through the Japanese occupation and the Korean war.

As his parents had done for him, he provided me the best he could. Instead of public schools, he sent me to Lick-Wilmerding, the only private high school in the city that met his standards. After I excelled there, Dad supported me through college and gloated on the prestige of having a Harvard son—something he knew would eventually impress his parents.

In his exile, he tried to teach me to avoid his own mistakes, so that we could both be exonerated in the next generation. It may not sound fair that I must carry his burden, but I understand that it's not about him. It's much more important than that. If I fail, like my father did, the family legacy would come to an absolute end.

I'm pretty sure that's what was going through Dad's mind when I walked Fiona back to her village that night. After I calmed them down and introduced them formally, my father pulled me aside. He repeated the edict he gave me before I'd left home: "Remember your family."

"Dad, she's just a friend. Really, it's nothing."

"Remember your family."

I finally escaped my father and went out to escort Fiona home, but she was already walking toward Sbeitla, almost out of sight down the unlit, unpaved road. Her long skirt, like a royal train, smoothed a path over the saline soil. The Shaheelee hurled dust everywhere, stinging my face and arms. When I caught up to Fiona, she said, "Jayyyysus Chroist! I can't believe I flashed me tits to your da! Grand first impression, wha?"

"Don't worry about it," I said. "It's not as if either one of us knew he was coming."

"Is he angry?"

"Only at me. He thinks I'm jeopardizing the family."

"Maaaad. Your da and you are absolutely mad with your wanky lineage," she said, smiling.

"Fiona, maybe if you had such a long family history, you'd understand."

"Bollocks, I say. It's all bollocks. Even if I had a family tree shoved all the way up me gee, I still wouldn't let a poxy ancestor dictate who I can and can't have children with."

We passed a grove of olive trees and entered a flat clearing. There was little protection from the wind except for the cacti fencing the road. Fiona reached out and held my hand.

"You have a choice, too," she said, her voice lapsing into the earnest tone she saved for work. "It's your life, not your family's. Why do you think I decided to work anywhere but in my homeland? I had to get out. If I were like you and decided to uphold my family line, I'd be another repressed Irish Catholic with dysfunctions and all. No, thank you!"

"That's easy for you to say, but I'm the first son and I have..."

"Pleeeeease," she playfully blurted as she wrapped her arms around my waist. "Not the first sonava sonava sonava again. I already know it. I luv ya anyway."

I pulled her close and kissed her.

"What I really want to know, though," Fiona continued, "is what's with yer family's obsession with willies? How come you don't record th' girls." She put her lips to my ear. "I think I know why," she whispered. "Maybe your ancestors were like you. None of them could own up, either!" She put her hands down into my front pockets. I bet none of them could admit they fancied who they shagged."

She began pulling me off the road.

"No, not here," I said.

"Come on, no one's around. Who'd be out on a night like this?"

She guided me into an alcove framed by prickly pear and kissed me with her tongue. The wind raged against the cactus walls as she undid my pants. She lifted up her skirt and lowered herself onto me. I rolled her on her back, because I always have to be on top, and soon, I pulled out just like the countless times before.

Afterward, at the outskirts of her village, we held each other. I turned my back to the wind to protect her from the whipping sand.

"I wish you could stay the evening," she said.

"I can't. Dad would really flip if I did."

"Well, let him flip away." She let go of our embrace and crossed her arms. "You're here with me so tell him there's a queue."

"What's the matter?"

"What's always the matter with you, Luv. Your precious pedigree. Because of it, all we do together is shag until you leg it home. How do you think that feels to me? Makes me wonder if you even care it's *me* you're with."

"Of course I care about you."

"You know what I mean. That you'll admit this is more than just sex. I don't think your bloody ancestors would mind to see you have some human emotions."

I stood silent. I wanted to tell her how much I adored her, how I collected her hairs off my clothes and put them in a small box under my bed, so a part of her would be near me at night, how she made me want to stray from my predestined future. But saying so would have been an admission to myself and my ancestors that my future was for me and my needs, and a deviation from the royal path set before me.

"Anyway, you ought to remember that you have another heritage, your mother's. And a perfectly good one it is, too." Then she said, lapsing into her brogue, "A good Irish boy the loikes of ya should be with a mad Irish woman loike meself."

She put my hand on her breast, squeezed and said, "Tits out fer y' da, Luv." Then she kissed me good night.

The Shaheelee raged through the next morning; its ageless power has been eroding the Roman ruins in Sbeitla for centuries. The wind comes from deep down in the Sahara where it picks up speed and knocks off flecks from felled structures that are older than my family's recorded history. I took Dad out into the fury to go to the *hammam*, the bathhouse. The Shaheelee caked our skin and howled past our ears all the way to the *hammam's* front door. We entered.

Inside it was quiet, warm and serene. The front room had a low ceiling supported by columns pilfered from neighboring ruins. The old towel man behind the counter had traditional Berber tattoos on his creviced chin. He was drinking a Diet Coke. He gave me two towels. My father and I undressed, and I showed him how to knot the towel around his waist. We walked into the steam room. Humidity caressed our bodies. We sat down on a raised platform in the middle of the room and took audience with the rich and poor of Wled Malik, all sitting on benches against the white tiled walls.

"*Salem oualleykoom*," I was greeted through the steam from around the room.

"*Oalleykoom assalem*," I greeted back. I introduced my father and men began lining up to meet him.

"What are they saying?" asked Dad.

"They're thanking you for having me. They're saying I've helped their village a lot. They're blessing us."

"Blessing?"

"Yes, like, 'May God protect you, May God be beneficent to you, May God provide for you.'"

We moved into the hot pool. Another body entered the pool across from us.

"Hello, Mr. Nolan. Nice to meet your father," said smiley Abdel-quessem in his heavily accented English, by far the best of all the kids. He practiced with me all the time.

"Dad, this is Abdel-quessem." Dad nodded his head.

"I welcome you to Son of King," he said to Dad.

"Excuse me?"

"He's welcoming you to the village. Wled Malik translated means Son of King."

"Very auspicious name. Thank you," said Dad.

"I think you and Mr. Nolan look same," said Abdel-quessem.

"Except for the nose, Abdel-quessem. Illa l'xsham."

"I think Mr. Nolan is good man," he said to my father. "I ask, 'Why you come to Wled Malik?' and he say 'To help.' I ask, 'Where is your family?' His family far away. I not able to do same. I not want to leave family."

"Wise boy," said Dad, without looking at me.

"You speak Korea language?"

Dad nodded.

"Why not Mr. Nolan?" Sometimes Abdel-quessem didn't know when to stop practicing.

"That's a good question," said Dad.

"Mr. Nolan say to me, must know my past, then I know me, then I know future. I think, if I live in U.S.A., like Mr. Nolan live here, I must know Arabic. Must know."

"You teach them well," Dad said to me.

"So, I say to Mr. Nolan, 'Mr. Nolan must know Korea language. Must learn.'"

"You should listen to him, Jae-Hyun," said Dad, grinning. "He knows what's important."

"Then I say to Mr. Nolan, 'Also must know Irish language. Must learn. Must learn both. Must know past.'"

Dad's face turned dour.

I returned Dad's smile and said, "Should I still be listening to him, Dad?"

He stared ahead as if he hadn't heard me.

We got out of the pool and I led Dad to the scrub room. The scrubber, a big, toweled man with rough cloth mitts, finished scraping a bather clean. Dad declined and went back to the steam room. I lay down on the raised, tiled platform and the scrubber began. For four days I hadn't washed and was saturated with dirt, grime and sand. With slow easy sweeps of his hand, the scrubber stripped off that ancient coating from my neck, chest, back, arms, legs, until I was left reddened with nothing but new skin.

Dad and I walked back home accompanied by the whistling call of the Shaheelee. I moved ahead and he followed close, like a shadow that clung to me even without sunlight.

We passed by the whitewashed primary school, a long, flat-roofed structure partitioned into fourths, and I thought of the many evenings that Fiona had taught prenatal care in those classrooms, and how she would continue her work, even after I'd left.

Dad matched my stride.

"This sandstorm is pretty bad," I said. "I bet it's difficult to drive through."

Dad maintained his pace and didn't reply.

"So when is your flight?" I asked.

"I told you already." he said, as if he were spitting.

"You may want to take a bus today instead of early tomorrow. If the sandstorm gets worse, the bus could get delayed or canceled, and I don't want you to miss your plane."

"I don't think wind can cancel a bus."

"Well, around here it can. Sometimes."

Dad's feet pounded the ground like fists. His strides grew longer, and he pulled ahead of me. We finally reached my house. As I unlocked the door, Dad bitterly said, "So if I go today, will your *friend* visit as soon as I leave?"

Before I could reply, his right hand shot up to halt my words. He entered the house as if it had belonged to him.

In the living room, he took off his coat, threw it on a chair and stomped into my room. He returned with his bag and pulled out a folder. He sat down on one of the flower-print foam mattresses that I used as a couch.

"Here, I brought this for you," he said. He opened the folder and an assortment of glossy brochures and papers slid onto the floor.

"What is it?"

"It's our future. It's the information on jobs and schools in Korea that I gathered while you goofed off here." Dad pushed the folder between us. "You should be prepared before coming home."

The top packet's black cover dully reflected Dad's face, distorting it as if under the rippled surface of water. I opened the packet and saw one of my potential futures.

"Couldn't this have waited?" I said. "You didn't have to come all the way out here for this. I'll be back soon enough."

"You shouldn't waste any more time. You have important responsibilities." He picked up a pamphlet. "Look. Look at this school. You can get a Ph.D. while you learn Korean..."

"Dad."

"...but if you want to work, these companies..."

"Dad."

"...will teach you..."

"Dad!"

He stopped. Authority gathered in his face. "Do not speak to your father in that tone."

"I'm sorry. It's just...I want to enjoy the rest of my time here without worrying about the future."

"Jae-Hyun, you should look forward to the future. It will bring great things. You are not like others; you are of royal descent. Your ancestors are written about in history books. They are depending on you."

"I know, I know. You don't have to worry about me. I'm not going to let them down. It's just lately I was wondering what things would be like if Mom were alive?"

"What do you mean?"

"Well, I wonder what she would've thought about all of this?"

"This?"

"Yes. Your plans for my future."

Dad breathed heavily, each inhale and exhale a sign of his composed anger. His fingers rolled the pamphlet into a thin tube; he held one end and pointed the other toward me.

"This is not my plan. It is yours. This is what you wanted to do with your life. It's what we agreed upon isn't it?"

I didn't answer. I avoided his gaze and looked around the living room, glancing at the items I'd put on the walls to make it my home: a satellite photo of the world, a print of Van Gogh's dying sunflowers, a wedding shawl from a colonial town that had once thrived on the coast.

"It's your plan. Isn't it?" repeated Dad.

I remained still. Dad waited for me to speak. I kept on looking above his head at the shawl, its faded red and green geometric shapes, its random tears in the weave, no longer useful though its beauty remained intact. All for show.

"I'll look at this later," I mumbled, and pushed the papers back into a pile and closed the folder.

The pamphlet dropped from Dad's hand. He slowly shook his head. He stood up and said, "I'm going to take your suggestion and leave today. I'll leave these materials for you." Then he shuffled to the bedroom to pack.

In the late afternoon, we silently waited at the café that doubled as a bus stop. For an hour, we watched the sky darken with dust. The bus finally arrived. We ran to it, shielding our faces from the wind.

My father patted my shoulder. "It was good to see you."

"Yeah, I'm glad you came."

He went up the bus steps, and at the top, turned around.

I waved and said, "I'll see you in a couple of months."

"Jae-Hyun, please, I do not want an illegitimate grandson."

The door shut, and the bus drove off.

In the distance, through the hazy sandstorm, the glare from the bus's tail-lights looked like a pair of miniature wings. When it disappeared at the point where horizon met heaven, I turned around and ran.

When I entered her classroom, Fiona was in her uniform, sitting on a high chair. I walked through the circle of women around her and fell to my knees.

"*Salem oualleykoom, Si Nolan.*"

She was distant and courtly in front of her students. I coughed up sand and could barely catch my breath.

"*Labas?*" she asked.

"No. *Moosh labas.* I'm not well at all."

"What's wrong?" she quickly asked, "Is it your father?"

"No. He's all right. It's just me," I wheezed.

The Shaheelee was in a fury outside. The shutters bashed against the window frames. Even the corner support columns trembled in the wind.

"I wanted to talk to you," I said, trying not to sound desperate.

"I think now is not the best time to have a discussion," she said, her voice curtly formal. "It would be wise to continue this conversation after my class. In private. Can you wait outside until we're done? It's almost over."

I didn't answer her. Though I knew better, I leaned my head into her knees and hugged her legs.

"Nolan, stop. Nolan, not in front of everyone. Nolan!"

She tapped my arm with her notepad but I couldn't stop. I hugged her tighter. "Nolan."

Tap tap tap. Tap tap tap. Tap...tap...tap.... I felt her muscles loosen.

"Nolan?" she whispered. She put her hand on my head and sighed. "You wee lamb. Don't worry, everything will be grand."

I let go of her legs and looked up.

"I don't think so," I said.

"Of course it will, Luv." Her hand caressed my hair. "You're here with me." She pursed her lips and blew me a kiss. "You're here with me."

I buried my head into her lap and felt safe. For a moment, I absolved myself from my familial duty. I wanted to stay like that, with Fiona, in that room, forever, even though the building swayed, back and forth, to and fro, under an unrelenting wind that would one day knock it down.

IKHYUN KIM

n [prob. alter ME *chine* crack, fissure] 1535

in 1666, as lingering
doubts as to the inevitable
end of the world
swept seaward
over snowcapped waves
toward home,
Isaac Newton let
light slip into a dark
room through a chink
in a blind and fall
obliquely on one face of
a triangular glass prism

in a favorite episode
of Wonder Woman
an alien being
shrinks down
grown men
and women and
traps them in
triangular glass prisms

unable to escape, his
dollhouse stammers are
useless protestation against
the sixty cycle hum of

the frost-free refrigerator
upon which we find him, the first
victim, in his light, permeable,
un-chinked prism, waiting to be
saved by Lynda Carter

Oh, if you only had
blonde hair, my sweet creature,
you could be Ms. Minnesota, or
at least compete for the honor.

Out here, no one would throw stones at
your "invisible" glass airplane or
comment on your rack. Instead,
like you, we parse and sieve with
deft precision, identify and record
difference to love our
constant sameness.

At a job interview, she
states, "Your English is so
good." It is her portable
interferometer talking, measuring the
speed of my response in
relation to the speed at which
human discomfort grows. So sensitive
is this instrument "it can
measure the growth of a plant
from second to second."

Its inventor, three years old
from Prussia, Americanized
by San Francisco and Civil War,
trained at Annapolis,
crowned first American
Nobel Prize in 1907,

Albert Abraham Michelson took
three mirrors and forever cleared
space of luminiferous ether,
defined one meter in Paris,
stamped and signed Relativity's manifest,
but made a poor seaman. Perhaps he
did not have a stomach for the vagaries
of seawater, its buoyant ripple led by
moon and wind and tectonic thrust.

The reflection
of light
off an object
or mirror
is so very
important.

Like the sound of bullets
off Feminum bracelets
it defines
a slit of space
<a ~ in the curtain> that
may leave one vulnerable and
an act of filling in
such spaces (as by caulking)
<~ a log cabin>, kneading
into it, erasing every trace of
ever having been imperfect

JI SUNG KIM
The Smell of Stars

In this coffin, we ride to paradise or hell?

I lie on a scratchy wool blanket through which I feel the aluminum grooves of a van that smells like unwashed pits, my head sandwiched between a pair of shoes and the metal wall. The motor runs its noisy tattle. The driver shepherds the steering wheel, wagering a game of brake, accelerate, tumble.

From the outside, we are a van cruising a green mountain under chiffon clouds befitting angels. The sun hovers to etch the tint of each substance with exacting pleasure. Butterflies flutter above cobblestoned streets against the tropical rain. Later, the horizon will separate heaven and earth, glowing stripes of tiger red, weightless.

Only God with his X-ray vision can see us. I made an offering to the Catholic church and the Buddhist temple before my departure. I pray to the moon deity of bygone days. I seek prosperity from all views.

Inside. Twilight never leaves.

The floorboard of unfinished plywood, stapled together, bisects this home. It holds the tension of hiding. Above lies the cargo. The cages of hens, no roosters. More than a few birds to each cell. Birds without beaks or claws. Adjacent are boxes of mangoes, avocados. So precious in Korea, at first, I reacted with glee. They abrade against kin in their own slosh. Their heaviness curves our chests. The floorboard presses our crinkled bones.

I hear talking beneath the engine's roar, if I concentrate. But I can't make out what they intend to do or achieve. I don't know their meaning. And when the engine stops, silence unfurls. Even the chickens stop clucking. There could be cops in uniform who strip us naked for our cash, their black leather soles breaking our fingers if we don't comply. If it has happened before, it may happen again, this time actualized on someone like me. I want to protect myself from calamity, from the control others exert.

Voices. Deterge me. Sores of the clammy mind.

"You think that in America, you'll find yourself. But you're wrong. You can't run away from these things, even if it happened 10 years ago," says the friend.

"You have nothing to do with how your mother died. You didn't cause your father to kill himself or your mother. He thought he had killed you. But he hadn't. You survived him. He went crazy after the IMF crisis. He wasn't himself," says the fortune-teller.

"We aren't sure if she's telling the truth. Why would this upstanding businessman, a banker, kill himself and his wife? The daughter could have shot them both and then shot herself. You can't trust her type," says the cop.

My limbs have swirled off poundage. I do not recognize me as me. I panic that my body is not mine, that my thoughts are a distraction from detecting the truth, that I have been incorporated into a metropolis inhabited by ghosts. They've made a nest in my armpits. They've pitched tents under my fingernails. The ghosts skip from the Ankle County to the Town of Thigh, drinking my blood like intoxicated fleas. They want my identity. They want my chance. They think that by crossing the border, I will be born again, as if our van is in labor, rushing to deliver.

I count my activities in the van. Sleep. Swell and shrink stomach to facilitate breathing. I close the right eye, the left, then both, over and over again to redirect a perfunctory awareness of pain. I feel cars are crashing along the avenue of my back. My neck feels like a balloon plastered by papier-mâché.

The air smacks of blood, waste and rot, the reek of clients. Balls of white feathers and black jelly. Dust and hair. The floorboard's chips mix with my sweat. I crunch it like gum, brushing teeth with sandpaper.

Confined by hope, our desperate consciousness breathes shallow heartbeats, scavenging air between bodies. It immobilizes our limbs. It erases our fluttering eyelids and flattens strands of hair. Partitioned from each other by our feet, a fog of privacy. We are an accordion of lullabies in our passage to dreams. We are a symmetry of head-feet yin-yang, mirroring agony and expectation.

A soap opera broadcast in all the languages, starring the better life, by availability. Ride a van, hop freight trains, contort to cargo ships, walk a million miles. Run. Factor time and weather, menace and chance. Done it all to hit the borderland. Adults. Children. Babies. Fetuses. A load of cliff-hangers: to be or not to be?

My stomach keeps calling for at least a bowl of rice and a cup of water. Not a bowl. One handful. One drink. The dial tuned to hunger, my life takes on a cooking-show affair. A woman stands behind a voluptuous countertop. The food has been chopped and placed in porcelain bowls. She makes all my favorite foods like broiled beef in garlic, sugar, soy sauce. She prepares seaweed soup with oysters. She concocts cod egg stew with finger-length chunks of green onion. I love her.

I approach her, but each time I step forward, she glides back. The food follows her, like pets on a leash. I tell her, you are rain to a drought. You are a persimmon tree whose fruits fall rotting.

She answers with betrayal. She feeds the dogs as I watch. She says this food is not fit for consumption; it's disguised dog food. Still, I wish she let me decide whether or not to eat it. My stomach whimpers like a puppy. Two puppies.

As I lay captive, my mother's perfume coils my body. Her scent of gardenias, menstruation, kimchi threads shut my nostrils. A foam of sighs surf the roof of my mouth.

Mother says, that ghosts haunt dirty spaces, like spider-webbed ceilings and snot-wiped crevices. She asks, Do you think rich people have ghosts?

No, they pay people to clean up after them. It's poor people like us, the ones who are too busy working, the ones whose homes are too small, who ghosts penetrate. Ghosts don't like being seen. They like dirt and night. When you clean your house and your body, the ghosts get upset. They put up a fight. They don't want you to be clean. They do mean tricks to drive you crazy. That's what ghosts do.

This is the lecture she gave me as a child, to frighten me into a finger-lickable house, spotless like a sheet of paper. Ghosts, cursed spirits reincarnated as germs. Occasionally, I rebelled, just to refuse the matrix. Binging a house ravaged, exhibition of reckless stacks.

In the van, I spot what mother submitted. I feel an otherworldly presence in the corpse of insects. The crustaceous jerky crawls toward my mouth, even though I am sure I squashed the critter.

I wonder if ghosts have a nationality. Do they transgress the limitations of language and customs for a universal ghost talk? Can they leave their place of death for a vacation across latitude and longitude? Or are they tied to the soil, like vampires, thwarting humans from fulfilling their paltry goals? There are good ghosts. Those are called spirits.

My mother disguises herself at times as spirit and at other times as ghost. I can't make her out with finality. She eludes indentation. She likes to hide in the telephone. The phone will ring. I will pick up the receiver. If no one answers, I suspect she might have dialed my number. Come on, Mom! Cracking jokes as always.

Van wall, me, feet and the face. A woman's face.

Through the tiny cracks that filter in light, I see the rays that illuminate her eyes, nose and mouth. I hold her features like a mirror and a knife. She shines, metallic. Her face has the folds of a desert's waves, those double dune cheeks. Eyebrows grow thorns for eyes of roses. Nose swoops like a comet. Lips flake fish scales.

Maybe she's 27 like me. Maybe she needs a paying job to fling money to her family. Maybe her family is there and she was last. Maybe she's done this before, crossing from edge to edge to edge. Her expectations sinking in her birth country, she drafts her future to materialize a vitamin makeover. Faulty improvisation is not a treachery, but a matter of public concern.

The others know. I hear whispering.

Before getting on the van, I smiled at all the women and nodded at the men so that they could not accuse me of being aloof. Even the reticent foreigner can assess body language. In her smile, I saw sadness and pride. Eyes cast down, her skin like polished gold, she reminds me of Maria. I feel safer looking at her optic stars. Brown on the outside and yellow in the inside, like grandfather's. Such pair of eyes half a world away.

We can become friends, talking friends. We'll speak American. Reminisce the van's farting. Escaping the quicksand. Van on the brink of a nervous collapse, ha, ha. Or will this taboo drive us apart, a needle at the base of our feet?

We are both women. Did she grow up doing the dishes, too, unlike her brothers? Was she taught that the whole qualified on her virginity? Does she feign, and feel, like I do?

Does she ever consider how she would differ if she had been born a man? I think about it. I don't want to be a man. But I register the slights that discern man's trip from woman's. For one, men don't get pregnant. Just when I thought I knew the way, I have been tripped. I consider the odds of pregnancy. Before leaving Korea, I met a man I seized with temporary lunacy. Bailing out from my daily clock, I hunched I would disappear from all that I had staked as real. I attempted one last jab before going extinct. I fished for no other interest, until the baby questions started munching. In the Americas. I feel hungry and nauseous. I want to throw up. But I wait for my period.

Me and a baby. Uncle is shocked, but his grandfatherly desires edge out propriety. I live and work with his family, until the interlude comes for my child and I to hang paper ringlet chains from our own ceiling. When the child asks about the father, I will not package his myth with pop-song fatalism. No scenes of a devastated love story chopped into firewood by quack parents. Our future will not taste like the trailing smoke of exhaust pipes.

Squished against the side, where the floorboard is one piece, and not the stapled part, I am set apart from the group. I float like a kite, accustomed to the van's deep whistle and bumpy motion. When the van steers disorder, the turbulence of all ten bodies heap on me like a hill of blankets. My head bangs epileptic, leaving multiple knots of cactus. My eyeballs feel they have lost a boxing match. My jaw is a grinding factory when I'm not looking.

Some people find dreams closer to truth than the waking world. Dreams hold their own reality, with consistent inconsistencies. Entering its story, I become a character in the belly of disposable fiction.

I am a bride at a wedding ceremony held inside a department store with four walls and a ceiling made up of glass. The department store has advertised the event. Many people swarm. I was about to get married to someone I had just met and forgotten. I didn't worry about it because I'd see the groom soon enough. But the groom was late. So late that the sun had set and the store closed. I was about to extricate myself from the bridal dress in the unflattering shade of beige, when the music started. Down the aisle walked another bride, a cloud of tulle covering her face.

In my excitement, I cried out, Who are you?

The bride lifted her veil. I recognized her as Maria.

I asked the minister, who looked and sounded like President Clinton of the United States, Is it all right for me to marry a woman?

He said not to bother because it was not the woman I was really marrying and took out a full-length mirror where I saw us bisected down the middle, in clothing and biology, as man and woman.

Maria turned to me and said, I want to tell you that I don't want to marry you, not because you're a Korean, but because you're not the person I had, in love.

I asked, Do you know anyone who has money and a green card?

Our wedding gowns disintegrated at the seams and the diamonds in our tiara are exposed as plastic. President Clinton explained that the day wasn't wasted because he knew of green card holders and that if we signed the contract, we could meet our grooms right now. Easily, without deciding to preview, we signed the paper.

From out of nowhere a pack of wolves began chasing us. We were on a field. We climbed a fence, giving all of our effort. We thought we had out tricked the pack, but we saw that they had found an open gate and had gained on us. They were closer than before.

Seeing a lake, we dived in, swimming across the shore where we were met by a deserted highway. Relieved, we walked together, hand in hand. From the horizon behind us, a lone truck trailed us. Soon, we were surrounded by trucks.

I whisper to her, You can't pretend to love me?

Chicken blood soaks the plywood above her forehead. Green and white feces dangle and red drops bounce off her brow, streaming down her eyes. She blinks away the nuisance from her long lashes. A bead zigzags her constellation of raised moles. Now multiple veins traverse across her cheek, landing in her mouth. The nostrils clog, giving up. In the background, sweat weeps. Her cheek gestures to one shoulder. Her elbow wiggles, her fingers flex. Dried from gulping air through her throat, she gasps for saliva, her drink of choice. We catch our sweat to quench our cottony tongues. Hers has the quality of rust.

The rays nail her cornea with rainbow. She squints. Her lashes fend lazier. She tells the yellow glitter, Don't come anymore; seeing you is painful. Her eye-balls break out and enter the sky, incarnated as flames. She tilts her head to me. We look into each other's eyes, wearing our damp life savings, trapped on this island. I want to talk to her, but I can't. My mouth lacks moisture. Mere bacterial growth and hairy teeth.

I intensify my blink to let her know, I see you. No reply. Her receiver is off the hook. Her eyes are faucets releasing a stream of gaze she cannot shut. Why doesn't she shut her eyes? Every so often, I imagine her eyes closing. I listen to check her organs. I realize she is in a corner within herself, preparing for freedom through her open windows. Her body is a statue of organs in a female sac. Her lips have wilted, and I wheeze under her indecent eye. Breathing has become impossible, but my voice materializes.

I scream, *She's dead.*

Arms flailing, one hand bangs the aluminum while the other knocks away a pair of shoes. The shoes want to kick me till I'm dead. Maybe the shoes killed her for space. It knows I'm pregnant. I'm taking up space for two. The feet clamor, I'm stupid for coming on this trip, that I'll die. No one in Korea will know I didn't cross the Mexico-U.S. border. Instead, they'll envision a home of crystal frills. My promises will ricochet as deafening curses shrieked by the man-greed chimera swearing me to hell.

I pee, letting go. All over the world, one dream haunts the vacant stomach. The United States, a carnivore in a red bikini, creeps in the fleshy imagination of the movie, the bubbly soda, the thingamajig invention. I don't know where we are, where I am.

I had estranged my nerves from everything I had touched as poetry for this vile sequence. I had accepted to do the exceptional, to do what it took, no matter what, to achieve alienation. I felt unbearable. I had been feeling the absence of my character acutely in this new world, where I could hardly identify anything of myself, and of my people, in the mix around me. Then I met her.

The full-faced eyes of the woman I named after the virgin are faded tapestry. I feel a sharp pain stab my breast. Heartbeat accelerates to the head's throbbing. A warning tells me not to care, to shake off her aura like dust. Worthless to regret that I had not tried harder to exchange our hopes. Dehydrated by apathy, the virgin seeks faith in the kingdom of God. She levitates, supported by the cloud and the serpent. Why did she die? Each of us must decipher this message of life and death. We, her witnesses, shelter our anonymous loss, a loss that forms another brick in our yellow brick road. The road stretches with each risk taker leaping off the precipice. Employers beneath the ledge swarm, teasing the destitute with parachutes imprinted with dollar bills.

The van is parked near a house with a veranda covered by the tang of cow. One by one, we leave the van. Except her, in her last visual performance, whose limpness we drag. My palms closed, the smell of stars rise from my fingertips.

ROGER PARK
The Sardines

When he walked over the hill, the noise became louder and Manny saw that it was group of prisoners working in the fields. Hammers and pickaxes pounded the swollen earth as the men chanted in unison with low voices. They wore gray uniforms and were chained. Armed guards stood by them. Some of the prisoners were white, some were black. The guards, who were all white, carried rifles. A few of the prisoners stopped to watch the young Korean boy walking along the road, but the guards yelled at them to get back to work. Manny kept walking, and the singing grew faint.

The sun was a dizzy drop of butter in the summer sky. Manny jammed his hands in his tattered overalls and bent his neck over like a crane. From the position of the sun, he figured it was about noon, but time meant little more than night and day to him. He would forget where he had been and what he had seen. All he knew was that he was hungry again.

The dirt road went through a wide field of dried grass and then, after a few more miles, up a hill that sloped to a line of oak trees. As he approached the trees, he heard cicadas buzzing among the branches and the trickle of a stream. The smell of wild mint rushed into his nose. He tried to think of the Korean word for mint but couldn't remember.

Kneeling on the wet sand, Manny cupped his hands and drank from the stream. He dunked his head in the water and saw tiny fish darting around and pebbles on the bottom. When he raised his dripping head, he noticed a frog hanging on a reed. Manny froze and fixed his eyes on the frog. Then, in a one quick motion, he dove for the frog but missed.

"Ah hell!" he shouted as he splashed around the stream. Although he had missed a meal, the water felt good. Manny leaned back tried to float, but the water was only a few inches deep. He washed his face and drank a lot of water. Then he stood up, ran a hand through his thick black hair and headed for the road.

The road cut through some woods where the branches around him creaked in the wind. The hot summer sun soon dried his clothes. A Ford truck drove toward him as he walked. Manny waved at the truck, and it stopped in front of him.

"Something wrong, Son?" asked an old white man with a leathery face. He wore a red baseball cap.

"No, Sir. Where does this road go to?" Manny asked softly.

"Durnville. Speak up, Son. I can't hear you so well."

"How far is the town from here, Sir?" Manny asked.

"Maybe a few more miles," the man said. "I just came back from town for some supplies." He pointed a fat thumb at the back of the truck.

"You need any help at the farm?" Manny asked lifting his wiry arms to the sky. "I'm strong."

"I'm sorry. It's just me on the farm, and I don't need any help. But let me ask you something. You seem to be a nice Chinese boy. What the hell are you doing out here?"

"Looking for work."

"Well, so is a lot of folks. Sorry." He started the engine then stuck his head out the window. "Hey, you have a gun on you?"

"No."

The old man looked around and then said, "You should, because there's niggers around here." He threw the truck into gear and drove off. As the truck rolled by, Manny saw the crates in the back of the truck. Something glinted in the sun; it was a tin can. He read the label: sardines.

Up the road, there was a small country graveyard next to a grove of elms. An old white man in a moth-eaten black coat was digging a grave very slowly. He wore a tweed slouch cap with holes in it. A tiny pine coffin lay next to his feet.

Sunlight came through the leaves and spotted the headstones with patterns, which moved in same torpid pace as the gravedigger.

"You need any help here, Sir?" Manny asked quietly.

The man shook his head and pointed at his mouth. Manny took it to mean that the man couldn't speak. The man smiled and went back to work. Manny nodded and slowly stepped toward the road. As he walked by a pail near the man's tool, he glanced at the contents. On the bottom of the pail were a few crumbs and an empty tin of sardines.

Manny walked on the road to Durnville and began to think of sardines; he couldn't remember what they tasted like. He didn't know if they were salty, or if they had any taste at all. He remembered eating Korean-style fish at the orphanage in San Francisco, but that was many years ago. He shook his head, and the memory faded.

When he got to town, Manny asked a white man wearing a brown tie if he knew where he could find work.

"Cross the bridge and ask around in Niggertown," the man said curtly as he walked away. When Manny went over to the Negro part of town, the people told him they all worked on the other side of the bridge.

Manny crossed the bridge and went into a coffee shop. There were a few people in the coffee shop. They were all white. An old jukebox was playing a scratchy hillbilly record.

"You need something?" a woman behind the counter asked. She tapped her thick white fingers against the dark counter. The coffee shop smelled of bacon and coffee; Manny's stomach rumbled and reminded him of his hunger.

"Do you need any work done here, Ma'am?" Manny asked nervously, half whispering.

"What? I can't hear you." When Manny repeated his question a bit louder, she shook her head. "No. Sorry." Her mouth became a tight and straight line.

As Manny left the coffee shop a man at the far end of the counter hissed, "Chinamen belong in China."

Manny went behind the coffee shop. Nobody was around. He quickly opened the dumpster. There was a slice of white bread soaked in grease and dirt. He grabbed the piece and closed the dumpster lid. Then he jammed the bread into his pockets and ran up a hill topped with two oak trees. Manny sat down and pulled out the bread. He brushed off the dirt and ate the bread; it was stale, soggy, and had no taste. With his back against a tree, he stared at the sky and breathed through his nose. It was the first thing he had eaten all day, and he was still hungry.

In the general store, Manny wandered around until he found the sardines. He picked up a tin and weighed it in his hand. There was a picture of a fish on the label and a boat at sea.

"Can I help you, Son?" asked a white man in a plaid shirt. He had round glasses and held a clipboard.

Manny was going to ask him if he needed help, but just shook his head. "No, Sir."

"You speak English."

"Yes, Sir."

"That's Good. Do you live around here? I've never seen you before."

Manny hesitated before answering, "Yes, Sir." He didn't want them to know he was a vagrant, because the police would take him and send him to an orphanage or prison. "I just got hired to work on a farm," Manny mumbled as he felt his neck turn hot.

The man patted Manny on the back. "Oh, did Russell hire you? That's good for you. I told him he was getting too old to work the farm by himself."

"Yes, Sir." Manny went along with the lie. He felt the tin in his hands; his stomach growled. "These are for him." He raised the can to the store owner.

"OK, I'll put those down on his tab. What else did he forget and have you pick up?"

Manny looked around the store and saw all the food, but just answered, "Matches." He knew he could always use some matches.

"OK, matches, too." The store owner handed Manny a box of matches. He flipped a few pages on his clipboard and wrote something down with his pencil.

Manny began to walk out of the store. "Thank you."

"Hey! What's your name?" the man asked.

Manny turned around and said, "Manny."

"OK, Manny, I'll see you around."

Manny walked out of the store with a tin of sardines and a box of matches in his pocket. His face was hot, and he worried that store owner knew he was lying. He arched his shoulders as he walked away from the store, getting ready for the man to shoot him. But nothing happened.

Manny quickly walked away from town.

In a field and underneath a mulberry tree, Manny opened the tin of sardines and ate them. They were not salty at all, but very oily. He ate every single fish and afterward, he licked the oil off his hands like a cat. He rested his back on the soft grass and gazed at the great tree and the blue sky behind it. Clouds drifted by as birds darted across to catch insects. Soon he grew tired and fell asleep. He dreamed of different animals fighting with people. He tried to remember the names of the animals in Korean, but he couldn't. He saw mountains in the snow and didn't know if they were in Korea or in America. He saw ships on the sea and then frogs jumping into a fire.

When he woke up, it was night, and the sky was filled with stars; the glowing dots looked like the pebbles he had seen on the bottom of the stream. The night air smelled of jasmine. He didn't feel like sleeping anymore.

Manny got up and started walking.

He had walked several miles in the dark before he heard a faint siren in the distance. The noise grew louder, and he could see a car approaching. It was police car with a red light. Fear grabbed him: The police and the store owner were going to get him for stealing the sardines and matches. He ran into the some bushes and hid as the police car sped closer. He cursed himself for getting himself into trouble again. He didn't want to go back to jail. He remembered the time in Utah when some prisoners held an ice pick to him and raped him. His stomach tightened, and his legs began to shake. As he crouched down in the bushes, he pushed that bad memory, like so many other memories, away from his mind like a boat from a landing. As the car raced past him and through the leaves, Manny could see the red lights splashing around the trees. Instead of stopping in front of him, it had sped past him. They didn't see him.

Manny watched the car disappear over a hill, though he could still hear the siren. He got up and started running in the opposite direction but through the woods. He ran with all his strength as bushes and thorns scraped at his thin body. His chest hurt, but he kept running. Finally, he stopped to catch his breath; his heart thrashed within his chest as he bent over and rested his hands on his knees.

In the distance, Manny saw a small farmhouse with a barn. He wondered if he would be able to hide in the barn. He approached the building very slowly and cautiously. Through the woods, he saw the faint glow of a few lights.

Suddenly, a group of men ran from the house and jumped into a truck. Manny hid behind a bush and recognized the truck; it was the same truck the old man on the road coming back from town drove. The truck started and tore through the gravel.

Manny stood up and approached the farm. He guessed that the old man was looking for him for stealing the sardines. He knew that the old man lived by himself, so there was nobody in the farmhouse. A new plan formed in Manny's head: Instead of hiding in the barn, he would break into the man's house, get some supplies and travel the back roads the rest of the night. He wiped the sweat from his forehead and walked to the farmhouse.

Manny opened the backdoor and walked into the kitchen. He found an empty flour sack and began filling it with tin cans of food, bread and fruit, anything that would fit in the bag. He went to the sink and washed his face. He cupped his hands and drank the cold water. He drank and felt good, relaxed.

"Oh, help me," somebody groaned in the front room.

Manny froze.

"Somebody help me," the voice called again. "Please call an ambulance."

Manny slowly peeked into the front room. There was a table, a rocking chair, a fireplace and a man lying on the floor. There was blood on the floor and covering his stomach. It was the old man in the truck Manny had met earlier in the day. The old man looked up and pointed at Manny behind the door. "Son, come here."

Manny put the sack down and slowly entered the room. "I'm sorry for stealing the sardines," he stammered.

The old man, with one hand over his bloody stomach, pointed toward the desk. "The phone," he whispered, "Call the police and get an ambulance and tell them it was the prisoners who broke into my house. It was the prisoners who stole my truck."

"I didn't mean to take them," Manny stammered. "I was hungry. I'm sorry. Don't send me to jail."

The old man blinked his eyes and groaned. "Just pick up the phone, please. I need a doctor."

Manny took a pillow from the rocking chair and placed it over the man's stomach. As soon as it touched him, it soaked the blood. Manny picked up the phone, and when the operator came on, he handed it to the man.

"This is Russell, send an ambulance. The escaped prisoners stabbed me and I'm dying. Hurry." He spoke into the phone. He handed the receiver to Manny, who hung up.

"Are you OK, Sir?" Manny asked.

"No, damn it! I'm dying!" the old man shouted. Manny coiled back. The old man raised a hand and spoke softly, "I'm sorry. I didn't mean to yell. I'm sorry. I'm thirsty. Get me a glass of water?"

Manny nodded and went into the kitchen. He poured a glass of water and saw the flour sack on the floor. The old man groaned from the next room as Manny stared at the sack. Manny went back to the living room and gave the man the glass of water. As the old man drank the water, Manny watched quietly. "The ambulance should be here soon, so I better leave," he told the old man.

"No, Son," said the old man. The pillow had slipped and a pool of blood on the floor was spreading. "You can't leave. Stay here…please."

Manny shook his head. "I can't go back to jail. I don't want to."

"What? You didn't do anything, Son. You're saving my life. Just stay here. Please."

Manny ran into the kitchen and grabbed the sack.

"Don't go, Son. Stay here. I'm dying," the old man groaned. Suddenly, he started to scream, "I'm dying! I'm dying!"

Manny turned around and ran out of the house. He threw the sack over his shoulder and as he left the yard, he could still hear the old man's screaming. The screams pounded into Manny's eardrums as he crossed the field, but he kept running. He gripped the sack tighter and ran faster. His heart thrashed in his chest, and the screaming of the man faded away. Manny heard his own heavy breathing and the tin cans clanking against each other in the sack. And as he ran, the sounds of the cans and his breathing became faint. Pretty soon, he didn't hear anything at all.

DENNIS KIM
writes of the child

between the legs of downtown
skyscrapers arching alloy necks
into cloud cover
high-rises clothed like
colossus, their bellies
swarming with the underlings
of corpulent and corporate interest
i run crooked
contradictions piled 21
years high on a spine
made of spit
and fishing line, i
teetering into the uncertain
maw of a 22nd, i
leap for the unborn promise
       of   You,
echobreath of ancestors
who have traveled up
the roots of evergreens
and flown into my coarse cropped hair
as pine needles and sap
and the hunger for You,

coming hummingbird
born to bear the restitched
shattered flags

of myriad pasts
into borderless futures
shitting on the belligerent
bald pates of WTO potentates
and their truckloads
of unfortunate working
goons whose truncheons and missiles
lap the heads of skyscrapers
miles above
but cannot touch You,
little one, tumbling down
                    the   funnel
                                        of the inevitable
                            shoulders tucked
                                    into the runandfly

You must scorn
the scorched earth
and desiccated checkerboard
of boxed options, soar
the way i dream my voice
does in sleep,

from the windswept perch
of an unseen future, see me,
baby boy,

pounding these words flat
to stretch them to cover

your broad bronze back

tracing your possible faces
between would-be lovers' shoulderblades

scribbling songs in the churning shadow
of police horses' curled and kicking legs

chipping at the leg of colossus
with this pen i found on the bus

"i write the world in which my seed
will be at ease inside his own skin"

i want to give you the world wrapped
in blue construction paper

no tenements
no nightsticks
no 1% rich
with clenched and gilded fists
and the unclothed earth eating
at the moldering dollar that hangs
out of it
no averted eyes on damplit streets
that would rather examine
the syringes in the sidewalk
cracks than see

You,
double helix miracle
of dirt and god
every riddled history
riding in the yellow pages
of your skin

there is no barbed
fence jagged enough
to ward these shadows
off and keep you in

perhaps there is no
prayer as profound
as the wish to simply
tear it down

CONTRIBUTORS

Dominic Choi was born in Korea and came to the United States when he was 4 years old. He lives in Arlington, Virginia and grew up in Alexandria. He attended West Virginia University, works as a marketing manager, is 29 years old and is currently single.

Kendra Chung grew up in Seoul, South Korea, and New Jersey. She lives in New York.

Jennifer Dobbs is a Korean American adoptee and a graduate student of poetry at the University of Pittsburgh's creative writing program. She teaches composition, women's studies, creative writing and poetry courses at the University of Pittsburgh and in the community. Her work has appeared in *5AM*, *Prosody* on 92.3 FM and in the forthcoming *The Cream City Review's 25th Anniversary Issue* and *Crazyhorse*.

Zoli Suek Kim Hall is a writer and artist living in Minneapolis. She received a 1999 Jerome Foundation Travel/Study Grant and participated as a panel member at the American Adoption Congress Conference in San Francisco. Her poems have been published in several local and national publications including the *Asian American Renaissance Journal: Sexual Orientations and Seeds from a Silent Tree; An Anthology by Korean Adoptees*. She will have work in an upcoming issue of *The Asian Pacific American Journal, Borderlands and Drumvoices Revue*. She is currently editing her chapbook entitled, "Portrait of an Orphan's Memoryscape."

Benjamin H. Han is finishing up undergraduate study at Wesleyan University in Middletown, Connecticut, with a senior honors thesis in English on the examination of the past and transitional spaces in Southeast Asian American literatures. He has intentions of pursuing a MFA in creative writing.

Sasha Hom was adopted from South Korea in 1975 and grew up in Berkeley. California. She currently lives in Oakland where she works as a dog walker/professional petcare provider while finishing her first book. She has been published in *A Ghosts at Heart's Edge*, *Hip Mama*, *The Sun* and *Going There: An Anthology of Essays on Creativity by Women of Color*.

Peggy Hong was born in Seoul, South Korea and raised in Hawaii and New York. A graduate of Barnard College at Columbia University, she is currently in Antioch University's MFA program, studying both poetry and fiction. She is the author of the poetry chapbook *The Sister Who Swallows the Ocean*, and her poetry has been in many journals and anthologies including *Rhino*, *Bamboo Ridge*, *Mothering Magazine* and *The Asian Pacific American Journal*. She is a recipient of Milwaukee County's Art Futures Artist Fellowship and until recently, she served as education coordinator at Woodland Pattern Book Center. Also a dancer, she teaches writing to children and adults, specializing in interdisciplinary, inter-arts approaches. She lives in Milwaukee, Wisconsin, with her husband and three children.

Suil Kang is a native of Seoul, South Korea, and came to the United States in 1977. She is married and has a 20-month-old daughter. She struggles to divide her time between writing, patent law and family.

Amy Kashiwabara was born in Seoul, Korea, in 1973. She was raised in New Jersey, but has lived in the San Francisco Bay Area for the last 10 years. She studied political science and creative writing at University of California at Berkeley. She now works as a lawyer. Her publications include the periodicals *Talus & Scree, the Berkeley Poetry Review* and *Lynx Eye*; the anthologies *Seeds from a Silent Tree: An Anthology By Korean Adoptees* and *Skin Deep: Women Writing on Color, Culture and Identity*; and the textbook *Scott Foresman's Literature and Integrated Studies*. Her first two volumes of poetry were published by Cyborg Press in San Francisco.

Dennis Sangmin Kim was born in Virginia and raised in Chicago's Koreatown and its suburbs. He currently lives in Chicago's South Side and writes poems. He is one of four founding members of I Was Born With Two Tongues, a pan-Asian spoken word collective. The Tongues have released a CD of music and poetry entitled *Broken Speak* and have toured extensively throughout the United States. He is one of the MC's in a hip-hop group called the Typical Cats. He coordinates an ongoing showcase of Asian American spoken word artists called Blinkwellz. Dennis is in love.

Eugenia SunHee Kim was a finalist in the 2001 F. Scott Fitzgerald Short Story Contest and has an essay in "The Spirit of Pregnancy" edited by Bonni Goldberg. A resident of Washington, DC, she's writing a novel that unfolds in a land she's never seen and is tweaking a collection of short stories.

Ikhyun Kim is an MA candidate in the English department at SUNY Buffalo. He worked at his parent's 7-Eleven food store, photocopied legal documents, distributed coupon books, taught ESL in Korea, and worked in Information Technologies and as a coordinator at a literary center. He received the Jack Kerouac School of Disembodied Poetics' 1997 Zora Neale Hurston Minority Scholarship Award. His poetry has appeared in *7 Poets in Heaven*, *Chain*, *Kiosk*, *Plum*, *Elevator: The Box Project* and in a forthcoming issue of the online journal, *Altitude*.

Junse Kim is the recipient of the 2001 Philip Roth Residence in Creative Writing at Bucknell University and the 2000 William Faulkner Award winner in the short story category. His fiction and creative nonfiction has been published in *ZYZZYVA*, *Onatario Review and Cimarron Review*.

Sue Kwock Kim has appeared in *Poetry*, *Paris Review*, *The Nation*, *The New Republic*, *Yale Review*, *BOMB*, *Threepenny Review*, *Salmagundi*, *New England Review*, *Ploughshares*, *Southwest Review*, *The Asian Pacific American Journal*, *Michigan Quarterly Review*, *MUAE* and other publications. She's received *The Nation* / "Discovery" Award and a Fulbright Scholarship as well as fellowships from the National Endowments for the Arts and Washington State Artist Trust. *Private Property*, a multimedia play she cowrote, was produced at the Edinburgh Festival Fringe and featured on BBC-TV. She is currently a Stegner Fellow at Stanford University.

Julia Lee was born and raised in Los Angeles. In 1998, she graduated from Princeton University with a degree in English. After graduation, she worked for a consulting firm and then entered high school teaching. Currently, she teaches English at Harvard-Westlake School in Los Angeles.

Mijin Lee is 22 years old and fresh out of college. She works with Asian American youths who seem more mature than most adults with their fearless honesty, inherent energy and prejaded days. Her title is health educator, but she feels more like an older sister. She is an oldest child who can't imagine life without her sister, a loyal friend who fervently keeps in touch with her friends—her second family of earth angels, a woman who admires strong women of color, an artist who thirsts for fearlessness of self and a daughter of God who learns how to love everyday.

Tina Y. Lee earned her BA from Yale University and an MFA from Sarah Lawrence College. Previous publication credits include *The River City Journal*, *Kalliope Magazine* and *The Susquehanna Review*.

Frances Park is the author of the novel, *When My Sister was Cleopatra Moon* (April 2000, Talk/Miramax Books); inspired by her Korean American experience in the '70s, the story was featured on *Good Morning America*. An upcoming novel, coauthored by her sister, Ginger, *To Swim Across the World*, is a fictionalized memoir of her parent's accounts growing up in Korea during the Japanese Occupation, World War II and the Korean War. She also coauthors children's books with Korean or Korean American themes. *My Freedom Trip* was based on her mother's escape from North to South Korea prior to the outbreak of the Korean War and won the 1999 International Reading Associations Children's Book Award. Three upcoming children's books will be published by Lee & Low, Orchard and National Geographic.

Ishle Yi Park worked as Arts-In-Education Director of the Asian American Writer's Workshop. She was a poetry editor for the *Asian Pacific American Journal*. Her work has been published in *New American Writing*, *DisOrient*, *Manoa*, *The Cream City Review*, *Roots & Culture* and *The NuyorAsian Anthology*. She is the recipient of a fiction grant from the New York Foundation of the Arts.

Jane Park was raised in Vancouver. Currently, she lives in Edmonton, Alberta Canada. She received her BAH in English and modern literature from Queens University, Kingston. She has written poems for the *Queens Undergraduate Review*. This is her first published short story.

Roger Park's creative work has been published in *Moon Rabbit Review*, *DisOrient* and *Insomnia*. A graduate from Trinity College in Hartford, Connecticut in 1993 with a BA in creative writing, he has studied under Hugh Ogden, Gary Snyder and Sam Hamill. He is a music, art and culture journalist based in Los Angeles. In the past he has worked as a gardener, TV movie executive, babysitter, an Internet startup entrepreneur, S&M video script supervisor, news wire reporter and various other jobs. He plays bass, banjo, guitar, cello, accordion and piano. He collects records and puppets and loves clowns.

N. Rain Noe is a New York-based freelance writer and author of "Love in a 10-Block Radius," a column on urban dating, posted biweekly on AsianAvenue.com. The ex-designer has written for several magazines people have actually heard of and several that people haven't. Fast approaching thirty, he lives downtown and enjoys parallel parking, coffee and sandwiches.

Soo Jin Oh is a writer living in New York. Her work has been published in *writing away here*, an anthology of Korean American writing, *Hanging Loose* and *Sojourner*.

Hun Ohm's short fiction has appeared in several literary magazines in the past few years, including *The Asian Pacific American Journal*, *Just a Moment*, *Gallimaufry*, *The Green Age Review* and *The New England Intercollegiate Literary Review*. He was a recipient of the 1997-98 Van Lier Fellowship for fiction. Originally from Seoul, Korea, he currently resides in Michigan where he is a student at the University of Michgan Law School.

Daisy Chun Rhodes is an author having written a book of historical significance, *Passages to Paradise: Early Korean Immigrant Narratives from Hawaii*, two years ago. She has also been published in literary magazines and national newspapers. A Hemingway first novel finalist and playwright, her play *I know About Olympus* has been produced on Florida's east coast. Obtaining her BA in creative writing from Eckerd College, she has had the privilege of working with James Michener. She has presented papers at the Asian Studies Conference and the Asian American Conference, and has also presented lectures at the University of Hawaii, Center for Korean Studies, University of Washington and the Korea Society in New York.

Sung Rno's plays include *Cleveland Raining, Gravity Falls From Trees, Drizzle and Other Stories, Principia, New World (the Columbus Variations), wAve* and *Yi Sang Counts to Thirteen.* They have been produced in regional theaters and colleges around the country and in Seoul, Korea. His works have appeared in the dramatic anthology *But Still, Like Air, I'll Rise* (edited by Velina Hasu Houston) and in poetry anthologies *Premonitions* (edited by Walter Lew) and *The Nuyorasian Anthology* (edited by Bino Realuyo). He is a graduate of Harvard and Brown Universities and is currently collaborating with the band Progress on a piece called WCBMB.

Sung Yung Shin was born in 1974 in Seoul, Korea, and like thousands of other in her generation, he was abandoned. Living at first in a Korean orphanage, then in foster care, she was eventually adopted by an American couple. She was raised in Chicago and has lived in Boston and Minneapolis, where she now resides with her husband and two children. She has a BA in English from Macalester College and is working on a Master of Teaching at the University of St. Thomas.

Carolyn Sun is a 27-year-old Korean Canadian American freelance writer who has a weekly column for AsianAvenue.com called "The Inside Scoop." She is also currently studying web design at Parson's School of Design. she has lived and breathed in Manhattan for the past three years, where she has done the traditional company grind for a publishing company, Simon & Schuster, before quitting and going freelance. Currently, she is working on the narration to an independent film, Haiku 17 and writing other freelance magazine commentary articles, which are mostly somethings about nothing at all. She has a forthcoming fictional memoir entitled *Coming of Asian* about a girl moving from a hick town to New York and her ridiculous and ordinary events along the way.

Thomas Teska was born in Pusan, Korea, in 1966 and was abandoned shortly thereafter. At the age of four, an American couple from Long Island, New York, adopted him. As the son of a Hungarian and German father and an English Czechoslovakian mother, Thomas was raised as American as apple pie. After high school, he attended the School of Visual Arts in New York, but then took some time off to travel to Korea to study the culture and language. He later finished his college degree and works at an advertising agency in Manhattan. He lives with his Chinese American wife in the Inwood section of New York City along with three cats and a dog, Casper, an extremely lucky and pampered Pekinese.

Stephanie Uys was adopted by an American family at the age of six from an orphanage in Seoul. She was raised in a small, blue-collar town in Northern Ohio. Her family includes three older brothers, and another adopted Korean girl. She attended Bowling Green State University and Colorado State University. She has been published in *Hayden's Ferry*, *Connecticut Review*, *Wisconsin Review*, *Poet Love* and others.